The
Self-Deceiving
Muse

Literature and Philosophy

A. J. Cascardi, General Editor

This series publishes books in a wide range of subjects in philosophy and literature, including studies of the social and historical issues that relate these two fields. Drawing on the resources of the Anglo-American and Continental traditions, the series is open to philosophically informed scholarship covering the entire range of contemporary critical thought.

ALREADY PUBLISHED:

J. M. Bernstein, *The Fate of Art: Aesthetic Alienation from Kant to Derrida and Adorno*
Peter Bürger, *The Decline of Modernism*
Mary E. Finn, *Writing the Incommensurable: Kierkegaard, Rossetti, and Hopkins*
Reed Way Dasenbrock, ed., *Literary Theory After Davidson*
David P. Haney, *William Wordsworth and the Hermeneutics of Incarnation*
David Jacobson, *Emerson's Pragmatic Vision: The Dance of the Eye*
Gray Kochhar-Lindgren, *Narcissus Transformed: The Textual Subject in Psychoanalysis and Literature*
Robert Steiner, *Toward a Grammar of Abstraction: Modernity, Wittgenstein, and the Paintings of Jackson Pollock*
Sylvia Walsh, *Living Poetically: Kierkegaard's Existential Aesthetics*
Michel Meyer, *Rhetoric, Language, and Reason*
Christie McDonald and Gary Wihl, eds., *Transformations in Personhood and Culture After Theory*
Charles Altieri, *Painterly Abstraction in Modernist American Poetry: The Contemporaneity of Modernism*
John C. O'Neal, *The Authority of Experience: Sensationist Theory in the French Enlightenment*
John O'Neill, ed., *Freud and the Passions*
Sheridan Hough, *Nietzsche's Noontide Friend: The Self as Metaphoric Double*
E. M. Dadlez, *What's Hecuba to Him? Fictional Events and Actual Emotions*
Hugh Roberts, *Shelley and the Chaos of History: A New Politics of Poetry*
Charles Altieri, *Postmodernisms Now: Essays on Contemporaneity in the Arts*
Arabella Lyon, *Intentions: Negotiated, Contested, and Ignored*
Jill Gordon, *Turning Toward Philosophy: Literary Device and Dramatic Structure in Plato's Dialogues*
Michel Meyer, *Philosophy and the Passions: Toward a History of Human Nature.* Translated by Robert F. Barsky
Reed Way Dasenbrock, *Truth and Consequences: Intentions, Conventions, and the New Thematics*
David P. Haney, *The Challenge of Coleridge: Ethics and Interpretation in Romanticism and Modern Philosophy*
Alan Singer, *Aesthetic Reason: Artworks and the Deliberative Ethos*
Tom Huhn, *Imitation and Society: The Persistence of Mimesis in the Aesthetics of Burke, Hogarth, and Kant*
Jennifer Anna Gosetti-Ferenci, *The Ecstatic Quotidian: Phenomenological Sightings in Modern Art and Literature*
Max Statkiewicz, *Rhapsody of Philosophy: Dialogues with Plato in Contemporary Thought*
David N. McNeill, *An Image of the Soul in Speech: Plato and the Problem of Socrates*

The Self-Deceiving Muse

Notice *and* Knowledge *in the* Work of Art

Alan Singer

The Pennsylvania State University Press
University Park, Pennsylvania

Library of Congress Cataloging-in-Publication Data

Singer, Alan, 1948–
The self-deceiving muse : notice and knowledge in the work of art / Alan Singer.
   p.   cm. — (Literature and philosophy)
Includes bibliographical references and index.
Summary: "Focuses on the phenomenon of self-deception, and proposes a radical revision of our commonplace understanding of it as a token of irrationality. Argues that self-deception can illuminate the rationalistic functions of character"—Provided by publisher.
ISBN 978-0-271-03721-9 (cloth : alk. paper)
ISBN 978-0-271-04846-8 (pbk. : alk. paper)

1. Self-deception.
2. Aesthetics.
I. Title.

BD439.S56 2010
128'.4—dc22
2010006199

Copyright © 2010 The Pennsylvania State University
All rights reserved
Printed in the United States of America
Published by The Pennsylvania State University Press,
University Park, PA 16802-1003

It is the policy of The Pennsylvania State University Press to use acid-free paper. Publications on uncoated stock satisfy the minimum requirements of American National Standard for Information Sciences—Permanence of Paper for Printed Library Material, ANSI Z39.48–1992.

For Rhea Singer (1926–2006)

I think it will be a good plan to turn my will in completely the opposite direction, and deceive myself, by pretending for a time that these former opinions are utterly false and imaginary.

René Descartes, *First Meditation*

The content uttered by spirit and uttered about itself is, then, the inversion and perversion of all conceptions and realities, a universal deception of itself and others. The shamelessness manifested in stating this deceit is just on that account the greatest truth.

—G. W. F. Hegel, *The Phenomenology of Mind*

A serious human life . . . can hardly begin until we see an element of illusion in what is really there and something real in fantasies about what might be there instead.

—Northrop Frye, *The Great Code: The Bible and Literature*

Contents

List of Illustrations   ix
Acknowledgments   xi

Introduction   1
1 The Self-Deceiving Muse   13
2 Illusionism and the Self-Deceiving I   47
3 Learning from Self-Deception   66
4 Being Out of Character / Normativizing Self-Deception   97
5 Picturing Self-Deception   138
6 Spelling Out the Viewer   164
7 Shameless Self-Deception   203

Bibliography   219
Index   225

Illustrations

1 Parmigianino, *Self-Portrait in a Convex Mirror*, c. 1524   70
2 Caravaggio, *Medusa*, 1596–98   87
3 Lorenzo Lotto, *Portrait of Andrea Odoni*, 1527   101
4 Tintoretto, *The Discovery of the Body of St. Mark*, 1565   147
5 Jeff Wall, *Milk*, 1984   156
6 Gerhard Richter, *Hanged*, 1988   172
7 Gerhard Richter, *Arrest I*, 1988   174
8 Gerhard Richter, *Confrontation 2*, 1988   176
9 Jacopo Pontormo, *The Visitation*, 1528–30   181
10 Bill Viola, *The Greeting*, 1985   185
11 Alba and the Deuces, from *A Zed and Two Noughts*, 1985, directed by Peter Greenaway   199

Acknowledgments

This book has been a richly collaborative exercise. Its twofold ambition—to achieve a cognitively dutiful and ethically responsible grasp of aesthetic experience—entails new construals of human character and agency. I have shared the stakes of this endeavor with many colleagues and students who believe that the prevailing theories of beauty or notions of aesthetic value predicated on prescriptive ethics, identity politics, or the postulate of an anti-aesthetic are inadequate to the purposes of artistic making and critical practice. This inadequacy is observable in the fields of literary study, philosophy, and art theory, where the agency of the artist is too frequently a casualty of our valuing the artwork. Furthermore, our evasion of the problems inherent to the agency of the artist has deleterious consequences for our own agency. This is especially true insofar as we wish to maintain that the artwork has worldly value consistent with the aims of practical rationality.

Above all, and over many years, I have benefited from the shrewd skepticism, critical acumen, and resourcefulness of Robert L. Caserio and Allen Dunn. I thank them both for their intellectual tirelessness, their commitment to ideas, and their extraordinary clarity of focus with respect to the technical arguments unfolding in these pages. Dan O'Hara has been a diligent reader of these pages and a source of much astute advice with respect to my clarifications of the structure of argument and the trajectory of thought. Charles Altieri's skeptical voice has sharpened my rethinking of the most intractable problems facing any attempt to theorize a cognitive aesthetic. Other critical minds have generously brought their intellectual energy to bear on this project. They include Phil Alperson, Brunella Antomarini, R. M. Berry, Jeffrey Di Leo, Richard Eldridge, and Susan Stewart. I am also indebted to my graduate students, in many seminars in aesthetic theory over the years, who have held the discussion to high standards of skepticism and self-scrutiny.

Finally, and as ever, my gratitude to Nora Pomerantz, companion and coworker in life, is unbounded.

Versions of some of the chapters that follow first appeared, although in very different forms, in journals and collections. I am grateful for permission to reprint that material here. The gist of chapter 1, and the germ of everything else in this book, first appeared in *Symplokē* 12, nos. 1–2 (2004). This article was subsequently reprinted in *Fiction's Present: Situating Contemporary Narrative Innovation*, edited by R. M. Berry and Jeffrey R. Di Leo (Albany: State University of New York, 2008). Portions of what is now chapter 3 appeared in *SubStance 120,* vol. 38, no. 3 (2009), reproduced courtesy of the University of Wisconsin Press. The discussion of works by Gerhard Richter, now contained in chapter 6, first appeared in "Skeptical Self-Deception," in *Soundings: An Interdisciplinary Journal* 85, nos. 3–4 (2002).

Introduction

The Problem

The Self-Deceiving Muse is an endeavor to rethink our relationship with an abiding character-type and ethical conundrum of life and art: the self-deceiver and the specter of irrationality with which such a character menaces our cognitive dignity. Typically, the self-deceiver is marked as an antagonist of reason. On this basis, self-deception is rendered stigmatic for characters in life and in the artistic fictions that purport to reflect lived experience. Judging in this way we assume that the self-deceiver knows better than he or she does. We fault his or her judgment. But our own judgment in this case may be the unintended consequence of an overly instrumental idea of reason. The idea that the self-deceiving character is simply and belligerently irrational is irresistible as long as we judge by the assumption that we know what right reasons are. But we might judge otherwise.

In *The Self-Deceiving Muse* I am not interested in stigmatizing the unreason of the self-deceiver. I do not for a moment deny that agents who act on reasons that have no correlation with their actual circumstance may do injury to themselves and others. But the flexibility of mind implicit in the self-deceiver's disposition to reason beyond the most immediate recognition of his or her circumstances presents another prospect. This mental disposition might be a resource of rational agency worth cultivating. In other words I want to explore that dimension of the self-deceiver's experience which prompts him or her to be especially sensitive to competing grounds of reason-giving. This sensitivity puts self-deception in league with active imagination and, I will show, consequently converges with aesthetic experience. In *The Self-Deceiving Muse* I thus strive to mitigate the mutual exclusion of moral and aesthetic choices that is typically prompted by the stigmatizing of self-deception. Instead, I want to take the phenomenon of self-deception as a crossable bridge between life and art—one that the artist and the ordinary rational man traverse in both directions. That is to say, the mark of self-deception need not be seen as the stigmata of an ethically burdensome irrationality so much as the discernment of human capacities for reasoning with which rationalist self-assertion has lost touch. We shall see how this might beneficently broaden the experiential reach of rationalistic character.

Philosophers have long asserted that the self-deceiver believes what he or she knows to be untrue: he or she knows that *P* but asserts that not-*P*. Hence the self-deceiver is tagged as an irrationalist.[1] But one could point out that the self-deceiver is in fact a notorious and indefatigable rationalizer. It is a commonplace that self-deception produces rationalization and rationalization produces self-deception.[2] Under these assumptions we can say that the self-deceiver is not just a person who believes what he or she knows to be untrue. Rather, the self-deceiver finds a reason to know something else, something more immediately self-explanatory with respect to the beliefs he or she must hold in order to be a self-preserving subject under the condition of changing circumstance. For this reason, one could argue, the self-deceiver is more conscientiously attuned to the possibilities for giving better reasons to buttress his or her beliefs than the already self-possessed believers who take their doxa to be self-evident. This is to say that the self-deceiver is an especially acute *noticer* of the circumstances in which he or she must avow the beliefs that guide his or her actions. In the course of time one can easily imagine that the self-deceiver is ever more anxiously aware that the reasons for his or her avowals of belief are increasingly inadequate to the changing circumstances of his or her existence. The more one attends to the available reasons for acting, the more one is conscious of the potential inadequacy of each of them. So the stigma, the mark of self-deception that arises from a suspicion of false knowledge, may in fact be the opening of a more capacious horizon of knowledge: unfolding in full proportion to the plot of agential existence. The stigma of self-deception might be mitigated by the transfigurative marking of time itself.

I am interested, therefore, in exploring the ways in which the self-deceiver's heightened powers of notice might dovetail with the imperative to notice ever

---

1. See Raphael Demos's influential overview in "Lying to Oneself," *Journal of Philosophy* 57 (1960): 588–95. This essay represents the orthodox view of self-deception that more recent work, including the present book, attempts to challenge.

2. This is a point of view shared by theorists of self-deception on both sides of the debate about the rationality of the self-deceiver.

more urgently over time. I take this narrative imperative to be a key underpinning of artistic composition generally speaking, as well as a condition of everyday life. Artworks typically urge us to know more than we already surmise. By seeking correlation between self-deception and aesthetic activity, I will endorse the view that we ought to think of the preeminent rationale for art as an unremitting inducement to notice more. On this basis, we can persuasively distinguish self-delusion and the deception of others from self-deception. The former do not dispose the subject to seek better reasons for avowing the beliefs that instantiate its commitments to action. As we shall see, self-deception is on the one hand constitutive of rationalistic subjectivity because the subject considers the need to accommodate more reasons commensurate with the prospect for noticing more aspects of experience. He or she is thereby disposed to knowing more in a quantitative sense. Once again, this makes a striking contrast with the deceiver of others, whose knowing more typically gets expressed as an antagonistic ratio of power vis-à-vis the other, rather than as a self-consciousness about the authority of one's own knowledge. So we can also say that the inherent lack of what Hegel might call self-certainty on the part of the self-deceiver is indistinguishable from the source of his or her potential wisdom. This follows a common Romantic belief shared by the English and German poets of the nineteenth century and post-Hegelian aestheticians: that the creativity of the artistic self constitutes knowing more in a qualitative sense because the *becoming of the self* is what is most conspicuously at stake in the act of creation.[3] This is of course especially true if one grants a susceptibility to the ever more urgent promptings that experience might give to the subject's power of notice. In other words, we do not need to choose between the quantitative and qualitative aspects of the self-deceiver's wisdom.

It is within this context that we must be especially mindful that the history of artistic production is a record of how deeply ingrained the philosophical prejudices against self-deception are in the humanistic practices of representing human selves. It is indeed uncontroversial to say that the self-deceiving mind is a common theme of both literary and visual art. But I want to forestall the conclusion that self-deception is merely an artistic theme, subject to contemptuous philosophical moralizing about the incontinent nature of the self-deceiver. Rather, and more important, I want to consider the possibility that

---

3. Here I am anticipating the discussion of the "Notional" dimension of self-deceiving experience in chapters 3 and 4. Also see Richard Eldridge's very astute *Persistence of Romanticism: Essays in Philosophy and Literature* (Cambridge: Cambridge University Press, 2001), in which he makes a compelling case for a self-transformative ethos as a crux of artistic meaning.

self-deception constitutes a crucial innovation in aesthetic practice that challenges the moral and practical opprobrium stacked against the self-deceiver according to standard views of rational normativity.

In order to mount this challenge to orthodox accounts of self-deception, I will examine the significance of self-deception as a form as well as a content of literary, painterly, filmic, and art-historical practice. My examples range from the first century to the present. But my point is not to confabulate a historical progress. Rather, these examples will shore up a theoretical framework for linking dynamics of aesthetic experience with dynamics of human self-understanding in the countless and inescapable situations where the human subject suffers a disjuncture between intentions and actions. The work will thus establish conceptual continuity between traditions of artistic practice and the philosophical traditions that treat the problem of self-deception as integral to the philosophy of mind in general. That mind, after all, exacerbates the post-Enlightenment antagonism toward self-deception that I seek to moderate here. I will therefore strive to illuminate artistic invention's complicity with modes of self-deception and to illuminate self-deception's centrality to the life of aesthetic production. The stake of self-deception in both realms will be seen as nothing less than the nature and fate of human character itself.

The Argument

Self-deception has been a thematic crux of literary art since the earliest classical tragedy in which plot reversal (*peripeteia*) forcefully figured the fate of the protagonist. One need only mention Oedipus, Don Quixote, Emma Bovary, and Humbert Humbert to realize the pervasiveness of the self-deceiving mind in the histories of the epic and the novel. The literary protagonists I have just named are seen to be self-deceived by virtue of their wishing to see more reasons than already suit their best sense of themselves as self-comprehending agents. This is, after all, an inescapable consequence of an Aristotelian reversal of fate. Similarly, painters conjure perceptual ambiguities and inducements to the perceptual uncertainty of the viewer that figure the reversibility of perspective. One might say therefore that the wish to see more is inextricable from the means of seeing that sustains the history of painting *tout court*. This has been the case since the notorious trompe l'oeil perpetrated in the contest between Zeuxis and Parrhasius. It has been apparent since the advent of Roman illusionist painting, and since Cimabue and Giotto first depicted the movement of bodies in space. In all of these cases, literary and painterly, the confidence about what one knows redounds to a second-order knowledge of what one knows one doesn't know. This is the knowledge that will count the most in the exploration that follows. Finally, it is worth considering that the theme of self-deception sketched out here makes the artwork a unique venue for examining the nature of the self without indulging the apocalyptic scenarios of post-Enlightenment disenchantment with the subject. By and large, these speculations have tended toward radical critiques of identity and selfhood that nullify human agency. Self-deception might then be characterized as a modality of human attention that is, at least potentially, agency-enhancing.

I am thus keenly aware of the counterintuitive nature of this enterprise. But I hope my reader will see that only by attending to the reasons why we stigmatize the self-deceiver, why we mark him or her as an unreliable witness, will we be able to expose the quality of heightened attentiveness that makes the self-deceiver such an interesting character in the first place. We have already noted how artworks that "treat" the hazards of human self-deception have served as vehicles for ethical admonition against the prospect of self-deception. Clearly I think too little has been made of the alternate possibility: that self-deception is not simply a moral flaw, the pretext for a cautionary that artworks perpetuate for the purpose of bolstering already authoritative belief systems. Self-deception might also, and more beneficently, be seen as a fulcrum of human learning. In that way it might also help us understand what constitutes formal innovation in artworks. After all, we commonly anticipate that new worlds of possibility for human action arise from the innovative artwork. It is on this basis that I wish to explore the possibility that the structures of experience that formally inventive artworks orchestrate for readers and viewers are coherent with the experience of self-deception. In other words I want to consider the prospect that what is most specific to the pragmatics of innovative aesthetic practice entails the kind of self-compromise epitomized in the circumstance of self-deception. For this reason, I have claimed that self-deception portends the kind of character transformation that is figured by Greek *peripeteia* in the forms of conventional emplotment. This challenge to intelligibility is part and parcel of what gives the innovative artwork its epistemic distinctiveness. We shall see, for example, in chapter 1, that a modality of self-deception is induced by Flaubert's innovative deployment of free indirect discourse. Flaubert's shuffling of perspectival horizons in this aesthetic gambit will remind the reader of better reasons for attending to the narrative actions that inform his or her authority as a reader. Such aesthetic practice intimates how much the stigma of self-deception might be a lever of insight rather than a blind spot of rational intent.

Because I will presume upon a close relation between our understanding of the dynamics of self-deceiving consciousness and the dynamics of aesthetic experience, I will have to demonstrate how—within both realms of inquiry—human frailty is a plausible site for linking aesthetic invention with ethical growth. By invoking ethical growth I am anticipating the necessary adaptation of character to circumstance. I refer to the prospect for sharing perspectives. Alternatively, our prejudice in favor of untroubled rationalist self-assertion risks isolation within what Hegel might call a deluded "sense certainty." This denotes a kind of temporal shortsightedness or a blindness toward the exigencies of the ensuing moment. I would maintain that where there is ethos, there is a portent of change. The orthodox view of self-deception as a failure of reason makes what is undeniably a human frailty too reductively tragic. I will consequently report a significant shift in philosophical thinking about self-deception that supports my recuperation of self-deception as an unexpected strength of character with which we might thwart this fate.

As I have already said, self-deceivers have long been treated simply as people who seem to believe and disbelieve the same proposition at the same time, as if only one time of belief were relevant. The self-deceiver's weakness would seem to be his or her capitulation to a time-induced logical contradiction. But more recent philosophical thinkers in this arena—Alfred Mele, Herbert Fingarette, Donald Davidson, Robert Audi, Amélie Rorty, and many others—support my challenge to the orthodox notion of self-deception as mere logical paradox. After outlining the thrust of more contemporary argument about the meaning of self-deception, I will offer a justification for seeing self-deception and rationalization as integral to, rather than antithetical to, each other. Insofar as the self-deceiving mind causes rationalization and rationalization produces self-deception, I will argue that reason-giving and self-deception are, in effect, reciprocating functions of mind. Self-deception is tantamount to the task of sorting out how to understand oneself through one's errors. This sorting seeks an emphatically contextual knowledge. It entails something like the broadening of contextual parameters for comprehending the worlds that artworks are expected to foster. To use Herbert Fingarette's terms, we might say that the self-deceiver "spells out" inferences from his or her experience that would otherwise go unnoticed and unconsidered as motives for action and belief.

Thus I am committed to advancing three counterintuitive propositions respecting self-deception as a feature of aesthetic production: (1) the self-deceiver—figured as a fictional character—knows that something more than sufficient reason for his or her action constitutes adequate warrant for that action; (2) the self-deceiver may thereby be characterized as possessing an anxious disposition toward the possibility of insufficient knowledge of the conditions for self-realizing action; and (3) as a consequence, self-deception is a condition for instantiating an unusually acute form of notice or vigilance with respect to the contingent circumstance of human action. Self-deception therefore entails an ever more perspicuous mustering of reasons that are incrementally responsive to conditions of change. As many recent theorists of self-deception make clear, such an account prompts us to see the possibility that the dispositions of the self-deceiver make him or her an exemplary character. The self-deceiver is an inherently compelling character because he or she is disposed to see what is not apparent. This makes the self-deceiver an unusually resourceful reason-giver. Moreover, the resourceful reason-giving of the self-deceiver helps explain what it is in the notion of character that makes Aristotle tie its ethical significance to action. Thus we are in a position to appreciate more fully why, in Aristotle's view, the actions of characters are our most dispositive access to the meaning of *mimesis*. In action we discover the warrant for a self-transformative initiative.

I thus treat the notion of character conceived under the sign of self-deception as a means to the end of better understanding what matters to us as self-transformative agents in our experience of the work of art. Consequently, each of the chapters that make up this book reflect upon the work of art in terms that are unfolded from the dynamics of self-deception: *spelling out,* so to speak, a more richly responsive attunement to worldly experiences. Reciprocally, the character of self-deception will be examined as a stake of aesthetic experience generally—at least with respect to those features of the artwork which elaborate the characterological dimensions of the reader or viewer. I make no attempt to treat the art-historical spectrum systematically or sequentially. Rather, as I have already made plain, my first concern is how self-deception is an occasion for broadening the scope of aesthetic experience on the registers of notice, attentiveness, and attunement with discrepant aspects of worldly experience. It therefore stands to reason that the artworks I have selected for discussion here will be expressly representative of these experiential registers.

Organization

My argument unfolds as follows.

Chapter 1, "The Self-Deceiving Muse: Fiction and the Rationalistic Dictates of the Present," reviews a wide range of contemporary philosophical thinking that revises orthodox moral judgments of the self-deceiver and tilts our understanding of self-deception in a more normative direction. This tilt correlates with novelistic representations that hold the idea of character accountable to a certain experience of present-ness, a state of acute responsiveness to changing experience.

I exemplify the philosophically inspired reorientation to orthodox moralizing accounts of self-deception by reading a literary text that only seems to reinforce the orthodoxy: Flaubert's *Madame Bovary*. Flaubert's text is especially apt and useful. Emma Bovary certainly typifies the morally judge-able self-deceiver and reveals the depth of our stake in character wherever we seek to judge self-deception. Typically, we condemn her self-deception as a willful blindness with respect to the immediate conditions of her existence. But this standard of self-deception is not reinforced by the formal orchestration of the novel. Flaubert anticipates precisely the good warrant for revising it. Such a revision of our thinking stands to enrich the prospects we can entertain for self-realizing character rather than depleting them. My reading of Flaubert, interpolated with new perspectives on self-deception and a view of their implications for theories of character in time, sets up the logic of the succeeding chapters. My interest in understanding how self-deception potentiates processes of self-realization will be seen as an opportunity for mapping a convergence of the philosophical stakes of rethinking self-deception with the ethical dimension of aesthetic experience. Ethos and *aesthesis* will be seen as joined in the rationalizing activity of the self-deceiver, much as they are joined in the protagonist of Aristotelian tragic plot.

Chapter 2, "Illusionism and the Self-Deceiving I," develops the theoretical and practical framework for seeing how self-deception might be understood as an auxiliary rationality rather than as a definitive instance of the irrational. I begin with a discussion of Hegel's "Notion," positing a self-deceptive moment within the "negation of the negation." Hegel's Notion is the relation of essence to being: where essence is the first negation of being, being is necessarily an illusion. I take illusionism in the visual arts as a useful topos for expanding upon the Hegelian insight. I then draw upon the postulates of philosophical inferentialism, best represented for my purposes in the work of Robert Brandom.

Inferentialism assumes that meaning is a give and take of linguistic usages, that concepts acquire their meaning through new perspectives of usage. By showing how inferentialism might be best appreciated as an exposition of the narrative nature of reasoning, I give more analytical framing to my earlier claim that our negotiations with illusionism entail a narrative rationality. All of this thinking, I argue, is coherent with what Harry Frankfurt has called a hierarchical model of agency: whereby we understand character to exist on a sliding scale of motivational biases. That is, the essence of character inheres in appreciating how our changing desires bear on our actions as a set of priorities to be constantly renegotiated. The chapter concludes with an account of how the inferentialist disposition and the shifting motivational biases that inform hierarchical agency fill out the experiential range of the self-deceiving character.

Chapter 3, "Learning from Self-Deception: Aesthetic Practices," makes the connection between self-deceiving practices and aesthetic practices more explicit. Through a close reading of illusionistic effects in Parmigianino's *Self-Portrait in a Convex Mirror,* and then in juxtaposition with the American poet John Ashbery's poem of the same title, I demonstrate how self-deception involves us in a quasi-Wittgensteinian game of giving and receiving reasons. This intimates a curriculum of learning to notice things aspectually. Such powers of notice, I argue, inhere in the concept of subjectivity that is the sine qua non of both literary and visual portraiture understood as an aesthetic practice. I then elaborate a view of the "portraiting" practices of Parmigianino and Ashbery by reading Caravaggio's famous shield painting, *Medusa.* The three pieces are seen to work as an ensemble. They are all instances of portraiture conditioned by an appreciation of illusionism that enhances powers of notice. They reveal qualities of subjective experience that familiar conceptions of character depend upon but frequently do not articulate. They give us occasion to contemplate further the game of giving and receiving reasons as coherent with self-deception. Inasmuch as paintings and poems foster premature readings, they promulgate inducements to imagining better reasons for reading further. The negotiations of such gamesmanship are revealed ultimately to have direct bearing on the ethical rewards of treating self-deception as a normative phenomenon. The ethical rewards at stake here depend upon our seeing normativity as a counter of self-recognition for the reader/viewer. Normativity portends a learning process that is, however, not governed by purely causal principles.

Chapter 4, "Being Out of Character / Normativizing Self-Deception," elaborates the relation between reason-giving and self-deception. Following from the premise that reason-giving is a source of normativity and from theories of rationality that are keyed to the aspect-dependency of human desires, this chapter explores the counterintuitive possibility that the paradigm of Enlightenment reason and the cultural "heroizing" of the Enlightenment character reveal, upon closer inspection, a furtive connection to self-deception. This prospect is exposed through an examination of how the Enlightenment character is a creature of plot. The temporal crises of narrative emplotment were already acknowledged to be a condition for the self-deceiving character in chapter 1. Chapter 4 reads three works of narrative fiction that are distinguished by their innovations of plot-making and their indebtedness to ideals of the Enlightenment character that would seem to obviate any interest in self-deception, except as a convenient whipping-boy of moralistic reason: *Don Quixote*, *Rameau's Nephew*, and *Lolita*. These novels serve as reference points for a reconsideration of the autonomy of rational ego, a Western ideal that gets its animus from the practices of portraiture discussed in chapter 2. It likewise portends narrative mastery of the world in tandem with the rise of the novel in the West. The history of the novel is seen to blur the line between the subject of modernity and the objectified cultural forms of modernity that endow that subject with the truths of reason. The three works by Cervantes, Diderot, and Nabokov span, and arguably epitomize, the history of the modern novel. More to the point, however, they display the novel's fascination with the self-deceiving character as a nemesis of Enlightenment reason. At the same time, they show how the novel gets much of its formal integrity from resources of mind that are attributable to this apparently flawed character type. So the self-deceiving protagonists of these literary narratives will serve to spell out how scenarios of human world-making and the frailties of the self-realizing Enlightenment ego reciprocate with one another.

Chapter 5, "Picturing Self-Deception," picks up the thread of temporality that underpins the rationality of the self-deceiver. Where chapter 4 drew upon the narrative resources of the novel to engage a diachronic rationality inherent to self-deception, chapters 5 and 6 demonstrate a complementarity of experience and knowledge on the visual registers of painting, photography, video/installation art, and cinema. Chapter 5 takes off from the earliest practices of visual illusionism in Roman wall painting. The argument is buttressed by E. H. Gombrich's insight that illusionism is fundamental to an understanding of the visual image generally. This insight furthermore intimates how the visual arts both clarify and dramatize the stakes of the self-deceiver in rational processes. Gombrich's idea that visual ambiguity is representable only in time, through a "switching" of the viewer from one visual system to another, furthers my account of the self-deceiver as possessed of enhanced powers of notice. It elaborates the ethical mandate I attribute to powers of notice in my earlier chapters. This ethical mandate is now revealed very starkly in the famous perceptual experiments conducted by Adelbert Ames during the 1940s and 1950s. It is given more specifically aesthetic grounding in visual readings of Tintoretto's *The Discovery of the Body of St. Mark* and of light box installations by the contemporary Canadian photographer Jeff Wall. These analyses focus on the resources of the visual arts for grasping the experience of viewing in terms that reflect the epistemic conditions of self-deception. Once again, they show us the ethical promise implicit in self-deception. By putting us in multi-dimensionally unstable spaces, Tintoretto and Wall lead us to know ourselves to be at a loss for explanatory resources about our motivational biases. In this circumstance we might say that the self is both deceived and knowledgeable at the same time. That is to say, we are prompted to *become* knowledgeable—if only by a kind of vertigo—of a better footing *yet to be found*.

Chapter 6, "Spelling Out the Viewer," carries the analysis of the viewer's aesthetic experience forward with emphasis on the ethical mandate to maximize human powers of notice. By now this mandate is well identified with the experience of the self-deceiving character. Readings of the work of the photorealist painter Gerhard Richter, the video/installation artist Bill Viola, and the filmmaker Peter Greenaway will unite my account of how self-deception is in league with ideals of the Enlightenment character, with a spelling out of the historical responsibilities implicit in powers of notice. The works by Richter, Viola, and Greenaway are all, in one way or another, reflections on the tragic fate of Enlightenment subjectivity. They also establish a framework for imagining how works of visual art that are so richly imbued with the qualities of the self-deceiving character proffer means by which the project of Enlightenment might go forward. Indeed, they show how it might go forward in a manner consistent with the proposals of Max Horkheimer and Theodor Adorno in *Dialectic of Enlightenment*.[4] In that influential text the authors anticipate a form of reasoning beyond instrumental reason. The visual artists featured in this chapter deploy perceptual strategies that depend upon the epistemic pathway paved by self-deception. The post-Enlightenment character that walks this path is arguably unencumbered by the Kant-inspired presumption that

---

4. Max Horkheimer and Theodor W. Adorno, *Dialectic of Enlightenment*, trans. John Cumming (New York: Continuum, 1990).

our performances are derived from a priori laws. Thus we will see that the dimensions of visuality revealed by Richter, Viola, and Greenaway are conducive to a mode of reasoning that is not co-opted by instrumentalist protocols of reason or deontological norms. The reasonings of the self-deceiver proffer a hope for a more humanizing rationalism.

Chapter 7, "Shameless Self-Deception," concludes the argument of this book. It takes off from Jeff Wall's identification with the Hegelian insight that self-consciousness is inherently self-deceiving: both shamelessly and productively so. This Hegelian attitude, first introduced in chapter 5, frames a discussion of how contemporary theorists of self-deception link this phenomenon to an anxiety about possessing the best reasons for one's actions. By this means I am able to tease out an admittedly counterintuitive dignity that might be credited to the self-deceiving character vis-à-vis the egoism of the Enlightenment reasoner.

This rationalist underpinning of self-deception then keeps faith with the idea that self-deception will be best understood as a normative phenomenon. Normativity matters in this context on a special condition: that the emphasis falls on norm-production rather than norm-adherence. Under this condition we might imagine that self-deception brings into play resources of mind—such as attentiveness, alertness, and a disposition to notice more than one knows—that would not otherwise animate our experience. That is to say, these resources would not come into play without the encumbrance of an anxiety about possessing the best reasons for taking up commitments. Self-deception then is an arena in which the hermeneutic will to face interpretive problems is fortified rather than threatened by experiential contingency. I maintain that it is on the threshold of this experience that the artwork comes to matter most for us. It matters for us as compulsive reason-givers. But more important, it matters for us as contenders with reasons not yet available to us within the bounds of our already all too reasonable knowledge of the world.

I

The Self-Deceiving Muse: Fiction and the Rationalistic Dictates of the Present

Uncharacteristic Character

We are interested in self-deception because we are interested in the self and its narrative counterpart, character. But character, I insist, is preeminently a threshold of human activity. Indeed, from the earliest Greek meditations on *akrasia*,[1] where it is assumed that the self can act against its best knowledge, we have reckoned with a deeply vexed self-understanding: that the threshold of self-knowledge is a slippery slope of imaginative inventiveness. The self-deceiving character has been emblematic of this knowledge. It has thus been a powerful motor of plot-making wherever the fate of character was seen to depend upon a human agent's prospect for better or worse knowledge about the choices for action. I am speaking very generally now of the human disposition to rationalize, the impulse to give better reasons for taking up commitments to action. To think about self-deception in these terms, however, is to risk the complicity of selfhood in an overly simple idea of fictionality: as a self-circumscribing realm of the imaginary. It is to confuse self-deception with mere delusion. This obscures the more beneficent exercise of imagination that inheres in self-deceiving rationalizations when we grasp the fictionality of the self-deceiver as a métier for bringing reasons to bear on actions.

It therefore makes sense to assess the place of self-deception in the historical drama of human self-realization by looking first at its place in the history of fiction making as an art form. In the realm of the aesthetic the self is typically seen to be cognate with characterization, not least in the imaginative entanglements of readers' lives with characters' lives. In the following pages I

---

1. See my discussion of how integral *akratic* reasoning might be deemed foundational for aesthetic practice in Alan Singer, *Aesthetic Reason: Artworks and the Deliberative Ethos* (University Park: Pennsylvania State University Press, 2003). See especially pages 98–102 with respect to how *akrasia* entails decision-making.

will argue that self and character are inextricably linked in the dynamics of self-deception that are always played out in the emplotment of a human life. Thus I will take the form of narrative emplotment in the novel as a point of departure—albeit heuristic—for wider speculation about the fate of the self-deceiving character. Moreover, I will do so without worrying about the distinction between fact and fiction. I will maintain that the very possibility of self-deception allows for a salutary blurring of that distinction. The more important touchstone of character for my argument is its susceptibility to a ceaselessly moving horizon of motivational knowledge within which all characters, fictional and otherwise, must act. This is the spur of human rationalization tout court.

So I start with the proposition that character in fiction, and specifically the condition of "present-ness" that the fictional character embodies (spatially and especially temporally), constitutes the best laboratory for inquiring into the self-deceiver's means of knowing. The present-ness of character in fictional narrative figures an inherently conflicted temporality. No one would dispute that plot conflict epitomizes tensions between moments in time as much as conflicts between persons. But our way of construing the thematic sense of narrative fictions, by emphasizing the conflict of personality, privileges the already formed dispositions of character. It transcends the disruptiveness of temporal immediacy, the quality of being present in the present. After all, novelistic dramatizations of the conflicts between personalities typically presuppose the well-formedness of those personalities. Such dramatizations invite the kind of abstract thinking that indulges a vicarious identification with character rather than a rigorous sharing of the vicissitudes of the character in time. Strictly thematic readings of character promote our treating character as propositional knowledge rather than as a site for our own engagements with the conditions of character formation. In other words, the focus upon plot conflict as a thematic armature of narrative inclines us to ignore the relative inchoateness of character in time. It inveigles us to lose sight of the possibility that character is too easily taken for granted as a repository of experience rather than as a threshold of experience. Particularly from the vantage point of the novel of the present, the novel since 1945—where character is an increasingly vexed proposition, a site of increasingly unstable orientations—it seems appropriate to refocus our attention. The present moment prompts us to consider how the novel—among many other art forms—has long harbored a notion of character that, in a manner of speaking, resists characterization insofar as it is responsive to the circumstance of present-ness. Free indirect discourse, as practiced by Flaubert, and stream-of-consciousness, as practiced by Joyce—not to mention their many postmodern variants—are tokens of this widely ignored dimension of character. I take the vivid present-ness of such characterization to be a crucial arena within which to assess our prospects for self-knowledge insofar as fictional form—in the verbal and, as we shall later see, in the visual arts—can hold us accountable to it.

That is to say, by reconsidering how the pressures of the present bear on fictional narrative (and implicitly, on fictional representation in other media), I intend to revise our notion of character. I wish to explore what I have already conceded to be a counterintuitive usefulness of character for modeling and remodeling human selves. By focusing on present-ness as the salient quality of character I conjure a distinctly *uncharacteristic character:* one that is inherently self-deceiving. I will take self-deception to be an inherent rather than an accidental quality of character. I think that popular assumptions about self-deception, which have made it a touchstone of the frailty of fictional characters and, on that basis, an abiding theme of the novel, have prevailed at the expense of a more complex view of ethos per se. By invoking an *uncharacteristic character* I want to explore the possibility that the condition of self-deception is both normative and imperative for sustaining our faith in the meaningfulness of selves over time. I will propose that only from the perspective of such a self-deceiving self can the ethical stakes of fiction be honestly derived. This is not because self-deception is simply equivalent to reflection over time, but because the self-deceiver is more acutely responsive to such change than the smugly rationalistic self-assertor. That responsiveness will be seen to be a warrant for observing a surprising continuity between the character formation of the reader and those characters animating the literary fictions in which the reader is involved. I ought to make one cautionary statement here. While I commence this inquiry with a focus on the novel, what I have to say will gain significance only insofar as the formal problematics of the novel can be generalized beyond the form of the novel. The novel has pride of place in this discussion chiefly because it is the artistic genre that has been most identified with our human adaptability to the exigencies of time and change.

In other words, in this chapter the novel will serve as a kind of locus classicus for the temporality upon which my view of the self-deceiving character is predicated. The link between the present-ness of character and its self-deceiving ethos is the very ongoingness of temporality. Temporal change is the most immediate threat to ego-identity. We are never more conscious of the frailty or instability of our ego ideals than in the midst of events whose outcome we cannot predict. On this score, there is little disputing that the self-deceiver is motivated to maintain a belief that promises self-realization: a self that can sustain its beliefs through the epistemic reversals of action. This bid for coherence between beliefs and lived experience—between beliefs and the reasons for the actions they prompt—nonetheless founders upon knowledge that the beliefs one is motivated to hold are often proved to be at odds with the facts in the course of their unfolding. What's more, these facts are quite often intractable to human will. The mind of the self-deceiver is thus torn between evidence that the world is one way and a desire that it be another way. The line that divides these visions of reality shifts as a variable of time. It threatens to divide character against itself.

According to the standard accounts I want to challenge here, an important threshold for recognizing self-deceiving character is this assumption: the self-deceiver knows that what he believes is contrary to the facts. Self-deception thus presents us with an insuperable irrationality. Our predisposition to value character insofar as we can understand it is radically thwarted by this characterization of self-deception. Indeed, it would seem to preclude any meaningful engagement with self-deceiving character altogether.

And yet the circumstance of a character seeming to believe what is false and acting accordingly, seeming to hold two contradictory beliefs at the same time, remains a fervent source of dramatic interest for us both in life and in fiction. The literary characters who exhibit the sign of self-deception also give a defining contour to the history of the novel. Self-deceivers are so pervasive in the canonical texts of narrative fiction that, from a certain perspective, self-deception seems to be what the novel is about. Cervantes' Don Quixote, Sterne's Tristram Shandy, Flaubert's Emma Bovary, Joyce's Stephen Dedalus, Conrad's Marlow, Ford's John Dowell, and Nabokov's Humbert Humbert: in one way or another all of these protagonists act at odds with what they know. They are self-deceivers in the sense that they seem to hold beliefs about their own motivations and acts that contradict their own accounts of motive and act. Thus, we are bound to conclude that self-deception—from one perspective, an epitome of irrationality—rationalizes the longevity of the genre as a métier of human self-understanding. In this susceptibility to paradox, the genre of the novel is painfully implicated in the predicament of its most exemplary and often its most tragically fated characters. Their self-understanding typically waits upon a plot resolution that would prove them unrecognizable to themselves. Such emplotment would, after all, entail a more capacious rationality than what is already compassed within their narrative universes.

And yet intellectual reflection on the problem seems to bifurcate. On the one hand, the paradox that seems to afflict the novel appears to deepen over the course of its history, as the history of the novel becomes increasingly intertwined with the fate of the self-deceiving character. On the other hand, philosophical debates about the status of self-deception vis-à-vis rationality have tended to underplay, even ameliorate, the paradox. Philosophers have achieved this result by putting argument on a path of inquiry that intersects with the novel's signature temporality. Certainly philosophical literalists have asserted that because self-deceivers believe and disbelieve a proposition *at the same time,* inquiry founders upon the "irreducibly paradoxical" nature of self-deception, proving further inquiry to be rationally "impossible."[2] But a recent turn in philosophical thinking has sought to obviate the preemptive characterization of the self-deceiver as merely irrational by insisting upon links between self-deception and processes of rationalization in general. In this new context of discussion carried on by Kent Bach, Alfred Mele, Amélie Rorty, Robert Audi, and others, rationalization is deemed to be a preeminently temporal phenomenon. For temporality entails a comprehension of how motivational biases of belief are fostered by changing circumstances of reflection.

This is to say that contemporary philosophical accounts encourage us to construe self-deception as a condition of present-ness in the following sense: one's reason for holding any particular belief in the present entails knowledge that one is beholden to another context of knowledge that one is presently unaware of. If one had different reasons, one would possess a different criterion of salience for picking out or construing the elements of context in which one's beliefs seemed to be warranted. When we posit self-deception, we typically imagine that others would see things differently than the self-deceiver, because others work within more relevant parameters of knowledge.[3] This is a presumption that the self-deceiver does not have all the relevant evidence by which to judge the advisability of the belief he holds. The only way to be undeceived would be to vacate the irrational self. This is the virtually suicidal gesture of making the present collapse tragically into the past, a stance that is perhaps epitomized in Othello's words of contrition for the self-deceived murder of Desdemona, which he punctuates with a self-dealt death blow:

---

2. See Robert Audi, "Self-Deception, Rationalization, and the Ethics of Belief," in *Moral Knowledge and Ethical Character* (Oxford: Oxford University Press, 1997), 131.

3. Alfred Mele gives one of the most persuasive explanations of "jointly sufficient conditions" for self-deception in *Self-Deception Unmasked* (Princeton: Princeton University Press, 2001), 117–21.

> And say besides, that in Aleppo once,
> Where a malignant and a turban'd Turk
> Beat a Venetian and traduc'd the state,
> I took by the throat the circumcised dog,
> And smote him—thus.
> (*Othello*, act 5, scene 2, lines 352–55)[4]

The power of Othello's words is their perfect coincidence with action, past with present. Can it be that the price of recognizing self-deception is so inexorably self-annihilation? More to the point, must it be the case that self-deception is mortally indebted to the past?

Our judging self-deception as a necessary sacrificing of the present to the past produces a somewhat irrational assumption that the only viable selves would have to be rational with respect to a single evidentiary ground for mustering belief. In other words the standard notion of self-deception cultivates a rather inflexible model of the rational self, one that I'd like to suggest is itself irrational with respect to real pressures of our normal experience in time. The question of how one gains access to evidence that the self-deceiver is blind to cannot be answered in a way that squares with real temporality if we treat self-deception as a static condition. If we deny the present-ness of the self by consigning it to a framework of judgment in which belief is an artifact of past experience, a self ensconced in a fixed repertoire of motives for belief, self-deception is effectively a form of self-cancellation.

Alternatively, I suggest that we view self-deception as an arena where we assess the unrealistic expectations imposed upon the self by its assimilation of inappropriate norms of rationality. By extension I want to say that the novel, in which self-deception figures so formatively, is most vital in its ways of dramatizing how we might best exploit this arena. The novel's predisposition to eventful successiveness favors characterizations born of changing circumstances of self-recognition. In a philosophical account that buttresses this view, Kent Bach observes that self-deception needs to be understood fundamentally in relation to an economy of attention: "Given our limited attentional and cognitive resources, we must be selective in what we consider in a given situation. Obviously, we cannot spend time and effort on each thing that might come to mind just to determine that it is not worth considering. Indeed, at every moment we implicitly but effectively judge that certain things are not worth

---

4. William Shakespeare, *Othello*, ed. Stephen Orgel (New York: Penguin, 2001).

considering simply by not considering them."[5] Bach makes clear to us that what we know is emphatically a function of our attentiveness and its volatile contingencies. The mind is, de facto, partitioned by virtue of its attention span. Bach is speaking of frames of reference that induce belief according to the limitedness of the scope of attentiveness they instantiate.

What's more to the point, Bach notes the paradoxical infinite regress to which we would be doomed if we had to posit an agency to take responsibility for the partitioning. After all, the duly partitioned mind must remain unconscious if it is to be duly self-deceived. Instead, Bach has recourse to an account of the attentional shifts of consciousness that can induce self-deception or govern an awareness of it that is fundamentally narrative. This account is coherent with how narrative order is the touchstone of rationality in the novel. Bach asserts the essentially diachronic nature of rationality. Apparent paradoxes in self-deception are thus seen to arise from "some sort of gap between what one is at a moment and what one is over time" (Bach, 187). If that gap is not taken into account, he implies, a single moment in time privileges criteria by which one judges rational fit between act and world. The rationality Bach endorses by contrast, like the genre of the novel itself, entails the necessity of transcending the current moment (187) in order to make salient evidentiary criteria—for belief in a particular course of action—that would not otherwise be apparent. As Bach says, rationality must be put "on a diachronic basis" (187) in the sense that one's actions are seen to change the context in which judgment of their rationality applies. Bach desires to keep faith with the conviction that "if mental action, like directing one's attention, is included along with physical action, we *are* continuously faced with the problem of what to do next" (185). This is the urgency of present-ness per se. The pressure to know what to do next implicitly changes one's access to the facts in which one discovered the imperative to do something in particular.

On this basis, Bach can characterize the self-deceiver as motivated and purposeful. But the self-deceiver is not an intentional agent per se. This is a function of his blindness toward a truth that, assuming other evidence precluded by his particular motive and purpose, would become apparent (see, especially, Bach, 165). Self-deceivers are able to act in a way that is blind to the "truth" because their view of the relevant evidence is prejudiced by motives and purposes whose validity depends upon a more relevant "truth" for them.

---

5. See Kent Bach, "(Apparent) Paradoxes of Self-Deception and Decision," in *Self-Deception and Paradoxes of Rationality*, ed. Jean-Pierre Dupuy (Stanford: Center for the Study of Language and Information, 1998), 170.

Most commonly this would be their desire to see themselves in a certain way, to sustain an ego ideal, which any other "truth" would compromise. Hence the man who wishes to see himself as not a cuckold will gather evidence from his observations of his wife's behavior quite selectively. Since Bach accepts that our attention is always inadequate to the range of relevant evidence available, it makes less sense to stigmatize the self-deceiver's behavior as irrational than to grant the rationalistic dynamics by which evidence becomes accessible to an agent. Bach focuses therefore on actions whose truthfulness is not pegged to parity with the information one has intentionally. It is rather pegged to the lack of parity between the information inhering in the intention and the information made accessible through action. This privileges a present-ness of mind that I am again bound to identify with the form of narrative fiction. After all, narrative forms starkly dramatize the question of what to do next by their relentless successiveness. Without this plot momentum, character would cease to be a crucible of rationalization. Similarly for Bach, the meaning of an action is not determined by the intentions that led up to it but by the changes in construing relevant intentions that the act occasions in its sheer successiveness. The cuckold who examines his wife's behavior in order to ascertain her guilt or innocence examines it in such a way as to preclude knowledge of her guilt. Rationality in this context is coordinate with the relative accessibility of evidence according to which the agent's intentionality would be ratified in his action. We can thus entertain the view that the information embodied in intention and the information embodied in action are incommensurable, but the disparity between them is not unintelligible.

In this respect Bach's position is coherent with Robert Audi's and Alfred Mele's idea that self-deception leads to rationalization and rationalization leads to self-deception. Rationalization in this case is understood "as a matter of appropriately responding to the reasons one has when one is suitably aware of them, and of some broadly instrumental relation they bear to something one wants" (Audi, 146). Wherever ego needs underlie rationalization, the occasion is favorable for self-deception. Whenever a self-deceiving intuition occurs, it induces rationalizations that enhance its plausibility. I have already established how the psychological terrain of such experience is contiguous with the forms of narrative fiction. But this furthermore points up a threshold of value-making in fiction that is overlooked in the literary critic's emphasis on self-deceiving character as merely a flaw of reason, a paradoxical tic of personality. As I proceed to elaborate how self-deception deepens our appreciation of the project of rationality, I will be setting the stage for less obvious claims about the pressures fiction can bring to bear formally upon the self, unbeknownst to itself as a nontraditional self-deceiver. Such claims will become especially apparent when we see the shortsightedness of working under the assumption that self-deception is non-normative. I will show that these formal pressures structure the very pragmatics of reading through which the humanist claims for fiction encourage us to seek ourselves in literary experience in the first place. The pursuit of self-knowledge remains the most durable of motives for valuing art. But the self that is privileged in this idealism may be the most self-deceived of all.

We must first understand what the rationalizing needs of self-deceivers presuppose about our notion of selves in general. As Bach has already reminded us, such needs are largely defensive, born of desires that are menaced by an unrequiting world. In this context "desire" is not a strictly emotive state, however. In a work on self-deception that seeks to discover what strength of mind can derive from defensiveness, Alfred Mele stipulates that "desires contribute to the production of motivationally biased beliefs" (*Self-Deception Unmasked*, 24). The working hypothesis that self-deception and rationalization are reciprocating activities is based on the psychological commonplace that we desire nothing without entertaining a strategic assumption about the available means of achieving the object of desire. This state of affairs constitutes a motive for belief in the efficacy of one's desires, relative to one's account of the world in which such desires are satisfiable. Such thinking entails what Mele calls a protocol for "hypothesis testing."[6] We are by this account deliberatively disposed to assess the costs of our erroneous judgment whenever we contemplate a belief to be acted upon. The costliness of erroneous decision-making induces us to improvise a calculus whereby we assign different evidentiary weight to different construals of the context of judgment. For example, it may be more costly for me to admit I am a self-deceiver than to admit that I have ignored manifest evidence contradicting my intention to act in a rational manner. Our hypothesis of what beliefs we will be prompted to hold as rational will be guided by available evidence; but what counts as available evidence will always be a function of our desire to hold certain beliefs. Hypothesis testing reveals that motivational biases are inescapable elements of rational deliberation and that rational deliberation is unthinkable without hypothesis testing.

---

6. Alfred Mele specifies that a judgment is a decisive best or better one if it settles the question "What (from what perspective of his [an agent's] own desires, beliefs, etc.) it is best or better to do given his circumstances." Mele, *Autonomous Agents: From Self-Control to Autonomy* (Oxford: Oxford University Press, 2001), 15.

Typically, as Robert Audi theorizes it, a person is in self-deception with respect to a proposition *P* if and only if (1) unconsciously he or she knows that not-*P*; (2) he or she avows *P*; and (3) he or she has at least one desire that explains why this belief that not-*P* is unconscious and why he or she persists in the avowal of *P*. The challenge is to explain how the self-deceiver is disposed to avow *P* even when presented with what he or she sees as evidence against it (Audi, 132). Audi here figures a notion of character that is quite complementary to novelistic representation. Hypothesis testing is the métier of novelistic characters. They are marked as dutiful bearers of motivational biases. In the course of plot complication these motivational biases are skewed from contexts of rationalization, but are at the same time susceptible to the revisionary force of adverse circumstance. The difference between the literary character, qua self-deceiver, and the characterization of self-deception as Audi schematizes it is this: the character who avows *P*, knowing that not-*P* is true, is not necessarily a character—like Othello—who feels bound to abdicate personal agency to ameliorate the problem. In ordinary circumstances—Othello's suicide notwithstanding—the costs of erroneous decision-making perpetually hang in the balance for those who persist in self-deceiving behavior. There is an ineliminable element of present-ness in Audi's dynamic. Because the disposition toward hypothesis testing is governed by the variable of a character's access to information, the shifting horizon of evidentiary knowledge, it perpetuates a deliberative process.

In other words, we could say Audi shows us how to think of the self-deceiver as a self-enhancing agency, or an agency-enhancing self. The notion of self-deception I am adopting here is thus linked to an abandonment of three commonplace assumptions: (1) that self-deception is an analogue of deceiving others; (2) that self-deception presupposes an ideal self to be betrayed; and (3) that self-deception is antithetical to truthfulness. All of these assumptions decouple the act of self-deception from the ongoing activities of the self-deceiving mind. Interestingly, Audi does not discredit the rationality of a reason upon which one acts, even if it is itself dependent on a self-deceived belief. What redeems the rationality of such decision-making is its contributing to a reduction of cognitive dissonance. One acts "to achieve greater harmony among one's beliefs and attitudes" (Audi, 151). The imperative assumed here to reduce dissonance, to serve the self-protective need of the hypothesis tester, is clearly a form of narrative implicature.

Jon Elster's idea that the self is always self-performative—by virtue of a dynamic that plays between our sense of possessing both inner and outer audiences—helps us see this narrative implicature. According to Elster, feeling the need to see oneself through the eyes of others in order to have credible eyes for one's self-image entails something like susceptibility to emotional role reversal. Elster comes to this discussion in his book on emotion, *Alchemies of the Mind*.[7] Here he wishes to distinguish between the ancient Greek idea of emotion as only the product of cognition and our modern understanding that emotions can also be objects of cognition. Where emotion is an object of cognition, it opens up an interplay of affective states whereby one is prompted to "second-order emotions" (Elster, *Alchemies*, 106). Emotions that instantiate a belief are, in turn, susceptible to emotional states that the belief fails to rationalize effectively. This is inevitable given the believer's need to reflect upon belief from a perspective external to the original emotion that formed the belief. Hypothesis testers, for example, full of the fear of erroneous decision-making, must constantly adjudicate their performance of self vis-à-vis what they want to see in themselves and what they can expect others to see in them. Elster invokes the violent confrontation of the eighteenth-century duel, a showy prop of narrative melodrama in the theater and especially in the novel, to make his point. In doing so he underlines the idea that rationality and emotion reciprocate by virtue of what Bach identifies as a gap between "what one is at a moment and what one is over time" (Bach, 187).

Elster characterizes the duel as a quintessential arena of self-assertion in which veilings, hiding one's emotions, and maskings, showing false emotions, are the métiers of self-assertion. The challenge was "not only to mask and veil one's own emotions, but to unmask and unveil, testing others to reveal their real emotions. Envy was expressed by backhanded compliments, and insults in the form of exaggerated politeness, intended to humiliate the victim and make him incapable of retaliating" (Elster, *Alchemies*, 107). Self-assertion in this case does not presuppose the form of selfhood. All of these behaviors are coordinated in a unique idea of the self: one that depends on the possibility of our augmenting contexts of evidence that will support a self-image over time. But the gap between "what one is at a moment and what one is over time" obtains here as a ratio of what one knows with respect to what one might know given other perspectives. The gap de facto figures a narrative structure. For we can approach those other perspectives only through the kind of diachronic rationality Bach promotes. One improvises a stratagem for best knowing the

---

7. Jon Elster's work in this context addresses self-deception only indirectly, insofar as it is a counter for the emotional dynamic of veiling and masking. See especially his discussion of veiling and masking in *Alchemies of Mind: Rationality and the Emotions* (Cambridge: Cambridge University Press, 1999), 96.

self in meeting the challenge of knowing what to do next. As I have already intimated, the gap portends that the motives governing one's self-image at any one time are beholden to what one doesn't know, given what the passage of time will necessitate.

Narratively speaking, it has typically been assumed that self-deception figures a character's loss of perspective: implicitly the loss of self. Plato in the *Phaedo* famously characterizes the soul's imprisonment in the desires of the body as a skewed and preemptive line of sight, blinding us to the preferable unrelativistic truth.[8] The soul is "bewitched." It collaborates with its own imprisonment within an unshakable and therefore ungovernable viewpoint. The invariability of the perspective is its susceptibility to self-deception. But in the context of the present discussion it might now be apt to say that self-deception is a way for the character to acquire new lines of perspective. This entails fostering an increasingly complex articulation of perspective out of an awareness of one's misperception of the adequacy of any original perspective. We could say that self-deception is both a motor and a métier of character transformation. For it occasions reflection upon one's misrecognition of the most relevant perspective informing one's beliefs.

David Sanford takes up this version of self-deception as the "contention that . . . being self-deceived consists in one's misapprehending the structure of one's attitudes, in one's taking the having of one attitude to explain the having of another when the true explanation is something else."[9] Sanford adduces the example of a father who wishes to maintain his belief that his son has not stolen the father's valuable stamp collection to pay a perilously mounting gambling debt. Presented with evidence of the crime, the father chooses to discount its credibility. The motive for his disbelief, Sanford explains, is his anticipating the perspective such belief would impose upon his rational will to avoid concluding that his son is indeed guilty. In other words, the real reason the father disbelieves the evidence has nothing to do with its evidentiary value per se, though this is the reason that ostensibly buttresses belief. Sanford characterizes the operative misperception on the part of the self-deceiver as a reversal of the "true direction of dependence" between the reason and the belief it sponsors (167). The father thinks that the inadequacy of the evidence is the reason for his belief in his son's innocence. But in reality it is because the father

---

8. See Benjamin Jowett, ed., *Euthyphro, Apology, Crito, Phaedo* (New York: Prometheus Books, 1988).
9. See David Sanford, "Self-Deception as Rationalization," in *Perspectives on Self-Deception,* ed. Brian P. McLaughlin and Amélie Oksenberg Rorty (Berkeley and Los Angeles: University of California Press, 1988), 169.

seeks to avoid the conclusion that his son is guilty that he judges the evidence to be inadequate.

In Sanford's nomenclature, the dispositive beliefs here are called "anticipating" and "ostensible." The father anticipates the inevitability of concluding his son's guilt if he accepts the evidence. The belief in the inadequacy of the evidence is hence an ostensible reason for discounting it. The terms "anticipating" and "ostensible" reference states of mind that hinge upon shifts in perspective. They in turn determine different construals of evidentiary grounds for belief. Anticipating and ostensible beliefs inevitably force a reckoning with the fact that "one's ostensible reason always functions differently from the way one takes it to function" (Sanford, 156). They assume a human propensity to take a desire for one thing to be the desire for another. They assume that whatever attitudes we hold are in turn held hostage to our ability to anticipate how they will survive our need to justify them under changing conditions of action. The reversal of the "direction of dependence" between reasons and beliefs is itself evidence of how the structure of one's attitudes follows the form of one's desires amidst a world of frustrating circumstance. One can misapprehend the structure of one's attitudes because one has capitulated to a desire that is blind to the viewpoint from which the perspective it imposes arose. In this circumstance we are like Sanford's troubled father. Anticipating the reason he would have for abandoning his belief in his son's innocence, the father adopts the belief that preempts any damaging suspicion. His self-deceiving rationalization in this case depends upon his not knowing what he has done. And yet I would argue that our very awareness of the reversibility of the relation between reasons and beliefs—even when we are unaware of it in any particular case—portends the possibility of knowing that one does not know. Indeed, this potential knowledge is the strongest incentive for our thinking about self-deception as something more than making invidious judgments about human character. This critical prospect intimates how the modalities of self-deception might be viewed more beneficently than we are moralistically predisposed to do. Clearly, if we follow Sanford's thought that the misapprehending of the structure of one's attitudes does "not require inconsistent beliefs or a belief in conflict with what one really knows" (169), we are open to thinking about self-deception as something more than the paradoxical denying of what one knows unconsciously to be true.

The attunement to reversals of perspective that is so crucial to Sanford's account of the rationality of self-deception takes us back to the narrative implicature of the self-deceiving mind and to the condition of present-ness without which such reversals are inconceivable. Sanford prompts us to see a resemblance between the "misapprehension of the structure of one's attitudes" and the reversals of narrative plot insofar as both occasion a testing of the stakes of one's knowledge. Both dramatize the urgency of the question of what to do next by emphasizing the reversibility/revocability of the present moment. One is never more present to oneself than in the circumstance of knowing that there is something one does not know. The self-deceiver knows this more than a person of unproblematic self-knowledge by virtue of being tethered—however unconsciously—to a context other than the one he or she acknowledges as the operative motivational bias of belief. His or her misapprehension of the structure of his or her attitudes is implicitly "apprehensive" or "anticipatory" with respect to another motivational context threatening to be made present in an ensuing moment of time. It could be said, therefore, that the present-ness of the self-deceiver is more alive to the past and the future than the subject of nostalgic retrospection or the subject of hopeful fantasy could possibly be.

This is to say that self-deception attunes us to complexities of present-ness that we might otherwise rationalize or narrate away in our submission to the most confident Enlightenment fables of self-understanding. Enlightenment self-knowers are, after all, distinguished by presuming that, unlike the self-deceiver, they know very well the structure of their attitudes: they are the measure of their intentions and their intentions are the measure of the world. And yet, as I have already pointed out, the preponderance of self-deceiving characters in the history of the novel—a form for representing the world that we cannot forget is made in the image of the Enlightenment subject—suggests a furtive lack of confidence in the self-knower. I would even entertain the idea that the form of the novel itself arises out of that lack of confidence. Hence its historical necessity. The prevalence of the theme of self-deception in the history of the novel may even be the source of the novel's unique imaginative energies with respect to the Enlightenment subject that conferred formal integrity on the genre in the first place.[10]

Herbert Fingarette, in a classic text on self-deception, proceeds from the premise that we only really understand self-deception when we de-emphasize the

---

10. Much of what I am assuming here is borne out by Bakhtin's analysis of the dialogics of novelistic discourse. See especially *Problems of Dostoevsky's Poetics*, trans. Caryl Emerson (Minneapolis: University of Minnesota Press, 1984), for Bakhtin's well-known account of the carnivalesque reversals. These are precipitated out of overly self-confident and stultifying rationalistic imperatives. While I do not subscribe to the Bakhtinian idealization of *heteroglossia* that ensues in his argument, he does seem to anticipate my own sense of the novel as antagonistic to the Enlightenment reflexes of mind that underwrite its canonicity.

relation of consciousness to knowledge and emphasize its relation to action.[11] This proposition has its basis in a decidedly non-Enlightenment conceit of character. It accords with my own previously stated suspicions of any construal of narrative fiction that emphasizes the conflict of personalities in plot so as to privilege "the already formed dispositions of character which transcend the disruptiveness of temporal immediacy, of being present in the present." To the contrary, Fingarette thinks of character, not in terms of the inviolable intentionality of the autonomous Enlightenment subject, but in terms of self-avowals that the subject can make within the horizon of changing circumstance. Fingarette's hypothesis is built upon the premise that human identity is bounded by the framework of avowal, an act of identification. But the subject is formed out of what he calls an "identification as." The force of "as" here relates the identificatory subject to any number of possible contexts of self-avowal, in stark contrast to what Fingarette dubs an "identification with." "Identification with" denotes a nature that is only exemplified rather than instantiated in its actions. One "identifies with" what is already decided. Thus Fingarette does not presuppose an "already well formed self" (Fingarette, 70). "Identification as" is constitutive of the subject, not representative of the subject. As Fingarette puts it: "I have changed the 'with' to 'as' in my phrase because I want to stress what one *is* as a result of identification and to eliminate the element of duality which remains implicit in the usual use of 'identify with'" (69). "Identification as" is a trumping of "identification with" in this sense: the self "identifying as" is known to itself by an acceptance or rejection of the circumstance in which an avowal of one's identity is most presently operative. As Fingarette stipulates, "Identification [as] is the name of a development which is thought of as constitutive of a self" (70). By contrast, "identification with" entails a *was* not an *is*.

It would be fair to say that in narrative plot "identity as" is virtually epiphenomenal of plot reversal. We must be careful, of course, not to treat the premise as a springboard for leaping to the postulate of a self that is indeterminately in flux, a perpetually self-reinventing persona. This would likely lead to madness or mere lying. Rather, reversal figures selves that are constrained to choose the terms of self-recognition in relation to the range of successive perspectives within which they might find a better purpose for themselves. This is roughly the circumstance of Audi's hypothesis tester in the ineluctable instance when

---

11. See the latest edition of Herbert Fingarette's *Self-Deception*, with a new chapter (Berkeley and Los Angeles: University of California Press, 2000). See especially page 64 for elaboration of this point.

motivational biases reveal their shortcomings with respect to the exigencies of actions they cannot rationalize. This has the effect both of exposing the self's dependency upon motivational biases and of acknowledging the plurality of evidentiary grounds supporting motivational biases that are bound to complicate the prospect of one's further actions. In other words these counters of reversibility suggest that "identity as" might be the formal feature of the novel that most predisposes the genre to the theme of self-deception. But beyond this, it intimates how the theme of self-deception, with respect to the artifice of character, is potentially "remedied" by the structural form of the novel. Hence the special attunement to present-ness entailed by the novel's complicity with self-deception. I am alleging, in effect, that the theme of self-deception—that is also the burden of conflict weighing upon character—has a beneficent corollary in the cognitive features of the reading experience that the formal devices of the novel command.

Revising Self-Deception in *Madame Bovary*

Now I want to examine the exemplarity of these formal devices with respect to a novel that is almost totemic for the theme of self-deception. Flaubert's *Madame Bovary* is, at the same time, a watershed for a historical view of the novel that discerns, in its formal particularity, a discipline of cognitive attentiveness.[12] We will recall that such discipline is precisely what Bach asserts is the substrate of our existence under the pressure of asking ourselves what to do next. Flaubert's aesthetic credo, that "ideas are actions," is clarion in his correspondence with Louise Colet.[13] Couched as it is in his despair that his work will not be entertaining enough for the general public, it captures a vital concern for this author and for anyone who knows the human susceptibility to self-deception. Flaubert fears that the cognitive responsibilities governing our attentiveness to the world and, concomitantly, the authenticity of our standing within the world are jeopardized by our most lax habits of mind. Such after all is the ethical tension that, by the most conventional accounts, epitomizes the self-deceiving mind. The classic self-deceiver, asserting belief in what he knows to be counter to the facts of his experience (albeit unconsciously),

---

12. Gustave Flaubert, *Madame Bovary*, trans. Paul de Man (New York: W. W. Norton, 1965).
13. See the excerpt from the letter dated January 15, 1853, in the Norton Critical Edition of *Madame Bovary*, 313–14. This letter is excerpted from *The Selected Letters of Gustave Flaubert*, trans. and ed. Francis Steegmuller (New York: Farrar, Straus, and Giroux, 1953).

is abdicating the cognitive vigilance that would hold him accountable to himself. Emma Bovary is, culturally speaking, iconic for this cognitive abdication.

And yet the substance of my discussion so far urges the necessity of modifying the most "conventional accounts" of the self-deceiver. We have seen how Sanford modulates the definition of self-deception: he shifts from the assertion of beliefs in contradiction of one's knowledge of evidentiary grounds to positing a misapprehension of the structure of one's attitudes. This modulation is conversant with Fingarette's sense of how identity is an act of self-avowal deeply implicated in the circumstances of choosing between evidentiary grounds for belief. As a consequence of these "rethinkings" we might take a more nuanced view of Flaubert's representation of the self-deceiver. In doing so we might gain a perspective upon its more general relevance to aesthetic practice. This is the case particularly in light of my earlier expectation that we see, in self-deception, prospects for the enhancement of agency. I have neither the scope nor the ambition for a full-scale reading of Flaubert's text here. What's more, such a treatment of the work would be divergent from my purpose. I wish to show how the thematic representation of self-deception in Flaubert's aesthetic practice is in fact continuous with the un-self-deceived knowledge of self-deception that he makes available to any reader of *Madame Bovary* who scrupulously honors the novel's formal constraints.

I have already asserted that attentiveness is what the artwork in general contributes most dispositively to the quality and the meaning of life. This is what links the complexity of aesthetic form to the dynamics of self-deception—so long as it is not crudely construed as a default of truthfulness about what one knows. With this understanding then my rather narrow focus on the famous agricultural fair scene from Flaubert's novel may seem especially apt.

The multitiered ironic structure of the scene, not to mention the double-tiered mise-en-scène of the action, is the hallmark of its reputation as a stylistic tour de force. The courtship between the two protagonists of Flaubert's narrative episode is staged as an elaborate upstairs/downstairs affair. The self-exalting lovers court each other from the vantage point of a balcony that overlooks the ground. There the pompous and officious feting of agricultural labors reveals how such earthly labor impoverishes human life. Our shifting back and forth from balcony to ground level perpetually threatens a loss of perspective that prompts us to misread the continuities of action in the two discrete but juxtaposed loci of action, and to reawaken us to the knowledge of what we do not know. This in turn torques the motor of the narrative. As I have already indicated, irony and self-deception have in common the expectation of knowing what one doesn't already know. That has been my motive for seeing self-deception in more beneficent terms than self-asserting moral judgment typically allows. The other stylistic element that links Flaubert's aesthetic practice to the dynamics of self-deception is his making present-ness the modus operandi of expository development in the scene. The agricultural fair scene unfolds out of a knowledge of the simultaneity of actions. The flirtation of Emma and Rodolphe ensues as a rhythmic accompaniment to the ceremonial rites of the civic event: the oratorical benedictions over the virtues of the laboring peasantry, the bestowal of prizes for the most self-sacrificing toil upon the land. These are sites of unrelenting ironic reversals.

Irony, like self-deception, depends on a heightening of the self-consciousness of present-ness per se. Irony, like standard accounts of self-deception, taunts us with the impossible cohabitation of incommensurable but simultaneous contexts of knowledge. Such pressure to be present to two diverse venues of self-understanding is a spur to our attentiveness to the particularities of our life-circumstance generally. It correlates directly with Flaubert's challenge to his own reader's attentiveness. The reader must become attuned to the text's abrupt shifts of point of view, out of which the ironic momentum of the scene arises. Nevertheless, I must also point out that Flaubert's aesthetic practice requires our going beyond a simple analogy between irony and self-deception. Otherwise we will be unable to appreciate how his self-deceiving characters tell us something important about the ethical work of the novel. Irony situates us vividly in the present but resolves itself by vacating that moment of valuation. I want to suggest that self-deception articulates the present moment with what *ensues* as unprecedented value.

First, however, we must see how the actions that make Flaubert's novel such a touchstone for the theme of self-deception are, on that basis, as convincingly distinct from standard accounts of self-deception as I am suggesting they need to be. If we are to understand self-deception as a resource of rational self-possession in artworks, then the self-deception epitomized in the lovers' flirtation must in no way involve an attempt to deceive others. Neither should the self-deception support any analogy between self-deception and the deception of others. Such an analogy would certainly not apply to Rodolphe's self-deprecation of his clothing and leisure existence, or to Emma's affectation of humility. It is emphatically not apt with respect to the self-deception of the civic leaders who see their exploitation of the peasantry as beneficent patronage.

The self-deception in Flaubert's narrative is more richly intelligible in light of its exposing a broader range of human experiences than standard accounts of self-deception license. In this regard, we might note Herbert Fingarette's sense of urgency about assimilating our understanding of self-deception to ordinary experience—or as he puts it, "how the mind ordinarily and familiarly works" (162). Fingarette reminds us that we are mistaken when we fault the self-deceiver for not taking account of everything within his or her field of attention. He is pointing to the simple fact that the *context* of our self-understanding is never coextensive with the *content* of our self-understanding. This is so not because we are simply negligent, but because the relevant context—as Kent Bach and Alfred Mele already make quite clear—is broader and deeper than any conceivable limited perspective can encompass.

Flaubert dramatizes this circumstance of knowledge—which strikes me as the sine qua non of narrative emplotment—in two ways. First, at the level of characterization, we are insistently reminded that Rodolphe and Emma are striving to see themselves in each other's eyes. They are indeed looking to see before either one of them can be objectively seen. They refuse to be seen without the self-deceiving screen of imagining how they might be seen to be at their best. But neither wants to see the spectacle of his or her own hypocrisy. In other words, anticipating and ostensible beliefs come into play. Each wishes to be seen as the object of romantic desire and anticipates the evidence of reciprocity. Furthermore, each accepts the ostensible evidence that they are above the lustful intent that their anticipation embodies but their decorous speech belies. Rather, the decorous speech serves as an ostensible reason for believing in the anticipatory goals of romantic consummation.

Second, but just as important for my purposes, I want to emphasize how the reader is implicated in the same formal dynamic as the characters, but with a difference. My proposal here will be that some remedy for the problems of self-deception, insofar as they are thematized in the novel, can be found in the formal devices of this particular novel: not coincidentally this remediation is effected by Flaubert's maximizing the reversibility of the direction of dependency of reasons and beliefs as it obtains between character and reader. Flaubert's text plays upon this reversibility in a way that invites us to broaden the scope of reason to include self-deception. Rationality, in this regard, begins to focus the challenge of our attentiveness to what we do not know as a productive self-discipline.

As Amélie Rorty proposes, in an essay that lends some unexpected dignity to the self-deceiving self, one who is self-deceived is caught sustaining two pictures of reality that exist in a relation of superimposition with respect to each other: there is a picture of the self as a unified panoptical rational integrator and a picture of the self as atomized in the conflicting subsystems of desire and knowledge.[14] For Rorty, the intractability of self-deception betokens a power of mind, not a weakness. Rorty observes that "only a presumptively integrated person who interprets her system-of-relatively-independent-subsystems through the first *picture of the self,* only a person who treats the independence of her constituent subsystems as failures of integration, is capable of self-deception. Not everyone has the special talents and capacities for self-deception. It is a disease only the presumptively strong minded can suffer" (25). Rorty seems to think that what motivates the self-deceiver—in the urgency and earnestness of her compulsion to integrate—invites a degree of self-consciousness that would be unthinkable without the scruple of panoptical attentiveness. Capacities of critical reflection are thus entailed by the possibility of self-deception where the presupposition of an integrated self actively contends with discrepant subsystems of desire and knowledge. After all, the presumptively integrated self cannot be its own integrator. Hence it must know more about itself than it can give an account of in the immediacy of giving account. This is an inescapable warrant for critical self-reflection. The ideal aspired to here, the demand that must be served, denotes a resource of rationality that might not be tapped by the kind of mere rational self-assertion that the characters in Flaubert's scene otherwise seem egotistically habituated to. I therefore want to consider the possibility that the special talents Rorty extols as features of this rationality are nurtured by Flaubert's aesthetic practice so as to make us, the readers, "suffer" Rorty's notion of strong-mindedness. Such strong-mindedness, I will argue, allows us to feel the urgency of Kent Bach's formative question, what to do next? in a way that will sustain our sense of ourselves as plausibly rational agents.

Again, we must acknowledge the relevance of the present both to the recognition of self-deception as a normative condition and to the novel's attunement with the deliberative predicament occasioned by such knowledge. The question of what to do next only has urgency in the present. I want to show how Flaubert's orchestration of the agricultural fair scene marks progress by forcing us to ask ourselves, time and again, are we still in the moment, or are we in the next moment? This is corollary to the self-aware self-deceiver's question, do I know what I'm doing or saying? Sanford's notion of self-deception as a misapprehension of the structure of one's attitudes is epistemically coincident with this question and is likewise a crux of the reader's comprehension of Flaubert's method.

14. See Amélie Oksenberg Rorty, "The Deceptive Self: Liars, Layers, and Lairs," in *Perspectives on Self-Deception,* ed. Brian P. McLaughlin and Amélie Oksenberg Rorty (Berkeley and Los Angeles: University of California Press, 1988), 11–28.

In order to get at this crux, I will focus on Flaubert's alternation of the action between above-ground and below-ground venues. Flaubert's use of overlapping phrases and "rhyming" actions, in order to cue shifts of perspective, ensures that we will continue to question whether or not time has passed, whether or not space is continuous. By this means, he induces an unusually high standard of attentiveness. Present-ness becomes a condition of reflective scrupulousness for Flaubert's reader. To sample the pattern of Flaubert's practice, we need only begin a reading of the agricultural fair scene at the beginning. Rodolphe voices the sentiment that "a day comes" (Flaubert, *Madame Bovary*, 103) when happiness is realized. But his utopian aria is interrupted by the councilor, holding forth in the ceremony under way beneath the lovers' perch. The councilor is proclaiming that agricultural laborers are "men of progress," whose happiness comes through waiting out the storms of political change. The councilor's phrase "men of progress," his paean to forward-thinking human enterprises, punctually chimes with Rodolphe's progressive view of happiness in the ensuing moment of narration. Rodolphe says: "A day comes" when true love reveals itself by opening the horizon of one's despair. For emphasis, Rodolphe puts his hand over his eyes, blinding himself to his own blindness. The councilor immediately resumes below with allusion to the blindness of men imprisoned in the prejudices of old-fashioned thinking. He ends by heralding progress as a "duty" to serve the good of all. Conspicuously, "Duty" is the very next word out of Rodolphe's mouth. But he confesses being "sick of the word" (103). The effect is a deceptive continuity of action and thematic meaning between the action on the balcony and the action on the fairground.

Each of these strategic overlaps of word and deed reveals the shifting dependency of reasons and beliefs as a fulcrum of knowledge that ultimately divides the characters from the reader. While the self-deception on display here is merely descriptive of the characters' terminally developed personalities, it constitutes for the reader something like a further development of the critical capacities that Rorty hints are inherent to self-deceptive practice. By showing us a deceptive continuity of time and action, a perpetual present in the overlappings of similar but distinct actions and dialogue, Flaubert foregrounds the present-ness of our own decision-making. Flaubert is alerting us to the way that the remarks by the councilor, Rodolphe, and Emma are consistently expressing thoughts that can be taken quite differently if one shifts one's perspective. The present is the occasion for realizing the perspectival stakes of such shiftiness.

Because the relation of dependency between reason and belief is an operative variable of meaning here, we must put some pressure on it. For example, the councilor's paean to the progress of agriculture obtrudes between Rodolphe's two appeals to the coming of a "new day." In the first appeal Emma's hopeful belief in the possibility of her happiness appears to be aroused by reason of Rodolphe's confession of the torments of his own soul. Not coincidentally, these torments flow from the "world's point of view," which judges his passions harshly. As I have already suggested, point of view is the crucial stake of Flaubert's aesthetic practice here. The intrinsic instability of point of view is what the circumstance of self-deception highlights. Accordingly, Rodolphe re-presents his torment as a belief that the world's bad opinion of him gives him reason to refrain from seducing Emma. By the same token, Rodolphe's self-sacrifice would be reason for his belief in the just reward of Emma's surrender to his passionate need. On the other hand, Emma's willingness to believe in his unhappiness is a reason for her to entertain the possibility of fulfilling her own romantic fantasy, as if her own act of generosity toward one so needy as Rodolphe would be reason enough to believe in the necessity to consummate their love.

But after the interruption of the councilor's paean to progress, the argument has progressed to a new and different vantage point. The new day coming, when "one is near despair," is occasioned, according to Rodolphe, by a realization that "you feel the need of . . . giving everything, sacrificing everything to this person" (Flaubert, *Madame Bovary*, 103). This was the sentiment that we previously surmised bolstered Emma's reason for wanting to believe in the absolute generosity of the true lover suffering the scourge of social judgment. Emma was especially vulnerable to the thought of this generosity because it indulged her own best self-image. Now it is purveyed as Rodolphe's belief and, in turn, is revealed to be his reason for presuming upon Emma's vulnerability to such lovely sentiment. Of course Rodolphe's espousing the belief that one would give oneself helplessly is a good reason for sustaining his faith in Emma's susceptibility to seduction. But it reverses the direction of dependency of the belief stated earlier as a reason for selflessness. We recognize, after all, that he is now seeing his own personal need as the reason for the belief.

The deceptive continuity between Rodolphe's gesture of putting his hand over his face, with the councilor's invocation of "blindness" in the next overlapping effect, again reveals a reversal of the direction of dependency of reason and belief. But the revelation now hinges on the reader's self-conscious assumption of a "duty." I want to suggest that this is a duty not unlike that alluded to by both Rodolphe and the councilor. It is a duty that links the councilor's invocation of blindness to our possibility of seeing beyond the critical blindness that both he and Rodolphe epitomize. So it is a duty that we cannot shirk, as Rodolphe admits to doing, without risking complicity with Rodolphe's bad faith. The motion of Rodolphe's hand, characterized as the gesture of "a man about to faint," reveals a reason that is immediately belied by the narrator and, in that way, instantiates a scruple of the relevant duty. The reason, which we are told the gesture "suits," is Rodolphe's declaration that the recognition of love—that selfless desire!—is like the bedazzlement one experiences "if one went out from the darkness into the light" (Flaubert, *Madame Bovary*, 103). Following the action of Rodolphe's hand with the kind of heightened attentiveness that I have said self-deception induces, the narrator observes that the gesture is only completed when, lowered from the eyes, the hand is allowed to "fall on Emma's" hand (103). So we can see that what looked like a reason that would determine Rodolphe's belief in himself as selfless is in fact dependent on a belief in Emma's vulnerability. That vulnerability is, in turn, a plausible reason for the self-dramatizing gesture, which would denote a belief on Rodolphe's part, in his own pathos. Without the pathos he has to confront something like rapaciousness as his only reason for acting.

Or to put it another way, we can see that Rodolphe's belief in the bedazzlement of selfless love can serve him as a reason to impose that bedazzling ego-strengthened self upon another person—in a manner that resembles anything but love. In the immediate circumstance, this reason is of course propped up by Rodolphe's vociferous protest against the hypocrisy of a society that reviles love. We are inveigled to indulge the belief that society's persecutions of the lover would be a reason for Rodolphe's sexual aggressiveness toward Emma. But because we have already witnessed the hypocrisies entailed by the reversal in the direction of dependency between his reasons and beliefs, I think we are now imposed upon by the duty to reverse our own sympathies. In the more familiar terms of narrative emplotment, I would say that we feel the pressure to be more actively present in the fictive moment. Furthermore, we are encouraged to become present in precisely the manner of the self-deceiver in her vigilant assessment of competing evidentiary grounds for self-justifying beliefs (implicitly modes of action). I have already noted that this is an effect potentiated by Flaubert's strategy of shifting between the action on the balcony and the action on the fairground. We are impelled to attend more critically to the interpretive choices that the reversibility of the direction between reasons and beliefs proliferate. We are cued to understand that the shifts of evidentiary ground that are dramatized in the characters' jockeying for some self-justifying high ground—effectively mocked in the loftiness of the protagonists' physical perspective overlooking the ceremonies of the fair—are material to our way of being good readers of this text.

But it would be an oversimplification to say that we are merely meant to judge Rodolphe and Emma harshly, which is to say self-righteously. In other words, my point here is not simply to denote an occasion for ironic reversal, which is certainly a well-honored register of Flaubert's aesthetic success. Rather, the dynamic of a more compelling complication of human experience is being unfolded. It calls our rationality to account, even in the midst of what seems like tragicomic self-deception on the parts of the characters. In each instance of the reversal of dependency between reason and belief, there is evidence that the characters misapprehend the structure of their attitudes precisely because they see, in the successive moments of present time, more circumstantial evidence for reasoning further. Whatever else Rodolphe, Emma, and even the councilor are doing, they are sharpening their responsiveness to the condition of knowing themselves knowing themselves. They are sharpening their responsiveness to the task of mustering reasons to believe in themselves as acting in accordance with their need to be themselves. This shows the warrant for accepting, as Sanford says, that real self-deception requires an "element of rationalization" (167). Sanford's point here honors the caveat that such rationalization is creative until it becomes too self-serving. By this I mean that the self becomes too much an artifact of its own creativity rather than a modality of artfulness; it becomes an artifact of pastness rather than a counter of present-ness. I am most interested here in the way that self-service can risk the dissolution of selfhood with respect to the temporal exigencies that narrative art otherwise motivates us to respect.

This brings me back to our duty as readers and to the warrant for treating self-deception as a tool of rationalistic enterprise in a way that is ultimately divergent from the characters' fates in Flaubert's novel. I now want to suggest that the effect of Flaubert's aesthetic practice depends on actualizing the present-ness of the reader, producing a self that is especially sensitive to its relation to what it does not yet know about itself. Consider how Rodolphe, in his anticipation of Emma's response (she vacillates, takes up the devil's advocacy, if only for show), is prompted to entertain a range of ostensible reasons. Just as his ostensible reasons are thwarted by the moments of uncertainty that require him to adapt his anticipating beliefs, so Flaubert's reader also anticipates what ostensible reason for sympathy or ironic contempt will be forthcoming vis-à-vis Rodolphe and Emma. The alternations and overlappings of the action on the balcony and the fairground figure a present-ness that is perpetually challenging the self-knowledge of the reader even as it is conjuring the false appearance of simultaneity and stasis. So any idea that the reader's self is able to escape the uncertainties of the present more successfully than Flaubert's protagonists would seem to be self-deceived in the most conventional sense. To the contrary, Flaubert is interested in something more. I think Flaubert is tutoring the reader to become proficient at grasping self-deception as a modality of durable selfhood. This is something the characters know without being aware that they know it. The lack of self-consciousness about what informs their self-consciousness disposes them to repetitious behaviors. More to the point, it makes them prisoners of their facticity. The reader, however, transcends that facticity in a manner that is not prone to the stasis of repetition.

The point is perhaps made most effectively by a culminating episode of the agricultural fair scene that interestingly dovetails and contrasts with Jean Paul Sartre's account of bad faith (*mauvaise foi*) in *Being and Nothingness*.[15] Not coincidentally, Sartre's description of *mauvaise foi* has become bedrock for the conventional notions of self-deception I want to complicate. I am referring to the moment when Emma has permitted Rodolphe to cover her hand with his. She remains as impassive in that grip as she remains unresponsive to the beliefs that buttress Rodolphe's reasons for acting in this way. She even considers the justness of society's curbing the enthusiasms of passionate love. She says, "One must . . . to some extent bow to the opinion of the world and accept its morality" (Flaubert, *Madame Bovary*, 104). Conspicuously, however, she does not remove her hand. This behavior, which transcends the facticity of physical reality, the physical touch, permits her consciousness to fly above her bodily existence on the wings of abstract moralizing. The logic is immediately echoed by Rodolphe's postulate of a two-tiered morality: "the petty one of small men" and "the eternal that is about us and above like . . . the blue heavens that give us light" (104). When Emma's fingers move, it would seem involuntarily ("Perhaps she was trying to take it away or perhaps she was answering his pressure, at any rate, she moved her fingers"), Rodolphe avows his recognition that there is a reason for his belief in her, and hence a warrant to avow "I am yours!" Flaubert's final flourish, "Their fingers intertwined"

---

15. See Jean-Paul Sartre, *Being and Nothingness: An Essay on Phenomenological Ontology*, trans. Hazel E. Barnes (New York: Washington Square Press, 1973), 96–105 (the opening of chapter 2).

(107), unequivocally puts the burden upon what Amélie Rorty might call the reader's critical capacities, since the characters have just so conspicuously abdicated theirs.

It is hard to believe that Sartre did not have this moment from Flaubert in mind when he illustrated *mauvaise foi* by conjuring up the predicament of a woman who consents to a first date with a man knowing that his intentions are carnal. The moment of "truth" arises when, in the midst of his verbal seductions ("'I find you so attractive!'"), he takes her hand. The woman's challenge is to defer the moment of decision in which she would have to avow a belief that she cannot muster reasons to enact. Rather than withdraw her hand, she treats the physical contact as an accident. She ignores the implicit consent to flirt by shifting the direction of conversation: "She draws her companion up to the most lofty regions of sentimental speculation; she speaks of Life, of her life, she shows herself in her essential aspect—a personality, a consciousness."[16] Sartre argues that she "knows" what she is doing. She is entertaining two incompatible, contradictory aspects of human being, a facticity and a transcendence of that facticity. As Sartre says, "Bad faith seeks to affirm their identity while preserving their differences" (98). This would seem to be a classic case of the self-deceiver who would wish to be in two places of knowing at once, thus depreciating the value of such knowledge. This is the very paradigm I have been challenging. I have argued that it is too inflexible to yield behavior that might come into rational synch with the temporality that makes the world real to us. So there must be some way to reconcile facticity and transcendence. But it could not simply be a capitulation to the purity of either one of them. Nor could it be the unconvincing possibility of a synthesis between them that Sartre himself contemplates in somewhat bad faith.

In order to approach this possibility of reconciliation we need to compare Flaubert's and Sartre's exemplars of self-deception. As I have said, Rodolphe and Emma know what they do not seem to know. This is because they lack the self-consciousness of present-ness that the narrator's juxtapositions proffer to the reader. These juxtapositions are fulcrums for the reversal of direction of reasons and beliefs affecting our sympathies for the characters. I would argue that Sartre relegates his flirtatious woman to the same lack of self-consciousness as Flaubert's characters exhibit. He similarly denies her the essential predicate of human decision-making. Herbert Fingarette, in a productive disagreement with Sartre's notion of self-deception, emphasizes that only where we

---

16. Ibid., 97.

see the self-deceiver as making an avowal to know, exhibiting a volitional self-consciousness, is he or she realizing the human capacity to make avowals. It is the capacity to make avowals upon which any defensible concept of identity subsists. To avow is to establish one's "personal identity in some specific respect" (Fingarette, 69), some specific "identification as." The importance of the phrase "in some specific respect" is, for Fingarette, the guarantor of some comparative judgment by which one will own up to a specific relation to the world by disavowing an alternative. It authorizes "one's existence as a particular person" (71). Certainly, if self-deception entails disavowal of what would thwart one's avowal, it is likely to open our eyes to the fact that we could see otherwise. We would thereby face the prospect of looking elsewhere to ground our beliefs. Otherwise one is simply not witness to how the avowals are implicated in a process of decision-making. This would be the case however inadequate we might judge the reasons and beliefs propelling human action vis-à-vis the fullest context of knowledge in which action is potentially meaningful.

Posing the question, "How do we get into the situation where we do not know what we know?" (93), Fingarette observes that Sartre's answer is too reductive: loss of consciousness. Indeed, Sartre says that putting oneself in *mauvaise foi* is like putting oneself to sleep (Sartre, 95–96). Fingarette thinks Sartre misses a crucial element of self-deception, namely, how not knowing still entails knowing something. After all, it entails making an avowal of which evidentiary ground is the least costly investment for staking belief in one's own identity. This would be the case even if one avowed the disavowal of the knowledge that would spare one self-deception. Fingarette thinks Sartre makes this mistake because Sartrean bad faith is compulsorily measured against an ideal of an authentic self that is fixed, that is to say, a "fixed system of the self" (Fingarette, 95–96). Flaubert, by contrast, exercises his reader's capacity for making avowals by insisting on the present-ness of our decision-making selves vis-à-vis the fixed system of self epitomized in his characters. Here it is important to note that I am presupposing an inviolable distinction between present-ness and mere immediacy.

Immediacy is the ethically empty placeholder of consciousness in which Sartre's flirtatious woman seeks refuge from time grasped as a duly intelligible rather than a sensationally mindless experience. Present-ness, like Fingarette's "identification as," entails active consciousness. The character who does not know what she knows can come to knowledge only through a decision to instantiate herself by an avowal of what knowledge she possesses. This is the case however contingent on shifting evidentiary grounds such knowledge may turn out to be. This presupposes a notion of human identity as perforce active. I would argue that while we see the activity of Flaubert's characters in their reversing of the direction of dependency between reasons and beliefs, we do not see our own complicity with them until we are forced into the same kind of decision-making. We are led to this in the experience of reading Flaubert's text wherever contextual parameters require an avowal of reading them from another viewpoint. I have staked my argument on the claim that this is what Flaubert's structuring of the agricultural fair scene accomplishes. In a sense narrative fiction generally involves this activity of adapting to new evidentiary grounds for one's avowals of what one knows one knows.

If, upon our first reading of *Madame Bovary,* we simply judge the characters to be acting in self-deceiving ways, without acknowledging/avowing our complicity in the mechanisms of such self-deception, we will make the mistake of thinking we stand outside the processes of rationalization. Flaubert inhibits this mistake by juxtaposing the balcony and ground levels of the agricultural fair scene. The alternating structure of the agricultural fair scene reveals us to be inside rather than outside—the outside of ironic distance—the predicament of the characters. We are hence that much more present to the fiction. The outside of ironic distance would be too much an indulgence of knowledge at the expense of action, specifically the act of reading. Our present-ness "inside" is a function of the fact that the forms of fictional narrative constitutively present the temporal dilemma of knowing that *one doesn't know yet.* This is also a quintessential predicament of living. Living is perforce living in the present. It demands recognition of our inexorable alternation between facticity and transcendence. Sartre's making the facticity and transcendence of the self-deceiving character (the creature of bad faith) mutually exclusive states fails to realize the possibility of their continuity through alternation. The virtue of seeing this continuity, as Fingarette has anticipated, is the possibility of accommodating a notion of character that is adaptable with respect to what knowledge he or she lacks. This knowledge, according to Fingarette, would be avowable under specifiable constraints of reasoning for better or worse.

The common criticism of Sartre's flirtatious woman is that she fetishizes the present by taking herself out of the time in which she would be too vividly reminded of the gravitational yearnings of her sexual body. But I think this explanation is just a way of taking the concept of the present itself out of time, of confusing immediacy and present-ness. Action, fully considered, precludes this oversimplification. Perhaps this is why, at the beginning of his book on self-deception, Fingarette calls for a "de-emphasis of the relation of consciousness to knowledge, and the emphasis of its relation to action" (64). With this admonition, Fingarette means for us to see the self-deceiver in tandem with agency-enhancing practices that I maintain have been the métier of the novelist since the genre's inception. Now we might even suspect the disingenuousness of Flaubert's confiding to Louise Colet his anxiety that not enough is happening in *Madame Bovary*. For the agricultural fair scene (Flaubert, *Madame Bovary*, 313–19) shows us how "ideas are actions," inasmuch as readers can be reminded of their agency in reading novels as a particular condition of human character.

So we have seen how the characters'—Emma's, Rodolphe's, the councilor's—words are actions. They constitute a fulcrum of reasoning across which the stakes of identity seesaw back and forth as a function of hypothesis testing and of the shifting of evidentiary grounds for motivational biases. If we can see this, then perhaps we can see something more. We are made aware that we see all this by means of our own participation in the protocols of hypothesis testing. Flaubert's alternation of viewpoints—challenging our orientation to what motivational biases may affect our sympathy with or antipathy toward the fictional characters whose own motivational biases are so labile—tells us something about the intrinsic fictionality of our own character as readers. We are as dependent as Flaubert's characters on apprehending how any misapprehension of our attitudes does not therefore presuppose a "fixed system of the self," one possessed of a finite repertoire of avowals. Rather, it denotes a repertoire constantly in need of expansion or new justifications.

Self-deception is curiously instrumental to such an enterprise. In fact, one might say that the reader of the novel form, historically speaking, has always been vividly present to the text in this capacity. But he has not always realized or accepted the duties of this human predicament. Flaubert insists upon spelling out our doing our duty in a way that not all novelists do. Flaubert's insistence is redeemed by our recognition that the human self that reads novels would certainly benefit from assuming such duties, from spelling them out. Certainly, Fingarette's theory of self-deception is predicated on the proposition that self-deceivers resist spelling out the conditions under which they act, the terms of their engagement with the world (Fingarette, 39). But this is because they are focusing upon other forms of engagement. This is not due to their passivity. They are agents, not victims, of self-deception. For they are bound by the necessity of instantiating themselves in avowals that preclude one instance of spelling out in favor of other circumstances that will presumably warrant a spelling out of their own.

What's more relevant for my purpose is that Fingarette links the mode of self-deception involved here to the willing suspension of disbelief that is commonly ascribed to the fictive reality of artworks. Fingarette declares: "The so-called 'suspension of disbelief' essential in the arts is in fact the focusing of attention on the artistic content of the work, and the systematic avoidance of focusing attention on its aesthetically non-relevant properties, even while still taking account of them" (175). The fluidity of motivational biases that underwrites our recognition of the emotional, psychological reality of fictional characters is likewise the means by which our willing suspension of disbelief is enabled. It is the indexical marker of our present-ness as readers. In other words, present-ness in this context is another name for the quality of attentiveness that the imperative of decision-making imposes. One feels the pressure of it when, in the course of instantiating one's self through one's avowals, one is confronted with the instability of ratios of information vis-à-vis what one knows and what one wants to know, between what one has reason to believe and what one believes for the reasons he can circumstantially muster. Thus to be present is to open the idea that knowledge of self-deception is a normative duty of what Audi calls "conscientious consciousness" (150). This consciousness is marked by its vigilance with respect to other motivational grounds.

The last line of Flaubert's novel is perhaps most dispositive for these claims. It occurs in quick succession with an equally swift montage of plot reversals that conclude the narrative action. The reasons that shore up Charles Bovary's highly theatrical bereavement are quickly undercut by the unexpected discovery of Leon's and Rodolphe's letters, his unexpected encounter with Rodolphe in which he is seduced to play Emma's part as the foil for Rodolphe's vanity, his utterly untheatricalized death, and the dispatching of his daughter to reside ultimately with a distant aunt. The avalanche of events induces a sense of forward inertia. This thrill of eventfulness is enhanced as the narrative shifts abruptly into the present tense. We learn of Charles, "He *was* [my emphasis] dead." We are told of the daughter: "She *is* [my emphasis] poor, and [the aunt] sends her to a cotton-mill to earn a living" (Flaubert, *Madame Bovary*, 255).

In the ultimate sentence of the novel, cast in most English translations in the present perfect tense (in French a forward-looking present tense), Flaubert crystallizes the disposition of knowledge in relation to action as it bears on the character of his reader. He furthermore illuminates how his reader's judgments of his characters raises the stakes of understanding the complexities of human character in general. We are peremptorily informed that Homais the pharmacist "has just been given the cross of the Legion of Honor" (Flaubert, *Madame Bovary*, 255). Flaubert's final form of address to the reader makes our knowledge that judgment is a function of what we do not know operative in a manner that joins the theme of self-deception with a practical capacity. Bach, Audi, Mele, and Fingarette all concur that this should be the direction of our thinking.

The ongoingness denoted in the shift to present tense is demonstrative of the reader's dependency on a time that ensues beyond the power of immediate self-understanding and—even more emphatically in this case—beyond the powers of the reader's desire to see justice done, which would be tantamount to being self-possessed. Homais's undeserved triumph, purveyed as the coincidence of the verb tense/temporality of the fictional world with the temporality of the labor of reading, implicates the act of reading in the knowledge that knowing more will be the imperative of knowing better. The present perfect and/or present tense signal our responsibility to the changing conditions of self-avowal that is a crucial threshold of the self-deceiving mind. Flaubert's closure in *Madame Bovary* coheres with my proposition that the way of being in narrative time requires a responsiveness to the conditions of self-deception—what Fingarette might call the locating of the self in avowal—as a sine qua non of ethical character. For in the narrative of *medias res,* the present-ness of reading, we know the inescapability of knowing that we need to know more. Being mindful of self-deception is a potentiation of powers of mind that are inescapably bound to the circumstance of present-ness. This is most acutely so where such knowing presses urgently upon the levers of ethical obligation.

Coda

To speak of ethical obligation in the shadow of Flaubertian form is to realize how swiftly that shadow moves in relation to contemporary narrative experimentation in the novel. As I indicated at the commencement of this argument—and particularly in the novel since 1945—character becomes increasingly a site for the intensification of present-ness and, in that respect, a marker for the transformation of novelistic form. If, as I have suggested in my reading of Flaubert, the novel has "long harbored a notion of character that has resisted characterization," it might be fitting to conclude with a quick survey of novelists for whom this notion portends a convergence of ethical obligation and aesthetic innovation. Since I have made self-deception a predicate of such a characterization of the novel, as well as the characters it harbors, I would take Samuel Beckett, John Hawkes, and Joseph McElroy as exemplary practitioners of the novel for whom knowing is an expressly transitive burden of narrating. What makes them exemplars for me is their common stake in compositional strategies that call the reader to account for the present-mindedness of misreading. This is more than plot reversal and certainly more than a typological illustration of the phenomenon of the self-deceiving mind. What these innovators always presuppose, in their formal enterprise, is the reader's characterization as one who must deny the lucidity of the evidentiary grounds for their reading correctly in order to read correctly. Self-deception and rationalization, as I have suggested throughout this chapter, become reciprocal mandates of self-realizing ambition. I will necessarily be brief in these sketches. The implications of what I am saying will unfold more fully in later chapters.

The Beckett of the last short novels—*Company, Worstward Ho!* and *Ill Seen, Ill Said*—deploys what I have elsewhere characterized as a "parsimonious syntax" whereby the eliding of syntactical elements (e.g., articles, prepositions) seems to render one's sense of narrative lucidity an artifact of a yet unrecognized error. Elsewhere I have asserted that the strategy of parsimonious syntax has the effect of instantiating a "self in error" (Singer, 91). But error, in this case, is not a malignant unintelligibility; it is a warrant for rationalization. Particularly in *Ill Seen, Ill Said* Beckett complements his syntactical strategy with the conjuring of an invisible interlocutor whose admonitions to the reader to go slow and be wary of error, render present-ness and contextual refiguration consonant with each other.[17] The admonitory refrain of the voice anticipating ineluctable error in Beckett's narrative devolves exclusively to the reader's fate. The reader knows how much the authority of one's reading is a function of *spelling out* (to use Fingarette's phrase) the conditions of one's knowledge claims.

John Hawkes and Joseph McElroy give us even more contemporary evidence that the possibilities of formal innovation in the novel depend—for the sustenance of its contemporaneity—upon the narration of the self through the labyrinth of self-deception. Hawkes I believe is too glibly acknowledged as an innovator by dint of his enthusiasm for the unreliable, self-deceiving narrator. I think in fact that the rhetorical pyrotechnics for which his self-deceiving first person narrators are renown obscure a more interesting and consequential innovation: this author's willingness to allow catachrestic figuration to complicate

---

17. Samuel Beckett, *Nohow On: Company, Ill Seen, Ill Said, Worstward Ho* (London: Calder, 1989).

a reader's prioritization of evidentiary contexts for discerning the boundaries between the narrator's imagination and the realities which it both constrains and by which is constrained. It is on this basis that Hawkes's fictions—particularly works like those which make up the triad of *The Blood Oranges, Death, Sleep and the Traveler,* and *Travesty*—present us with a narrator whom we suspect of self-deception in the conventional sense that I have been challenging. But this narrator's self-deceiving gestures reveal a risk of contamination to the reader. It is a contamination that is more virulent than mere knowledge that things are otherwise than the narrator is willing to admit. The excesses of imagistic elaboration that at times threaten to arrest the narrative plot nonetheless actualize a prospect for thinking that every elaboration of the figurative register portends our reckoning with the necessity of knowing more than we know.

Joseph McElroy's recent novel, *Actress in the House*,[18] offers the most vitally contemporary gloss upon self-deception as a mode of human creation in which present-ness is the sine qua non of aesthetic value. Such brief mention as I have space for here can hardly do justice to McElroy's innovation. But the hallmark of his métier is decisive for furthering the thinking I have attempted to provoke in this chapter and for grounding my own desire to keep faith with *fiction's present*. McElroy's novel proceeds by a kind of recursive syntax wherein the point of view frequently appears to be unmarked, unless one learns to read retrospectively. But the retrospect is neither backward looking nor nostalgic. Rather, it appears to be improvisational. A moment when McElroy has his protagonist physically poised in the narrator's thought of her is exemplary. Becca Lang is sexually present to the narrator. But in a syntactical instant she is traversing space and time beyond the boundaries of any individual body: "Becca was at the bureau drawers for a moment, the Sunday-night sour expression passed across the fine wide mouth, she was no pet to tend, and yet, almost naked in white underpants you could see the pale and shadowy behind through. That is what she was. She herself in the cab going downtown to the movie yesterday had betrayed a certain knowledge of Dutch Guyana. The once and 'former' Suriname the super hailed from" (McElroy, 310).

Each word doesn't so much fit the sentence as makes the sentence fit a world whose dimensions we are still learning to compass. We go back in time at least twice from the moment at the bureau drawers, to the moment in the cab, to the moment in world history, as if we are deceived at every point where we think we know what time it might be. Though the retrospect seems linear,

---

18. Joseph McElroy, *Actress in the House* (New York: Overlook, 2004).

we are really going forward on a trajectory of speculation about how best to incorporate what we do not comprehend at the moment, such as the fact that the "super" resides with and is custodian of Becca's residence. McElroy has always been a writer seeking to make thinking an ever more transitive enterprise by means of such contextual transits back and forth on divergent trajectories. In *Actress,* the entire plot is predicated on what may be false perception: that an actress on stage has been *actually* slapped, rather than merely represented to be so victimized. In McElroy's fiction the prospect of being so mistaken is the prospect of becoming connected to the world in ways that the stigma of mere error absolutely precludes.

What all of these fictions of the present have in common then is a vital rapport with the quandary of knowing one's self through the detours of the self-deceiving mind. They better acquaint us with the pressures that temporal experience brings to bear as we learn to bear its duration. The forms of the novel that are most responsive to the self-deceiving mind—rather than the novels in which the self-deceiving character is merely characterized—may be the most scrupulous witnesses to fiction's present. By attending to the formal imperatives of novels and paintings, photographs, videos and films, in the ensuing chapters of this work, we may match that scrupulousness by our effort to more fully realize the constructive powers of the self-deceiving mind. We shall see that whatever the artistic métier, self-deception portends an ethical, ethos-laden development of which only time can tell.

2

Illusionism and the Self-Deceiving I

Thinking Through Illusionism

If self-deception implies an ethos in time, we might gloss Hegel's "Notion" as a historical reference point for the development of that ethos. Hegel's "Notion," as elaborated in the *Science of Logic* (1812),[1] makes an interesting premise for considering the specifically ethical relation of knowledge to ignorance, without which any motive for countenancing self-deception as favorable or unfavorable is almost unimaginable. The Notion, after all, proffers a métier for self-superseding experience. In this way it furthers my assertions in chapter 1 about character development as a crux and counter of aesthetic value. For, with the Notion, Hegel famously presupposes a mode of subjective consciousness propelled by ignorance: one that is nonetheless experientially grounded in its own historical trajectory. On this assumption, subjective consciousness is always moving beyond its immediate powers of self-recognition, but never abdicates its responsibility to ongoing experience. If, as Hegel maintains, the Notion is the relation of being to essence, where essence is the first negation of being, being *de facto* becomes illusory being. And if the Notion proper is the second negation, or the negation of this negation (Hegel, *Logic,* 596), then the underlying stakes of Hegel's speculative inquiry demand something like a respect for illusionism. As Robert Pippin observes, "Essence and appearance . . . are not understood as separate beings, but as 'moments' of any being that reflection can identify and understand."[2] For Hegel reflective mind seems to entail the plot reversals of illusionism, that is to say, the transition from being to essence as the condition of its universal objectivity.

---

1. G. W. F. Hegel, *Hegel's Science of Logic,* trans. A. V. Miller (Atlantic Highlands, N.J.: Humanities Paperback Library, 1969).
2. Robert Pippin, *Hegel's Idealism: The Satisfactions of Self-Consciousness,* (Cambridge: Cambridge University Press, 1989), 202.

Inasmuch as essence and appearance are the controlling terms of Hegel's account of reflective consciousness, one could argue that the reflective capacity itself is implicated in a drama of self-deception. One might even risk the generalization that self-deception exhibits a Notional logic in the narrative articulations of literary and visual art forms. It is important to recall that Hegel's (and Fichte's) innovation in understanding subjective self-relation and selfhood is purveyed as a repudiation of Kant. Notional thinking challenges the idea that pure thought is conditioned upon an a priori form, a spontaneous self-relation that preempts narrative rationalization. Hence Hegel's emphatic distinction between appearance, understood as a subject without a predicate, or the "thing without qualities," and the determinate being of the subject, understood as the preserve of the Notion (*Logic*, 628). Hegel's corollary emphasis on determinacy over immediacy compels a shifting of our attention away from the Kantian predetermined forms of experience to the tribulations of formative activity tout court. Within this frame of reference, we can treat illusoriness as a métier of determinative subjectivity. If self-deception inheres in the rationalizing project of our contending with the illusoriness of subjective determination, perhaps it throws off the stigma of irrationality.

The underpinning of Hegel's critique of Kantian idealism is the assertion that one cannot represent the immediacy of experience as Kantian schemata purport to do. I would like to suggest that self-deception bears out this claim because its rationalistic/rationalizing trajectory can only be realized in the prospect of further determinations. The practice of trompe l'oeil illusionism in the history of visual arts offers a vivid dramatization of this exigency of self-deception. It might thereby serve as a stage for speculating upon the ethical and creative fruits unintentionally bequeathed to theorists of self-deception by Hegel's corrective to Kant. Illusionism is, after all, a representational practice that seeks something like the representation of immediacy without incurring the Kantian contradictions. Hegel famously and controversially aspires to an accounting of immediacy that is mediated: "an immediacy" that is representable, but within the "moment" of its representability, renders representation indecipherable as such (Pippin, *Hegel's Idealism*, 209).[3] Trompe l'oeil usefully presents this indecipherability as an ability of the viewer to see beyond the bounds of the immediacy that seeing denotes when we stand within the

---

3. Again Pippin reminds us that Hegel's success in this endeavor depends upon the notions of *Schein* and reflection. My interest in the visual conceit here presumes upon this assumption. In his preface to *Phenomenology of Spirit*, trans. A. V. Miller (Oxford: Oxford University Press, 1977), Hegel makes it quite clear that reflection presupposes Notional self-movement.

horizon of a unique objectification of reality. But trompe l'oeil renders that horizon permeable. Where we penetrate this horizon, the indecipherability of representation itself becomes the cipher of a new ability. It is one that we might fruitfully contemplate as Hegel's faith in the becoming of being, where becoming makes illusoriness coherent with actuality or *Wirklichkeit*.

The concept of *Wirklichkeit*, which preoccupies Hegel in book 2 of his *Science of Logic*, is preeminently a counter for a transumptive relationality. It compels our respect for all that belies immediate appearance and thereby makes us creatures of determinative consciousness. I want to speculate that this is where the experience of illusionism, such as trompe l'oeil, helps us see as our destiny that which we are otherwise predisposed to reject. We are naturally averse to the risks of accepting determination as the sine qua non of our ethical commitments in a world where commitments can be costly. We can, after all, be mistaken in our sense of what we are doing in taking up a commitment. Self-deception apprises us of this cost. Trompe l'oeil is, in one sense, a staging ground for such appraisals. Likewise, the crossroad at which we arrive in every instance of literary emplotment—from the moment of Oedipus's fateful confrontation with his father—puts us on the threshold of such self-deception. Self-deception assays the reader's willingness to run the risks of self-determination, *to bear the costs*. In this chapter and the next I want to think about how both the visual and literary registers of self-deceiving experience denote a substrate of human self-understanding that is inescapable in our ambition to claim a moral nature for ourselves, to bear the costs of not knowing what one is doing. I am suggesting that such an enterprise pegs our valuation of aesthetic objects to *bearing the costs* of determination or development. Such is the ethical crux of Hegelian self-consciousness after all.

Though it may sound heretical to say so, illusionism and trompe l'oeil in particular, which I obviously want to see as counters for self-deception, have their art-historical and their formal/practical roots in an idea of moral nature. It is a morality by which theologians sought to hold the power of illusion in check: iconoclasm. Iconoclasm,[4] like trompe l'oeil and self-deception, takes its authority from a dialectic of concealment and revelation. Iconoclasm, from its earliest manifestations as an instrument of Greco-Roman law, to the strictures of Judaic mysticism, to the early Christian sanctions against representations of divinity and the Counter-Reformational proscriptions against realistic

---

4. See Alain Besançon's *The Forbidden Image: An Intellectual History of Iconoclasm*, trans. Jane Marie Todd (Chicago: University of Chicago Press, 2009).

portrayals of the physical body, presents what it interdicts representations of. That is to say, in every historical instance of iconoclastic ideology what is *not* to be represented entails a protocol of concealment. But it is hopelessly contaminated by reference to what it would otherwise judge to be profane.[5]

While the term "trompe l'oeil" did not gain currency until the early nineteenth century (1803, in the *Petit Robert*),[6] illusoriness has been a locus of representational practice since the first images appeared on the cave walls at Chauvet and Lascaux. Broadly speaking, mimetic images are presentations of what is not there. There are art historians, however, who want to distinguish between illusionism and trompe l'oeil proper on the premise that trompe l'oeil is a culturally self-conscious "game" of deception. It is predicated on mimetic fidelity to perception, whereas illusionism does not presuppose a normative perceptual order from which we can stray or about which we can be mistaken.[7] Illusionism purports to be what it represents. But insofar as mimetic fidelity is necessarily delusive—by virtue of its meticulously unwitting annunciation of absence—it reveals as much as it conceals both about the world and the viewer of the world. The sharpness of any distinction between trompe l'oeil and illusionism is further blurred by the famous anecdote, out of Pliny the Elder, about the contest between Zeuxis and Parrhasius.

Parrhasius's trumping of his audience's expectations, by painting a curtain purporting to reveal a painting behind a curtain, belies, as Jacques Lacan points out—for reasons that are congruent with my own purpose—a trumping of illusionism itself.[8] As Lacan would have it, Pliny's anecdote is a powerful intimation that self-deception inheres in the desire structure of all representational practices: at least where desire figures itself in representations of the object world it seeks to possess. In this way Parrhasius's feat is transparently

---

5. Marie-José Mondzain's exhaustive exploration of Byzantine iconoclastic controversies in the eighth and ninth centuries supports my intimation of an inescapable dialectic of revelation and concealment. In *Image, Icon, Economy: The Byzantine Origins of the Contemporary Imaginary*, trans. Rico Franses (Stanford: Stanford University Press, 2004), Mondzain considers the ambition of the church to produce an account of the spiritual status of a religious image. The desire to authorize the image in a way that would not be susceptible to the charge of idolatry was resolved by a dual doctrine: the image, invisible.

6. See Marie-Louise D'Otrange Mastai, *Illusion in Art: Trompe l'Oeil, A History of Pictorial Illusionism* (New York: Abaris Books, 1975), 8.

7. See, for example, Eckhard Hollman, *A Trick of the Eye: Trompe l'oeil Masterpieces*, trans. Jürgen Tesch (New York: Prestel Publishing, 2004).

8. Lacan's exegesis of the anecdote is coordinate with his exposition of the "gaze" (*le regard*), where the stakes of subjectivity are caught up in the "deception" of *méconnaisance*. Though the consequences of this Lacanian self-deception lead in a different speculative direction than what I intend here, the stakes themselves are anchored in the same "illusion" of autonomous selfhood. See Jacques Lacan, *The Four Fundamentals of Psychoanalysis*, trans. Alan Sheridan (New York: W. W. Norton, 1973).

iconoclastic. Trompe l'oeil and illusionism both deprive us of a secure evidentiary ground for asserting our commitments to reality. But at the same time they hold us to account for our groundedness in the assertability of commitments. As Fingarette has advised us, we are the efficacy of our avowals.

In his *Optics* and *Rules for the Direction of Mind* (published posthumously in 1701),[9] Descartes exploited the illusoriness of vision in a way that reveals how the power of mind or *cogito* is inextricably bound to the kind of frailty of visual perception I have alluded to.[10] Descartes's sponsorship of mathematical experimentation with the illusionistic visual practice of anamorphic projection epitomizes his relevance to this argument about trompe l'oeil and illusionism.[11] Anamorphic projection specifically reveals the concealment of mind in the revelation and apprehension of appearances. Mirror anamorphosis in particular turns a flat unintelligible visual gestalt into a lucid three-dimensional representation of objects in space. In Descartes's deployment of a cylindrical mirror to reflect the "irrational" sensuous presentation figured upon the flat surface where the mirror is erected, he debunks mere visual perception. He shows us that visual form is antithetical to sensuous intuition. On the contrary, it is revealed to be a conceptual-technical construct.

But Descartes is an iconoclast with a difference. Unlike the iconoclasm of the Jewish mystics and the early Christian fathers, Descartes's *contemptus imago* is an assertion of the powers of the cogito. It is the faculty that knows what appearances belie. Descartes's anamorphic cylinder elicits knowledge of what is not there as an object of thought by heightening our attentiveness to the signifying properties of what is merely an object of thought. What implicates Descartes more deeply than theological iconoclasts in the experiential *terra firma* of appearance is his needing the concept of its illusoriness, and so needing a richer and richer imagination for the particular features of the apparent object's presentational aspects. After all, the negation of such features is the only leverage he has for limning what we must uncomfortably conclude are the correlative features of the cogito. In other words, Descartes makes appearances a register of fallible cognition. And yet such appearances figure the fallibility

---

9. René Descartes, *The Philosophical Writings of René Descartes*, vol. 2, trans. John Cottingham, Robert Toothoff, and Dugald Murdoch (New York: Cambridge University Press, 1984).

10. Dalia Judovitz gives the best overview of Descartes's way of implicating the Enlightenment subject in the register of visuality. She points out that the relocation of visual semblance within a mathematical schematism "constitutes a new point of view, based on the instrumentalization of both optics and pictorial perspective." Judovitz, "Vision, Representation, and Technology in Descartes," in *Modernity and the Hegemony of Vision*, ed. David Michael Levin (Berkeley and Los Angeles: University of California Press, 1993), 69.

11. See Jurgis Baltrušaitis, *Anamorphic Art* (New York: Harry N. Abrams, 1977).

of the cogito as a plausible occasion for my beneficent sense of self-deception: self-deception understood as the self-imposed mandate to know more. We will see in the final chapter of this work how the anxieties implicit in this knowledge of the cogito almost demand a discipline of self-deception if the self is going to be kept honest with itself.

Trompe l'oeil, which I take as a mode of illusoriness that is fully coordinate with anamorphosis and orthodox illusionism, is an occasion for knowing more because it is a pretext for seeing or sensing more than appearance portends. I began by referencing my argument to the Hegelian dialectic inherent to the Notion. This is because I believe Hegel gives us an excuse for thinking how important the expectation of knowledge is to the self-deceiver, who would otherwise merely appear to know less than he might—given the self-inhibiting irrationality of his predicament. On this basis I can more plausibly suggest how much sense it might make to see the self-deceiver as integral to a world of rationality that is not self-preemptively normative in the strict sense of unshakable conceptual prejudice. Seeing the self-deceiver as bound to know more in a Notional way will help us appreciate how our rational conceptualizing is itself beholden to worldly engagements at the level of sense and activity. On that threshold of experience we are always contending decisively with Kent Bach's defining question for the human subject: what do I do next? On the threshold of this question we keep faith with the mandate for normativity despite any doubts we may have about the "truthfulness" of any particular norms.

An emphasis on the visual arts, to be elaborated in the next chapter, and even more exhaustively in chapters 5 and 6, will make this point more compelling while strengthening links with the other métiers of aesthetic production. But first we must revisit Hegel's Notion proper and its teasing out of an unexpected coherence between self-deception and productive reflection. As I have already intimated, the Notion, whereby essence develops through its negation of determinate being, has (like the illusory mimesis of trompe l'oeil) its own specular or reflective dimension. Self-supersession is the fruit of its reflective labor. For Hegel something like the dynamic of concealment and revelation, which animates the vital conundrums of iconoclasm and visual illusionism in art, inheres in the development of self-consciousness through the negation of otherness.

Here, however, it is important to stipulate Hegel's refusal to countenance the negation of otherness such that otherness per se is taken into the self as a quality of its being. This is what Hegel rejects as a "spurious infinite" (Pippin, *Hegel's*

Idealism, 196). Hegel wants to ward off the threat that the otherness that is other to another would instantiate the self as indifferent: as merely other to an infinity of others. Quite to the contrary, further determinateness is what Hegel's phenomenology proffers to selfhood. Robert Pippin explains that "Hegel means instead to insist that properties immediately attributed to a thing must themselves be capable of some *contrastive work* [my emphasis], of excluding other properties concretely, and so of distinguishing the thing from other things that have such properties and that the thought of immediate *Dasein* cannot accomplish the task" (196).

Having a "contrastive effect" presupposes that a self-consciousness realizing its de facto illusory essence—through the negation of a specific being—precludes specific properties other than those of the object whose negation instantiates essence in the first place as illusory. As I suggested earlier, essence is perforce illusory. For the negation of a specific thing inheres in the knowledge of the limitations that obtain as the condition of the thing's being negated. Hence, other properties of other things are deemed not to be determinative. But they nonetheless may become determinative for other moments of self-realization. Essence, after all, says Hegel, "has *no determinate being;* but it must develop determinate being, for it is both *in itself* and *for itself,* itself, i.e., it *differentiates* the determinations which are *implicit* [*an sich*] in it" (*Logic,* 390). Hegel is thus emphatic that self-consciousnesss is a mode of determinate relationality with respect to what appears, as well as to what is excluded by that appearance. "Contrastive effect" is Hegel's hedge against indifference, that is to say, the "spurious infinite." Because he rejects the idea that a thing can be "indifferently" other than everything, he precludes the possibility that finite objects can be conceived as radically independent. Appearance (*Schein*) is a show of vanishing determinacy. This is so inasmuch as appearance is more than what it shows itself to be. Thus does it occasion contrastive relations as a condition of Notional truth. In the last chapter of the *Logic* we understand that essence and appearance therefore cannot be understood as separate beings but must be understood, in Pippin's words, as "'moments' of any being that reflection can identify and understand" (*Hegel's Idealism,* 202). The moments are orchestrated in a typical pattern of triplicity. First, the essence that issues from being through negation, seemingly as an opposite being, is deemed unessential. But it is more than just "unessential being." It is "*illusory being.*" And yet this illusory being is not something external to essence. Rather, "*The showing of this illusory being within essence itself is* reflection" (Hegel, *Logic,* 394).

So, reflection itself is unthinkable without the succession of moments that is sublated being.

In the previous chapter we saw how attuned these moments are to the prospect of *knowing more*. I identified this attunement as an imperative of the experience of present-ness (not to be confused with the purported immediacy of *Schein*). Therefore, we might now speculate upon the ethical stakes that I intimated were implicit in that experience. After all, "contrastive effects" ordain further determinations of knowledge according to which we are bound reflectively in the work of discriminating the various grounds of our judgment. I previously referred to this as the effective shifting of evidentiary grounds that is entailed by hypothesis testing. The negative determinacy of the Hegelian subject is a ratification of the idea that we are all irrepressible hypothesis testers. Reflecting upon any particular evidentiary ground, I do indeed become self-conscious of what ground I have excluded as a basis of judgment.

This is also why syllogism becomes such an important lever of Hegel's argument in the *Logic*. Syllogistic thinking is perforce a thinking through, qua contrastive effects. In syllogism, determinations are thinkable in their relationality but in such a way that we are never through with thinking. Neither does syllogism succumb to a "spurious infinite" of thought. Rather, syllogism helps Hegel shore up a distinction between the subject who judges and makes assertions and the subject of a propositional logic whereby what is asserted is preemptively isolated from its contingencies. A mere proposition can become a judgment only if asserted against some possibility of doubting it (Hegel, *Logic*, 235).

Within the form of syllogism we see the logical necessity of one conceptual scheme as standing in determinate relation to another. The Notion of a determinate relation here is to be understood *developmentally*, that is to say, as fostering developmental connections.

Robert Pippin summarizes this insight in a way that buttresses my desire to see that what might seem to be Hegel's unduly elusive account of a phenomenon of continuous determination actually has practical relevance for agents. Pippin fills in the most troublesome expositional gaps of Hegel's argument as follows:

> That is, if the correctness of propositions and . . . judgments depends on Notional criteria that change, then what was "true" relative to one moment in the Notion's development turns out not to be true relative to another. Since some prior Notion is not really an "alternative" to a

later one, but both are "necessary" in the Notion's full development, then both kinds of claims are indeed true, even if contradictory. (This is not a full-blown contradiction, since it is not the case that both judgments are true "in the same respect," but the rejection of bivalence is clear nevertheless.) (*Hegel's Idealism*, 240)

In other words, "Notional development" implies that the "correctness of propositions" has its own inferential trajectory with respect to contexts of explanation that are, in turn, the consequences of any specific propositional assertion. Hegel's rejection of bivalence mandates the kind of narrative successiveness to which I have tied the fate of the self-deceiver. The self-deceiver, by this account, is always a follower of inferences. He is consequently never merely a dupe of whatever knowledge serves the self of the moment.

I do not believe I distort the experiential vectors of Hegel's thinking, as they are invoked here, if I suggest their usefulness in locating the epistemic value of illusionism, for example, trompe l'oeil, vis-à-vis Notional truth. Both phenomena support an inferentialist imperative. This is cognate with the beneficent ethical prospect portended in my assumption that self-deception might serve as a framework for rationalization. Hegel's unequivocal preference for judgment over proposition is signaled, after all, by his sense that the latter merely evokes a standard by which an object can be judged "correct," while the former presumes upon a "truthfulness inherent to the 'agreement of an object with itself.'"[12] The more rigorous judgment inherent to Notional truth (*Wahrheit*) entails not a conformity of concept with a content but an elaboration of the range of applicability of the concept. Such elaboration of the concept is bound by inferential determinants in the manner of the very syllogistic reasoning upon which the Hegelian Notion is originally predicated. Likewise, it is bound by inferentialism's implicit laws of revelation and concealment.

The Inferentialist Impulse

Obviously, I consider inferentialism an important reference point for advancing the argument that we ought to appreciate self-deception as an ethical resource of self-realization in the verbal and visual arts. Therefore I want to be clear

---

12. Again it is useful to juxtapose Pippin's commentary (*Hegel's Idealism*, 239) with Hegel's words in *The Encyclopedia of Logic*, ed. H. S. Harris et al. (Indianapolis: Hackett, 1991), 237.

about how inferentialist thinking connects the realm of self-deception with the realm of viable and productive selfhood. For this reason I must briefly outline the recent work of Robert B. Brandom on this subject. Brandom's account of inferentialism is particularly apt for my purposes because he sets up an analytical framework for seeing complementarity between the self formed in the image of the artwork and the self imaged in the form of the artwork.

Brandom proposes replacing Kant's conception of a law, whereby rational will is the capacity "to derive performances from conceptions of law," with the proactive "acknowledgement of a commitment."[13] The making of commitments in this context is comparable to giving an assertion or making an avowal. Whereas for Kant law ought to be understood as what one is obligated to do in one's performance of any rational act, Brandom's "acknowledgement of a commitment" should be understood as "having the capacity to respond reliably to one's acknowledgment of a commitment . . . by differentially producing performances corresponding to the content of the commitment acknowledged" (Brandom, *Articulating Reasons,* 94). Brandom supplements the Kantian normative stricture by allowing for how acknowledgment of discursive commitments "makes a difference to what we go on to do" (94). As I have anticipated, Brandom's inferentialism then exhibits its own dynamic of revelation and concealment in the stipulation that if one gives commitments/assertions, one's acknowledgment of them does not count unless we take into account their consequences and unless those consequences entail further commitments that can be seen to be compatible (positively or negatively) with the inaugural commitments. This means that we must know how to see the differential criteria by which we square commitments with consequences in a context of "differentially" produced performances. The problem of learning how to see with such inferential radar is the epistemic armature of trompe l'oeil and illusionism in general. It is what makes these representational strategies so rich for inquiries into rational self-realization.

The usefulness of inferentialism for my purposes is best appreciated by noting Brandom's insistence upon grasping the uniqueness of human nature in terms of what he calls "sapience" rather than "sentience." The attribution of intentional states and beliefs denoted in the condition of sapience underscores our agency. Brandom's working assumption, that "sapients are agents, and acting is making-true" (*Articulating Reasons,* 158), indicates his Wittgensteinian

---

13. Robert B. Brandom, *Articulating Reasons: An Introduction to Inferentialism* (Cambridge: Harvard University Press, 2000), 94.

predisposition to see human life as an assertional game of giving reasons and accepting or receiving reasons. Brandom rejects the idea that a person can be known by attending to his or her beliefs. He admonishes us against believing in beliefs. To the contrary, he gives precedence in his deliberative protocol to *commitment* because it entails a disposition to act on a belief. As we have seen, commitments are preferable to him because they are undertaken in the acknowledgment that consequences flow (174). A "move" in an assertional game counts when it is suitably articulated by its consequential relations to other commitments. What's more, commitments are susceptible to substitutional strategies that accommodate the inevitable changing contexts of assertional game-playing. When such games hold the players accountable to the consequences of their assertions, the status of their commitments is manifestly altered.

Brandom wants a way to negotiate what he calls "doxastic gaps" (*Articulating Reasons*, 181) in our powers of logical inference. Doxastic gaps arise when we must extract information from what someone is saying when it seems incoherent with what can be said about what they're saying. Brandom's example is familiar to anyone who apprehends ironic potential in a statement. If I disagree with the characterization of the assertion that "the political freedom fighters liberated the village," I could interpolate scare quotes and produce a different or "substitutional" set of inferences. In effect, I would be undertaking new commitments with the same attribution: "Those 'patriotic freedom fighters' massacred the entire population" (Brandom, *Articulating Reasons*, 179). This line of reasoning arises directly out of inferentialism's ambition to show how logical vocabularies are significant insofar as they can make inferential commitments explicit, which is to say, make them relevant to other motivational frameworks. The underlying principle is that the semantic content of any sentence depends on the normative rules governing inferences to and from it: in other words *knowing more* than what the statement purveys as ostensibly expressible knowledge. As Brandom puts it, "When we try to understand the thought or discourse of others, the task can be divided initially into two parts: understanding what they are thinking or talking about and understanding what they are thinking or saying about it" (158). These are respectively the *propositional* and *representational* aspects of sapience. Brandom's stake in the distinction is clearly his preference for conceiving sapience as a counter of inference rather than as a counter of truth. The benefit of this stance, from his perspective as well as my own, is recognition of the social dimension of the propositional-representational dynamic of assertional game playing. In this dimension, as we have seen, "Representational locutions make explicit the sorting of commitments into those attributed and those undertaken—without which communication would be impossible, given differences in perspective" (183).

This sorting presupposes a divergence of or a multiplicity of perspectives. Once again, the concordant ratio of propositional to representational knowledge entails a dynamic of revelation and concealment. This dynamic is comparable to the effects of illusionism in general and trompe l'oeil and iconoclasm in particular. Inferentialism's acknowledgment of "doxastic gaps" and their licensing of substitutional commitments presents a complementary dynamic. All of these phenomena make us vividly present once again to the epistemic pressures of Kent Bach's motivating question respecting human agents for whom "knowing more" is constitutive of being epistemically responsible to one's agency: in short, asking oneself consciously, what do I do next? In each case we are aware that any prospect for rationalism implicates us in a two-part question: what reasons can we give for asserting a commitment and how do we earn entitlement to that commitment given the consequences that flow from our undertaking it?

In Brandom's inferentialism all assertional games of giving and accepting reasons are played with a provision for what he calls "score-keeping." This is simply the circumstance in which we acknowledge how, for example, the statement "the swatch is red" adds to one's score for the statement "the swatch is colored." Brandom is careful to point out that making one move obligates one to make another (*Articulating Reasons,* 190). That is to say, all such games are playable according to what Brandom calls rules of *"consequential commitment"* (191). A move always makes a difference with respect to previous assertional commitments. The project of knowing more, or what is more pertinent, knowing more about one's capacities with respect to undertaking commitments, can thus benefit from the principles of inferentialism. In my earlier account of self-deception I argued that even a person's mistaken conception of what is the case for him- or herself is an aspect of that person that we want to know about. Without such knowledge we would commit an error of idealization. Just so it is the case that inferences which do not merely follow from a precept of correctness make a demand upon the self to own the consequences of its commitment as the condition for any further self-assertion. We are brought to a threshold of acknowledging that commitment in these circumstances presupposes a quality of attentiveness to the world by which we are bound to know the "score" in Brandom's parlance. For we are bound to inquiry about what we will do with what we know.

So, in important ways trompe l'oeil and illusionism in general are dramatizations of our being so epistemically "bound." The truism of objectifying distance is of course what visual illusionism confounds. Subjects and objects are otherwise discernibly different by virtue of what distance obtrudes between them, by dint of the fixity of the viewer's epistemic orientation. I will shortly take up some specific illusionistic works from the visual arts that exemplify the point. I want to show how that agency is actually sustainable only through self-transformations that make distance a variable of one's desire to understand where one stands. This is alternative to establishing a standpoint that does not vary because one does not ask the question, how did I get here?

But first I must further stipulate how inferentialism guides us in this thinking. Inferentialism, after all, actively prevents the self from invoking the kind of self-serving distance from itself that idealizing modes of self-understanding confer, usually in the guise of solipsism or egoism. My account of self-deception so far maintains that the self-deceiver's claim that P, when not-P is the case, might seem to instantiate a distance or an estrangement of the self from reality. But I counter that the self-deceiver, unlike the solipsist or the egoist, possesses an inferential radar which tells him that P and not-P constitute a relation to the world inasmuch as they constitute a relation to each other. For the self-deceiver is, above all, a reflective agent driven by motivational biases that become apparent and intelligible on the horizon of new information about one's desire to maintain P or not-P. In other words, one's sense of self is invested in one's capacity for what Brandom calls "differentially" produced performances, that is to say, activity in the world.

I do not mean to invite an open-ended perspectivism with this view. For Brandom's inferentialism obliges us to think of one's self as possessed of tacit beliefs. Their intelligibility depends upon their being made explicit or, as Fingarette puts it, being "spelled out." This "making explicit" is, like Hegel's Notional truth, a world-directed rather than a logically recursive conceptual formalization. It is a unique engagement with the circumstances of social constraint. Making anything explicit entails acknowledging specific normative expectations that do or do not get met. They are in turn subject to modification, one way or the other, on the basis of what we have already noted Brandom calls score-keeping. Score-keeping could thus be said to induce a heightened attentiveness to the world. For within this framework one follows the direction of one's beliefs. One honors the travail of understanding how the reasons supporting such beliefs are occasioned by the circumstances of asserting them as prospective undertakings. The emphasis on what we go on to do, in our acknowledgment of discursive commitments, reveals how much inferentialism is implicated in an illusionistic dynamic of concealment and revelation, where knowing and doing modify each other's commitments.

The interconnectedness of knowing and doing presumed here is a phenomenalist privileging of understanding over the Cartesian ideal of knowledge. By putting the focus on the process of "uptake," or the grasping of representational purpose, inferentialism keeps us mindful of a salient fact: self-knowledge that is fostered out of the give and take between reasoning agents keeping score on each other—with respect to the possibilities of turning attributions of commitment into undertakings—is likely to produce revelation as a transitional phenomenon. The doxastic gap between commitment and entitlement always risks the knowledge of a kind of self-deception whereby one's not seeing one's lack of entitlement renders one's commitment simply irrational. Against the grain of this thinking, where ordinarily a conflict between commitment and an entitlement would illustrate a kind of causal functionalism, Brandom proposes a normative functionalism. What would have otherwise registered as merely inconsistent standpoints may now be seen as "incompatible commitments."[14] This is to say that normative functionalism adumbrates a prospective register of intelligibility. The presumption of incompatibility ordains the search for rules of compatibility.

Practical Agency

Intelligibility in this instance is coordinate with the epistemic adventure of trompe l'oeil and illusionism that Ernst Gombrich,[15] among others, has convincingly argued must count for us as a seminal moment of art history. In Gombrich's view, art is arguably a Greek invention. It is attributable to artists whose works are fittingly unavailable to us except by second-hand accounts, which is to say as emblems of incomplete knowledge. The works of Myron, Phidias, Zeuxis, and Apelles no longer exist. But, as Gombrich tells us, these works spoke

---

14. Here I draw upon Brandom's first exposition of the inferentialist project, *Making It Explicit: Reasoning, Representing and Discursive Commitment* (Cambridge: Harvard University Press, 1994), 160.

15. In *Art and Illusion: A Study in the Psychology of Pictorial Representation* (Princeton: Princeton University Press, 1989) Gombrich does not argue as strongly as I would that the cognitive challenges posed by conceiving art as linked to the "solution of problems" are inherent to the psychology and epistemic agency of self-deception. This is a point that I believe gets strong endorsement from rhetoricians like Quintilian. Nevertheless, I believe that Gombrich's rich historical account of this visual tradition, especially given his emphasis on Roman Illusionist painting and earlier Greek sculpture, supports my emphasis.

preeminently to the possibility of a completeness of knowledge where none was naturally apparent, especially in the self-problematizing mimesis of Nature exhibited by the works of these artists. Quintilian, for example, characterizes Myron's *Discobolos* as "particularly praiseworthy for its novelty and difficulty" (Gombrich, 141). Quintilian thus codifies "a standard of criticism that linked art with the solution of problems" (141). Quintilian is noticing how the struggle toward naturalistic imitation involves the discovery of hitherto unacknowledged and unacknowledgeable thresholds of technical innovation. I take Gombrich to be construing the central "problem" here as follows. The artist strives to make an image adequate to an omniscient standpoint which we can only inhabit honestly by exhibiting the problematic nature of the productive enterprise itself. Illusionistic representation makes the "solution" of the "problem" of perfect mimesis reveal its inadequacy to the task by exhibiting feats of naturalism to be the limits of artifice. We know well enough Plato's righteous indignation at the artist's pandering to the illusion of naturalistic appearance. But we also know Plato's own weakness for trading in the rhetorical métier of poetry—in book 10 of *The Republic*—in order to finesse his denunciation of the illusions poetry purveys. What we perhaps do not attend closely enough to is how, in each of these instances, the attempt to find a solution to the problem is problematic itself, and in a way that is governed by strong inferentialist imperatives.

Reflective consciousness, seeking an accommodation between the world and the self, must, in the context of inferentialist principles, depend upon a normative rational capacity: to ask oneself if one has found the appropriate terms of fit. Under the pressure of inferentialist principles, I would argue that this entails our making more explicit the reasons behind our belief that terms of fitness apply in the first place, or of how they apply. Spelling it out, as Fingarette would say, or making it explicit, as Brandom would say, presupposes an expectation of something like the ideal of total knowledge. Our recognition of the impossibility of this goal nonetheless makes us responsive to the scruple of soliciting other evidentiary grounds than those which secure our judgment of ourselves as rational inquirers.

I have already cautioned that this should not be mistaken for an unbridled Nietzschean perspectivism. This act of mind accords with what Richard Moran describes, in *Authority and Estrangement*,[16] as a necessary recognition of the special responsibilities of the first-person reflective consciousness. Moran notes

---

16. Richard Moran, *Authority and Estrangement: An Essay on Self-Knowledge* (Princeton: Princeton University Press, 2001).

that the first-person subject is uniquely responsible for itself insofar as it is subject "to its own possibilities of infirmity" (Moran, 144). As is the case with orthodox notions of self-deception, the integrity of the self is beholden to the knowledge that its limits are its vantage point of reflective lucidity. Likewise, its limits are always a source of new information. Again, the Notional logic of Hegelian self-consciousness seems to apply insofar as it instantiates such a developmental phenomenon. Both the Notion and inferentialism subsist upon new information. Furthermore, both seem to foster a sensitivity to second-order desires whereby what we know initially is revealed to be a transitional modality. This transitional modality is dependent upon and presumes upon our disposition—in knowing that we know—to claim our knowledge in a way that leads beyond whatever presuppositions are instantiated in it. I am in effect reprising the inferentialist distinction between ascribing a commitment and undertaking a commitment, where the consequence of undertaking a commitment constitutes access to new information. What seems crucial here is the value of understanding human agency in special terms. We must value it as a capacity to discern new evidentiary grounds and, by that means, to enhance consciousness of the scope of our motivations, fostering something like a higher-order motivation.[17] Hereafter, the presumption that someone who could reflect on his or her reasoning would always be in the process of modifying the determinants of his or her motivational activity gives credence to what Harry Frankfurt, in *The Importance of What We Care About*,[18] calls a hierarchical model of agency.

The hierarchical model of agency presupposes that agents cannot be motivated by desires they do not acknowledge. It thus presumes that we are constantly presented with occasions to reflect on already acknowledged desires, such that we no longer claim them as our strongest motive for action. The pursuit of higher-order motivations is not, strictly speaking, the negation of a motivating reason but its augmented scope of application. As J. David Velleman points out in *The Possibility of Practical Reason*, this promulgates an enhanced autonomy that does not come at the cost of a brutal instrumentalism or at the cost of a self preempting logic of reasons (*Practical Reason*, 12).

---

17. See J. David Velleman's point that seeking after higher-order motivations enhances autonomy by forestalling first-order motives. Velleman's moral psychology puts a premium on this autonomy, while I put a premium on reflective activity per se. See Velleman, *The Possibility of Practical Reason* (Oxford: Oxford University Press, 2000), 13–14.

18. Harry Frankfurt, *The Importance of What We Care About* (Cambridge: Cambridge University Press, 1988), 62–68.

When we permit an inflexible logic to govern our expectation that a belief can be justified as correct or incorrect, we are often begging the question of what serves as the standard of correctness for whatever reasons we commit to. Thinking of what that standard of correctness for action might be leads us into the temptation of thinking "that the norm of correctness for actions is that they should be supported by the strongest reasons. But this thought leads in a vicious circle. What counts as a reason for acting depends on what justifies action; which depends on what counts as correctness for action; which cannot depend, in turn, on what counts as a reason" (Velleman, *Practical Reason*, 15–16). Given the risk of circularity here, Velleman concludes that we cannot simply count upon justification by reasons to assess the correctness of action. On the contrary, action will be correct according to a standard that is independent of the concept of already self-elucidating reasons. Only under this condition will it sustain a "normative context in which reasons exist" because the norms of correctness are internal to the aim of the action (16–17), which is governed in its turn by a higher-order motivation. Higher-order motivations arise under the pressure of our noticing that there are new considerations that arise from one's attentiveness to the scene of action. These potentially supervene what one formerly considered one's best motive for acting. Or, to be more specific, they arise whenever our native inhibition against doing things without knowing what we are doing fails, as in the case of a Freudian parapraxis. At that point, Velleman maintains, a second-order aim of knowing kicks in to regulate what we do (23–24). This is to say that motive constitutively regulates action insofar as the new "considerations" to which one responds count implicitly as *reasons* for acting (18). The content of that higher-order motive consequently needs no concept of a reason. But what is the source of such a self in relation to a realm of social practice and how does it shape our understanding of what effect the individuated subject can have upon that realm? What kind of world of human practices is envisaged here?

As a corollary to this questioning of what counts as the most adequate métier of reflective self-realization, it is worth attending to Stephen Turner's work on social practice. Turner focuses on the intrinsic illusionism of our notion of what social practice is and on our dependency upon identifiable sets of social practices as the ground of rational agency. Turner wishes to demonstrate the unfoundedness of making social practices causal and foundational for any cogent account of human agency. In *The Social Theory of Practices* Turner poses a simple challenge to the notion that social practice is a secure ground of self-reflection for individual members of society.[19] I must, of course, point out that in such cases any self-deception would be reducible to an error of rule-following and disjunctive with rational practice. But Turner makes a commonplace sociological assumption: that practices have an individual substance and a historical substance. He then argues that there is no way of understanding the transmission from the individual to the collective or explaining how individual substance is shareable.

I do not have the space here to give an adequate exposition of the persuasiveness of Turner's skepticism. My more pressing concern is what Turner sees as the consequence of that skepticism. He apprises us of the need to begin thinking in new ways about what authority governs our individual actions, specifically with respect to the acquisition of new information. Turner wants to see the possibility that an unindividuated body of practices on which any individual activity rests, is not composed of "a mysterious collective object [normative social practices] but of those individual additions to what is explicit and public, such as writings and utterances and 'observances'" (Turner, *Social Theory*, 97). He wants us to see that it may be our simple *noticings* of things, our performance in the face of new information, utterances prompted by new circumstances, that effectively constitute the structure of society when we become habituated to them (104–5).

In ensuing chapters I will argue that there is certainly a family resemblance between these "additions" of new information and the intensification and proliferation of forms of attentiveness associated with self-deception and illusionism. These forms of attentiveness furthermore dispose us toward diversifying our repertoire of strategies for self-realization. Turner asks us to reject the illusionistic appearance of social practices as logical causes rather than habits improvised out of ad hoc, circumstantially conditioned noticings. He is, in effect, inviting us to attend to such "noticings" in the way we would whenever we are challenged by our acquisition of new information in the furtherance of deliberate human action. Turner admonishes us that this new information would be preempted if we considered the appearance of social practices to be causally substantial on the model of something like our susceptibility to an orthodox notion of self-deception.

---

19. Turner is working out of the analyses of Ferdinand Tönnies (1855–1936), best remembered for his putting a premium on reflective activity per se. See Velleman, *Practical Reason*, 13–14, for a demonstration of the incommensurability of community (*Gemeinschaft*) and society (*Gesellschaft*). Their incommensurability is for Turner a strong warrant for questioning the reality of social practices. See *The Social Theory of Practices: Tradition, Tacit Knowledge and Presuppositions* (Chicago: University of Chicago Press, 1994).

Turner believes we cannot know what practices are because we take them for granted as causal motors of action. This is the case because we cannot see that we cannot see the means of their transmission which would otherwise authorize their cultural authority. In other words, since Turner believes that there is no ascertainable basis for the transmission of practices that explains how we interiorize collective notions, or how individually ordained practices can be shared (*Social Theory*, 86), we must take a different tack. So-called normative practices of society must be reconceived of as a body of individual habits or behaviors that vary from case to case. Under that assumption, the intuition that practices are effectively the assimilation of new information to what we already know/do ("additions to what is explicit and public") lends credence to Turner's more radical and relevant proposition: that practices are nothing more than "explanatory constructions that solve specific problems of comparison and unmet expectations" (123). Such analysis focuses upon our blind spot with respect to evidentiary grounds that would portend other (which is to say, unintended) social, actantial trajectories of cultural identity. This necessitates something like the self-deceiver's improvisational contending with the question of what to do next, which Hegel, Brandom, and Velleman all hold to be crucial to the efficacy of human agents.

What's involved here, above all else, is an initiative to know how we are motivated in our pursuit of self-explanatory action. We take this initiative when any declaration of belief must be reconciled with the conditions of the intentional act it fosters and the consequences with which it must be subsequently reconciled. Our motivational biases hang in the balance where intentionality stakes itself in action. We will be moved to different intentional acts depending on what we notice about the variability of the conditions fostering our intentions.

3

Learning from Self-Deception: Aesthetic Practices

The Pedagogical Resources of Self-Deception

In this chapter I want to engage what I might now call the pedagogical resources of self-deception. I have been arguing that the trajectory of self or character is a variable of an individual's capacity for paying attention to the surrounding world. The capacity for paying attention, for what I have called "notice," is an important anchor of intentional subjectivity as I have presented it. Now I wish to look at several particularly instructive artworks where intentional subjectivity must come to grips with the shifting motivational grounds of the reader/viewer's powers of notice. Each of the works I will engage imposes a distinctive formal constraint upon the interpretive enterprise. Each causes the reader/viewer to notice more than his or her initial motive for attentiveness allowed. Each work dramatizes how what we do not immediately notice draws us into a self-conscious and contested relation with our motivational capacity for contemplating the object in the first place.

I begin with an indisputable touchstone for representing the struggle of subjective self-realization: Parmigianino's well-known *Self-Portrait in a Convex Mirror* (1524). I will complement my reading of Parmigianino's masterpiece with a reading of John Ashbery's equally well-known meditation upon it in his long poem of the same title. Ashbery's poem figures the very psychological conundrums that have made Parmigianino's painting such an enduring occasion for speculating upon the limits of self-portraiture and self. Accordingly, we shall see that both artists richly serve the purpose of my more general argument—namely, that the endurance of the self is a primary stake of self-deception. This point will be emphasized in the last section of the chapter. There I juxtapose the examples of Parmigianino and Ashbery with an instance of self-portraiture that seems to forbid representation of the self altogether: Caravaggio's *Medusa*

(1598). This image is an allusion to the mirror in which we seek ourselves. But because this painting is mounted upon the convex frame of a wooden shield and worked in an explicitly illusionist métier, Caravaggio presents the menace of the mythical gorgon in a way that both attracts and deflects our gaze. Caravaggio's ingenious invention thus will help us rethink the motivations that cause us to solicit our self-image in the intersubjective dynamic of recognition. We might see them as integral to self-deception.

In each of the examples gathered in this chapter, we therefore will focus upon the drama of our unstable motivations for self-understanding. We will see how this drama is made coherent with the elements of artistic composition. In each of these examples, the artist presents us with an awareness of ourselves caught in a seemingly mistaken apprehension about what most warrants our attention. I will stress that our apprehension of each particular in the aesthetic composition constitutes a rational choice among other particulars. I want to promote the idea that rational behavior, even or especially under the sign of self-deception, is always a question of knowing more fully what one is doing when one acts. I have already stated that this is the sine qua non of treating self-deception as a rational enterprise. I realize of course that with this formulation I am identifying interpretive activity in response to art with the dynamics of practical action in the world. This is arguably a counterintuitive procedure; but I will justify it in the analysis that follows.

In point of fact, knowing what one is doing when one acts is a well-established threshold for distinguishing between purposeful behavior—that is to say, the prospect of subjective autonomy in aiming to act—and feckless activity.[1] It sets up reflective understanding as a regulative principle along Hegelian Notional lines. But it also occasions a closer relation between principles of reason and the pragmatics of action theory than even Hegelian philosophy typically cultivates. It makes the pursuit of higher-order motivations a register for self-reflective powers of mind. Once more, it shows what might be gained by blurring the line between orthodox self-deception and autonomous rationality. Autonomy in this case is no longer a causal hegemony of reason. Rather, it is a process whereby the reasons for one's actions or interpretive gestures are

---

1. In *Art and Experience* (New York: Perigee, 2005), John Dewey makes a relevant observation about the "co-efficiency" of expression. The act of expressing is always in tension with "things in the environment that would otherwise be mere smooth channels or else blind obstructions" (60). In other words, knowing what one is doing, or aiming to do is always a coordination of mind with elements of experience. The motivational biases that inhere in meeting "things in the environment" are effectively coefficients in the process of self-realization.

achieved—rather than proved truthful—in the determination of the aims they pursue and insofar as those aims are remanded to higher-order motivational assessments.

As I've said, illusionism in the visual arts has always been a paradoxical creature of rational desires. After all, the visual illusion is always predicated upon the most orthodox mimeticism as witnessed in its cardinal exemplars: Parrhasius's curtain, Masaccio's *Trinity,* and Mantegna's oculus for the *Camera degli Sposi,* not to mention the Sistine Chapel and *The Last Judgment* in particular. So, however counterintuitive it might at first appear, I want to argue that illusionism (with all of its mirroring devices) shares with self-deception and with normative rationality a definitive challenge to reflective consciousness. It is the challenge to notice what considerations, or avowals, or motivational grounds one misses within the horizon of one's lucidity with regard to any particular subjective view of the world.

Whether judged as mere error or tragedy, the cost of missing noticings, or considerations, or avowals, or "motivational grounds"—which would modify one's expectation about the success or meaning of one's actions—must ultimately be tallied as a deficit of character. This would be true whether we are thinking of character as "dramatized" in the third-person terms of representational practice, or in the first-person terms of acting per se, especially as it bears on the act of reading or viewing. I accept the proposition that seems to be endorsed by Turner and Velleman, that we reference our commitments to act to the motivational grounds from which "good reasons" derive. We desire to act in accord with reasons. We might conclude then that there is something that is fundamentally self-deceiving in all rational conduct. If good reasons depend upon shifting motivational grounds, they are never good enough. They are always exposing the unnoticed liabilities of cogent perspective. We might therefore make a corollary claim to have discovered something fundamental about character: that character in philosophy and the arts, or perhaps character in philosophy *because of the influence of the arts,* presupposes the necessity of a process of change, whereby knowledge is mercilessly subordinated to action. I maintain that this is precisely what might save the unorthodox character of self-deception I am promoting in these pages from an infinite regress of self-doubt. It certainly preempts what would otherwise be our culturally tragic capitulation to the legacy of Cartesian relativism pervading standard poststructuralist accounts of the split or divided subject.

In this regard Velleman makes a useful distinction. Whenever we judge between competing motivational grounds, we should not confuse the judging agent's identity with either choice. The agent must posses an identity "apart from the substantive motives competing for influence over his behavior" (Velleman, *Practical Reason,* 142). This does not make identity nugatory. For, by the same token, we recognize that the agent's identity, as one possessing "the attitude that animates the activity of judging such competitions" (142) in the first place, is inescapable. Moreover, as in the case of Fingarette's "identification as," the identity that obtains here is not ideational. Rather, it is functional in the judging behavior.

Parmigianino's *Self-Portrait:* Painter and Viewer

It is this identity that is at stake for us in our seduction to the deceptively mirrory surface of Parmigianino's *Self-Portrait in a Convex Mirror.* The controlling conceit of the painting challenges the egotistical conceit of self-control on the parts of both painter and viewer in quite complementary ways. Painter and viewer do become mirror images of each other, though the image is perhaps too picture perfect. Nevertheless, our fullest engagement with Parmigianino's composition fosters a decidedly deeper knowledge of mirrors and mirrorings, showing us reflective depths that we might not have expected to see, even in such flawless glass. For Parmigianino's self-portrait figures the process of self-identification by thwarting the simple expectation of all subjective mirror dwellers: that we can tell the difference between illusion and reality while ignoring the difference. This is all very much in the mode of the self-deceiver who sustains faith in P and not-P at the same time. But this involves more than a quaintly literary suspension of disbelief. Parmigianino's intricate device quite simply inhibits our motivation to see its convexity as an illusion that is sufficiently illusionary. The conventional mirror, flat in its pursuit of the perfect illusion, purports to represent three dimensions. The wooden armature upon which Parmigianino's painting is wrapped *is* unequivocally three-dimensional. In other words, it asserts the illusion and denies the illusion at once. The canvas bears out the three-dimensional reality behind the illusion without giving it any representational bearing. The canvas appears to us as the reflective surface qua surface, as if we could see the mirror image in illusionary depth. But it also appears to us, in all its material opacity, as the tain of a conventional mirror. It thus imposes a requirement upon us: that we demonstrate how we know the

Fig. 1 Parmigianino (Francesco Mazzola), *Self-Portrait in a Convex Mirror* (*Self-Portrait at the Mirror*), c. 1524. Kunsthistorisches Museum, Vienna, Austria/Ali Meyer/The Bridgeman Art Library.

means of our moving between competing registers of self-comprehension in asserting commitments about what we see.

It is a problem that might remind us of Plato's mirror in book 10 of *The Republic*.[2] Plato's mirror reveals the world in all of its dimensions by rounding them off into a single admonitory conceptual conceit: mimesis is illusion. Indeed Socrates' inferentially convex mirror—a flat mirror turned in every

---

2. See book 10 of *The Republic,* trans. G. R. F. Ferrari and Tom Griffith (Cambridge: Cambridge University Press, 2000).

direction to represent the world—is a portrait of Glaucon's foolishness. We perceive this when the student narcissistically takes the bait of Socrates question, "Do you not see that there is a way in which you could make them [all the items of the natural world] yourself?" (Plato, *Republic,* 78). In a sense Glaucon succumbs to the verbal trompe l'oeil of Socrates' rhetoric. Glaucon's rejoinder, "What way?" (78) brings him full circle, so to speak, to the realization that he is a creature of the image-based mimetic knowledge of the world that Socrates' question mocks by mimesis.

Socrates' rhetorical ploy joins Parmigianino's project by revealing Glaucon's blind spot to be premature agreement. Glaucon succumbs to an overly enthusiastic mirroring of his teacher's willfully and deceptively premature deduction. It marks Glaucon's failure to notice or consider how well his motivational bias preempts other purposes inherent to the purpose of his acting upon such motives. When Plato deflates Glaucon's egotistical expectation by explaining how a mirror turned in the hand makes all of the round world, we know the obscurity of Socrates' wisdom as the self-evidence of Glaucon's inattentiveness. Parmigianino's painting stages occasions for noticing and considering what its presentational powers (acknowledged by Vasari as an artful copy of the world; or as he puts it, "All you saw in the glass")[3] otherwise seem to obscure. The illusionary feat that galvanizes Parmigianino's self-portrait persuades us that self-realization is both the painting's theme, as is undoubtedly the case with all self-portraits, and its motive, with the caveat that motive always portends a yet unrealized self.

The painting was originally intended to be the artist's professional passport from his home town of Parma into the art world of early sixteenth-century Rome, then flourishing under the patronage of Clement V.[4] It was intended to present the painter as more than his visage and thereby as deserving of the patronage and regard reserved for manifestations of extraordinary skill. To achieve this end, the formal plan of the canvas advertises noticings and considerations that the conventional eye is bound to miss. Just as convexity makes objects seem closer than they are, especially at the "distorting" perimeter, theme

---

3. See Giorgio Vasari, *Vasari's Lives of the Painters, Sculptors, and Architects,* trans. Edmund Fuller (New York: Dell, 1968), 347–403.
4. See David Ekserdjian, *Parmigianino* (New Haven: Yale University Press, 2006), in particular the introduction. David Franklin's *The Art of Parmigianino* (New Haven: Yale University Press, 2004) similarly emphasizes the painter's adeptness for refining the surface of the picture plane. Relatively less attention is typically paid to the intellectual/experiential stakes of composition.

and motive here reveal their own reflective harmonics. We have seen that inferentialism prompts one to know more than one knows by coming to understand what one ought to do. Inferentialism, therefore, looks to the consequences of what one does for a principled rationality about how to go on. Just so, convexity in Parmigianino's self-portrait seems to be governed by what Brandom calls "rules of consequentialism." The possibility of seeing otherwise contradictory things at the same time in this painting eludes orthodox notions of self-deception. It likewise escapes the irony of Socrates' invocation of the illusionary mirror, not to mention the predicament that Plato thereby imposes upon Glaucon. Parmigianino purveys a world that depends for its lucidity upon something like a comparative or contrastive assessment of what he shows. What we see entails a ranking of the consequences our way of seeing incurs.

In other words, the contrastive effects propagated in Parmigianino's self-portrait figure the subjective *activity* of ranking our motivational grounds for reading ourselves into the picture/mirror/reflection. For example, our first expectation of self-image is one to which we are seduced by our easy recognition of the aspect of convexity itself. This familiar self-serving reflective surface to which we are drawn for its self-magnifying prospect (the self is the center and the substrate of visual resolution/lucidity) is supplanted by our recognition that the relevant moment of viewing is not ours, not *this* moment. For it is the painter's visage that has been reflected. A dimension of present-ness therefore obtrudes in order to keep things in motion, so to speak, to apprise us of the necessity of other considerations that might enhance our viewing.

It is of course counterintuitive to speak of keeping the elements of a picture, especially a self-portrait, in motion. But with this idiom I am calling attention to the way a painting's knowability is a variable of the subjective viewer's positionality: not just a privileged point of perspectival lucidity—the centrality of the self—but a decision-making imperative. It is the imperative to satisfy oneself about one's good reasons for choosing a particular vantage point, which the convex mirror, by its intrinsically distorting properties, otherwise appears to preempt. Parmigianino's painting seems designed to animate critical thinking with respect to this fact. Correlatively, it reminds us of Brandom's and Velleman's admonition that if we want to understand the rationality of what the subject decides in choosing vantage points of seeing, we must take careful account of what happens as we appreciate the potential for seeing more.

As we have already noted, theorists of self-deception value what we learn about the subject in the subject's coming to learn that there are other reasons, or higher-order motivations, that it has not yet considered. Just so, Parmigianino's conceit of convexity intensifies our awareness that the distorted and yet elaborately realized details of the peripheral surface of his canvas portend another register of yet uncomprehended lucidity for which one must be prepared to entertain other reasons. This is the painting's chief occasion for what Pippin calls "contrastive effects." The eye is constantly prompted to go back and forth between what can be seen nakedly, so to speak, with the eye and what requires the rationalizations of relative value via the mediations of mind and the instantiation of the "I."

For example, the enormous hand extended toward the viewer in the foreground of Parmigianino's portrait obscures our view of the head. In effect, its equivalent scale renders the head less head-like. We are forced to think again about how we must traverse the distance between the hand and the head to give each its representational due, especially as the mind and the hand are reciprocating human powers. In Parmigianino's painting the knowledge of each is a function of the deferral of both to another moment of measurement. Like Velleman, Parmigianino attunes us to how autonomous subjectivity must reconcile itself with the stance of future-directed decision-making, where reasons are not beholden to prior decisions about what reasons should count.

It may seem curious to speak of the increments of our responsiveness to a visual composition in terms of reasons and *better reasons*. It turns the painting into a kind of greeting of hitherto unmet prospects. But the mirror conceit that is Parmigianino's armature, both practically and conceptually, already presupposes a critical mandate. Reflection is both conative and cognitive in this aesthetic milieu. One desires to see what one expects and one expects to modify one's expectation of what sight will satisfy desire, based on the epistemic exigencies or disappointments that looking makes us vulnerable to.

In this case, as our vision moves out from the undistorted figure of the painter, we look increasingly *without* our eyes. For example, we construe the slivers of highlight in the upper left, glinting like the reflection of a light source above the surface of a globe, to be the window in the painter's studio. It is a window on a world that is perhaps as round as the curvature of his convex surface. But we know this ironically: by recognition of the denaturing rectilinearity that is both the hallmark of Leon Battista Alberti's illusionism (perspectivalism) and stark evidence of the inferentialism that such illusion depends on. For in this case we know the window pane by the barest metonymic hint of its square sash and leading. We are urged to a similar decoding of the arch framing the painter's head as a horizontally beamed and perhaps coffered ceiling, in short, a flat geometrical plane. Finally, we infer the curved line on the right periphery of the bulging eye of the painting to be the frame of the source mirror itself, flattened on this margin and presenting its back to our view. This effect literalizes the tain of reflection. The realization occurs in tandem with our inference that the painter contemplates what is visible in the mirror as the very depth which the tain at once produces and obscures.

Compassing all of these particulars, we may be reminded of how inferentialism guides us to think in terms of the game of giving and accepting reasons. For Brandom's scruple of score-keeping in such games requires our recognition that each "noticing" accumulates obligations to notice more. In Parmigianino's visual construct, each object that we see as a cognitive distortion depends upon what we see conatively. This is true both in the naturalism of the portrait proper and in the apparently distorting representation of the medium of convexity. For the representation of convex distortion, undistorted in that representation, is naturalized along different perspectival (perceptual) and conceptual lines than is the central figure of the painter. These lines nonetheless converge experientially with the naturalism of the portraited artist in our most careless viewing of the picture: where we notice only what is already elucidated by the conventions of portraiture *before we look*.

Just as the painter, especially the self-portraitist, aspires to an ideal viewpoint—the correlative of his self-idealizing image and craftsmanship—the viewer aspires to a privilege above other views. I believe that Parmigianino's painting pegs this aspiration to something like the game of giving and receiving reasons. Or to put in terms of the mise-en-scène of the painting itself, Parmigianino makes the viewer's success, with respect to other views, depend upon his developing a capacity to notice or consider what the aspiring "I" would not be disposed to see. In the mise-en-scène of the painting, the eye trumps the "I." It coerces a retrospective view on the part of the viewer. This is a kind of parody of our face in the mirror itself, whereby we are contemplating what we know has already been reversed. It has thereby already caught us up in a temporal process that the image by itself refuses to be a counter of recognition for. It is a view that reveals the trajectory of meaning, projecting out from the surface, to be something like a recurring moment: one for which we must take responsibility by adapting to the temporal pressures of seeing into the future, seeing or judging by recognition of the consequences of seeing one way. The power of the painting, in this regard, is its revelation of a subjective viewer's capacities to be a self-sustaining viewer.

Ashbery's Rationalizing Speculum

Almost five hundred and fifty years later, in John Ashbery's "Self-Portrait in a Convex Mirror,"[5] Parmigianino's painting is observed to be an occasion for projections of the self beyond a strictly self-serving point of view.[6] The poet characterizes Parmigianino's painting as a suturing of foreground and horizon "In one piece of surface" (Ashbery, 72). The image is subsequently figured as "a wave breaking on a rock, giving up / Its shape in a gesture which expresses that shape" (73). The image is thus posed as a counter for the truism that "Each person / Has one big theory to explain the universe. / But it doesn't tell the whole story" (81). The image is a marker for the present that "we are always escaping from / And falling back into, as the waterwheel of days / Pursues its uneventful, even serene course" (78–79). Most emblematically, when Ashbery attends to the artist's anamorphically enlarged hand—both representative of and part of the curvature of the painting's surface—he appreciates how the painting is the métier of a kind of recurring gesture: "a recurring wave of arrival" (68). Each of these figures is a marker for the recurrence of self-deception in the painting, but in a way that subtly differs from the effects of the painting itself. This is because the power Ashbery's poem wields seems to depend on detaching the painting from the act of viewing. The painting itself is objectified. Nevertheless, we will see that the painting's seeming deference to the effect on the subjective viewer—so prominently featured in my previous discussion of the painting—and the poet's early objectification of the power of the painting—featured as an account of the painter's self-deceiving artistry/trickery—are both, to some extent, self-deceiving and limited views.

Ashbery takes his consciousness of the painter's intentionality to be straightforwardly problematic. It dramatizes the painter's wish to represent that what he knows requires a more capacious representational practice than he already has in hand. It portends another moment of time, another consideration upon which his practice can be predicated and according to which it must be revised. The self-deceived mind is thus represented in the poem as an object distinct

---

5. John Ashbery, *Self-Portrait in a Convex Mirror: Poems* (New York: Penguin, 1990).

6. Both Ashbery's poem and Parmigianino's portrait benefit from much valuable critical commentary occasioned specifically by Ashbery's engagement with the painting. Charles Altieri, Marjorie Perloff, David Lehman, and Douglas Crase have written astutely about how the verbal and the visual interact. My contribution has less to do with the specific dialogue between poem and painting. Obviously, I am more focused upon how a viewer/reader's engagements draw us into the dynamic of self-deception. My stake in this conversation is very specifically tied to my own notion of uncharacteristic character.

from the subjective self-deceptions that we have seen the painting induces in its viewer. Or at least this is initially the case.

Ashbery indulges in something like a judgment upon self-deception that presupposes our most conventionalized attitude toward it as a character flaw located in the painter's practice, his practical mind. But the work of the poem takes us beyond that conventionalized attitude in ways that are coherent with the more recent philosophical rehabilitations of self-deception upon which my thinking here subsists. The ramifications of this self-deception, where disappointment for the artist is revealed to be an "unintended" but beneficent discovery for the viewer, are already apparent in the motif of surprise and discovery that dominates Ashbery's poem. Ashbery notes how the painter surprises his audience with the revelation that *they* do not appear in the mirror-mirroring canvas. In addition we are told that the painter has meant quite explicitly to "amaze" potential patrons. We are prompted to understand that this is unimaginable without rendering a shock to the imagination of the patron. This induces the correlative surprise that the patron's connoisseurship is inadequate to his experience: thus risking the very patronage the painter solicits by this gesture. Finally, we surprise the painter by crashing his studio where the "secret" of the work behind the work is on display.

In each of these instances, Ashbery makes us once more witness to and complicit in something like a game of giving and accepting reasons. But we are also more detached witnesses to this game than we were standing before the painting itself. For this reason we are also more responsive to the rationalizing premise that higher-order motivations obtain. This premise, as I have already argued, is corollary to the game of giving and accepting reasons. I do not mean to suggest that the poem promulgates a unique protocol of questions and answers. More to the point, it makes our expectation that all formally innovative works of art presuppose such a protocol a more self-conscious proposition. Hence the poem involves us in a dramatically escalating responsiveness to the presentational particulars of the painting without portending a resolution of our focus upon them simply because the painter already has. In doing so the painter may have missed seeing himself in the mirror of his artistic ambition. But my purpose here is not so simple as concluding that the painter's self-deception is the reader's self-possession.

The questions and answers animated in the logical movements of Ashbery's poem evoke a reading self that seems particularly attuned to inferentialist principles. This is especially the case with respect to the idea, advanced earlier, that the rationality of a motive inheres in a subject's being motivated in the first place. Following Velleman's assumptions about practical reason, we must assume that motive regulates action insofar as it embodies the subject's responsiveness to considerations that will, in turn, count as reasons for acting.[7] The making explicit or spelling out of the subject's commitments is crucial here. For it evokes a sense of how commitments make a difference to the subject's standing vis-à-vis what is attributable to him on the basis of something like Brandom's rules of consequential commitment. Accordingly, we shall see how the poem prompts considerations that help us rationalize the painting as an elaboration of the viewer's subjectivity. If, as I've suggested, the eye trumps the I in the painting, Ashbery's poem struggles to embody that I and bring it into its properly dialectical relation with the eye that brought it into play. In other words, the poem's form of contemplating the viewer's relation to the painting entails dramatizing the kind of self-questioning that the game of giving and receiving reasons animates in most intersubjective contexts. In this case, we understand that painting and poet are the relevant counters of reflective activity. Such is the poem's access to the rationalistic potential that I claim inheres in self-deception. It reminds us that, in the absence of self-deception, self-questioning lacks its strongest motive.

Our approach to this view of the poem is facilitated by Ashbery's early posing of the painter's ambition (albeit refracted by Vasari's account) as a contrary epistemic enterprise: to deploy the rule of art in order to "perfect and rule out the extraneous / Forever" (Ashbery, 72). Unlike the confident self-possession of the painting, the poem, so self-conscious about reflecting the painting in its mirror-title, makes us see that the practices of the painter only have significance for us because they are ruled by encounters with the "extraneous." Indeed, the tain of the mirror would appear to be the touchstone of the extraneous if we could see it, make it explicit, spell out its inferable existence. As such it proffers a touchstone for our experience of the poem: the extraneous rendered dispositive. It might be fair to say that the tain of the mirror is the conceptual armature of the poem's presentational strategies as the convex surface was the armature for the painting.

After all, Ashbery privileges the conceit of the presentational over the representational in his excavation of the mirror's tain. He figures the distinction in the poem's point of departure: the pathos of the painter's soul. For the first

---

7. Here Velleman (*Practical Reason*, 18) seems coordinate with Brandom's claim in *Articulating Reasons*: "Having a rational will, then can be understood as having the capacity to respond reliably to one's acknowledgement of a commitment . . . by differentially producing performances corresponding to the content of the commitment acknowledged." See Brandom, *Articulating Reasons*, 94.

awestruck viewers of the painting, Pope Clement and his court, the "reason" for the painting is presumed to be the liberation of the soul. The would-be manifestation of the soul is the medium of convexity here. Literally, it is a bringing forward of a desired object, a bringing into spatial presence. Convexity, like the illusionism of depth, which is also (however inversely) a vital element of Parmigianino's composition, nonetheless licenses the mobility of the viewing subject. The curvilinearity of the painting alternately shuttles us toward and away from the picture plane, which induces competing but reciprocating views. We must see center and circumference as proportionate focal lengths. The effect incites the antithesis of that stupefaction which the poet tells us, again according to Vasari, was the immediate effect of the painting on its first audience. They saw the soul in a way that immobilized them. Mobility, on the contrary, is the acknowledgment of a present-ness that is not merely presence. It is not soul-like, in the sense that the desire for the representation of the soul, like all metaphysical longing, is a desire for arrest. And this is precisely the difficulty that the painting posed for its historical audience. They saw that

> the soul has to stay where it is.
> Even though restless, hearing raindrops at the pane,
> The singing of autumn leaves thrashed by the wind,
> Longing to be free, outside, but it must stay
> Posing in this place. It must move
> As little as possible. This is what the portrait says. . . .
> The secret is too plain. The pity of it smarts.
> Makes hot tears spurt: that the soul is not a soul,
> Has no secret, is small, and it fits
> Its hollow perfectly; its room, our moments of attention.
>
> (Ashbery, 69)

The painting that seeks to represent the liberation of the soul panders to presence and obscures the affinity of the presentational with present-ness. It is a veritable echo of Hegel's rejection of the Kantian "I," understood as a self-sustaining representation. Hegel judgmentally identifies this I with the concept of "soul." From this viewpoint it would be equivalent to treating the Notion as a mere inherent property of subjective consciousness. The Notion would thereby be rendered inert with respect to the possibility of its freedom (Hegel, *Logic*, 585). Likewise, Ashbery's poem prompts our search for an alternative to the self-defeatism of believing that the meaning of the artwork depends on its possessing and manifesting soul. He gives animus to our (and possibly Parmigianino's) disappointment that the soul is an immobilized captive of its own invocation. For he makes us see that any "stupefied" expectation of the soul's imminent appearance in the painting was an evasion of the responsibilities of mobility. In this way, the painting prompts its audience to commitments that the poem shows us will not survive any single attribution. The poem's prompting us to higher-order motivations for understanding how to attribute the commitments inspired by the painting is revealed to be our only practicable mode of soul-like ascent.

If the soul is mortified in the narrow space of "our moments of attention," Ashbery can begin to make us think of how to reconcile its "ascent" with the succession of moments of attention: or to use the parlance of this moment in the poem, other "rooms" that make up the mansion of consciousness. By their intrinsic incommensurability, different moments are distinct. They confront us with something like the doxastic gaps that Brandom's inferentialism is designed to negotiate. Inasmuch as doxastic gaps denote the differential between what one thinks and how one might think about what one thinks (that is to say, between a commitment and its terms of attainment and entitlement), we might observe in Parmigianino's painting a mirroring or speculative resemblance between doxastic gaps and the illusionistic practice. The resemblance is cued by the poet's own bringing of the concept of speculation "(from the Latin *speculum,* mirror)" (Ashbery, 69) to the task of passing from one room of consciousness to the next in the attentional moments concatenated by the poem. The "room" in which the painter's soul is held within the visual bounds of convexity, owing to that convexity, reveals an apt ambiguity: there is a

> window or mirror on the right, even
> As a gauge of the weather, which in French is
> *Le temps,* the word for time, and which
> Follows a course wherein changes are merely
> Features of the whole.
>
> (Ashbery, 70)

Between "speculation" and "speculum" the distance of time distorts doxastic perspective. Knowing both the intentional purport of a commitment and the conditions of its assertability—which is to say the assessment of one's entitlement to it as a commitment—constrains us to normativize distortion itself.

That is to say, the etymological gap between "speculation" and "speculum" is equivalent to the temporal gap and correlative distortion registered by the punning dimension of "Le temps," with respect to the weather in the window: the weather in the window is both an image reflected in the glass and a reminder that weather itself is a medium of human temporality, hence a reflective surface in its own right.

Having to grant that in these cases "changes are merely / Features of the whole," demands that we treat the whole in entirely functional terms. I suggested earlier that Brandom's functional normativism allows us to derive performances "differentially" on the basis of how the acknowledgment of our commitments is responsive to changes in their contents. But we must keep in mind that, for Brandom, commitments have normative rational content only insofar as they are susceptible to acknowledgment: for what we commit to must make a difference to what we go on to do. Implicitly, for Brandom, a concept has content as a side effect of the way it is treated.[8] Ashbery's poem seems to subscribe to this "normative functionalism" in a way that I have alleged links it to the trompe l'oeil and illusionist tradition, for which Parmigianino's painting is a marker.

So, not unexpectedly, the semantic inferences of speculation, and the conceptual content it is freighted with, become a fulcrum of the poem's readability. Such readability is a variant of the game of giving and receiving reasons.[9] The poem is a treatment of the concept of speculation while serving as a speculum for the attentive mind. I have already noted that the game of giving and receiving reasons is typically operative in intersubjective contexts. But insofar as giving and receiving reasons is predicated on assertional claims and the circumstances of their entitlement, that is to say, the likelihood that they will be attributed, Ashbery seems to appreciate that the same dynamic is operative here. The self that wants to believe in itself, the self that the poet looks to see in the mirror of the poem, can be reflected in the poem as the poet's attempts to make attributional claims vis-à-vis the painting. In doing so the poet examines the way the painter's self-assertions succumb to failed attributions on the part of the viewer/audience for the painting. These failed attributions in turn incite the poet's/reader's struggle to articulate better attributional grounds, or

---

8. In *Making It Explicit* Brandom is clear that the concept of a commitment could be conferred on intentional states by "properties *implicit* in the way those states are treated in practice. According to such a conception, the conferral of content might be a side effect of the way they are treated, not requiring that anyone explicitly intend to confer it by their behavior" (147).

9. Brandom takes this concept from the work of Wilfred Sellars.

to discern higher-order motivations, in order to better substantiate his own commitments to reading productively.

After all, we are all fundamentally self-assertors. It follows that others will attribute to us the commitments that stand to make those assertions significant. The affinity with Hegelian self-recognition, and the necessary mobility of the subject intrinsic to Notional thinking, cannot be ignored. Therefore, I would like to suggest that asserting a commitment is always inferring something like the belief that self-deception is inescapable. For asserting a commitment always depends upon the possibility that it is not attributable, thus putting the subject on a trajectory of transition from one condition of self-realization to another. For this reason I see both Parmigianino and Ashbery, and in a moment I will see Caravaggio, as helping to show the necessity of normativizing self-deception. Furthermore, we should appreciate at this point how the idea that we are primordial assertors is in harmony with Hegel's ambition to prove that we are primordially creatures of determination in our Notional nature. We might then say that assertion and determination dovetail in an expectation of human productivity.

Ashbery's poem, insofar as it promotes the normativization of self-deception, clearly makes human productivity a crux of its own aesthetic efficacy. Once we appreciate the painter's/audience's conventional self-deception about the painting's power to represent the soul, we begin to understand the self-productive burdens of selfhood. We do so in a way that has less to do with the idea of social constructedness and more to do with the risks of presuming upon specific human *technes* of self-knowledge. Ashbery makes the reader's point of departure in the poem the revealed "soullessness" of the painting. This revealed "soullessness" is tantamount to the self-deception exposed by the poet's baring the devices of projection that would otherwise seem to represent the self in three dimensions. Thus we can see the "Notional" thrust of the poem as the crucial métier of what meanings it can enact. Since Ashbery tells us that the painting moves by the logic of "a *bizarria*," or distortion, away from ideal beauty—but without merely negating the commitments assertable under the claim of beauty—we see the kinship between the Notional, determinative force of the painting and the poem even more clearly. In the poem distortion itself is naturalized in our discovery of the substitutability of the attributional grounds that ideal beauty gives way to. While the painting seemed to show us this phenomenon, almost exclusively as a mirror of the viewer's subjectivity, the poet initially presented it as a phenomenon objectifiable in the painting/painter qua object. But, in the full course of the poem's development, its very temporal duration gives the phenomenon of distortion a more dialectical cast. Perhaps this is only appropriate on such familiar Hegelian terrain. But Ashbery takes us beyond the familiar Hegelian landmarks.

Ashbery shows us how the "amazement" that "stupefied" the pope and his court, that arrested the soldiers who might otherwise have terminated the painter's work when they discovered him in his workshop during the sack of Rome, might give way to a different order of surprise. It would be one that is less a touchstone for human paralysis than a threshold for human animus:

> The picture is almost finished,
> The surprise almost over, as when one looks out,
> Startled by a snowfall which even now is
> Ending in specks and sparkles of snow.
> It happened while you were inside, asleep,
> And there is no reason why you should have
> Been awake for it, except that the day
> Is ending and it will be hard for you
> To get to sleep tonight, at least until late.
> (Ashbery, 74–75)

Here the poem literally turns away from the objective phenomenon of the painting to a subjective consciousness that is not merely or fetishistically consciousness of the painting itself. This turning away is a counter for the kind of present-ness (in the present we are always turning elsewhere) that is made available to us by countenancing self-deception as a modality of reasoning. That is to say, our surprise "almost over" gives way to the realization that such naked self-deception as occasioned it will be superseded by knowledge of what constitutes our susceptibility to such surprise. The nap, which both made the snowfall seem a dream and is predicted to inhibit the sleep of dreams, conjures precisely the kind of mirror conceit that has just been debunked by the poet as a wayward specularity. The poet goes on to speculate that our yearning, and the painter's, for "naturalness" (82) beyond deception is the talisman of an "inner calm" which is itself illusionary in the achievement of naturalistic effect: "a frozen gesture of welcome etched / On the air materializing behind it" (82).

The alternative to "inner calm" is presently enacted in the poet's rejection of the distorted hand at the bottom of the painting, which was the marker of its fallibility:

Therefore I beseech you, withdraw that hand,
Offer it no longer as shield or greeting,
The shield of a greeting, Francesco:
There is room for one bullet in the chamber:
Our looking through the wrong end
Of the telescope as you fall back at a speed
Faster than that of light to flatten ultimately
Among the features of the room
                                    (Ashbery, 82)

The hand has been a "shield" in the sense that it deflected the charge of apparent distortion by the painter: the painter's hand is empirical evidence of the curvature of the mirror. We were oriented to the wrong register of reality if we focused on the distortion as merely a mirror reflection. The un-naturalistic effect is more perfectly naturalistic than we thought. In that understanding, the painting "greets" our expectation of parity with the painter's reality. It augurs for a perfect reflection of the painter's ego by the viewer's ego, though in reality such reflection entails, on the viewer's part, an assimilation of hitherto unclaimed reasons. Indeed, a shield (which the convexity of the mirror calls to mind in any case) is a defense against the necessity of greeting the other. Reciprocally, the formal greeting or salutation is oftentimes a shield against an overly candid revelation of self. The duplicity here is a warrant for knowing the self as mobilized in its self-deceiving gestures. Contrarily, as I have noted, sheer amazement at the miracle of naturalistic reflection arrests human agency, making the subject a prisoner of its "room," as the painter's soul is a prisoner of the representational métier of the painting. The oxymoron of the "shield of a greeting" only strengthens our sense of being present upon a threshold of asserting commitments in expectation of unknowable consequences. We are nonetheless confident of the necessity of our responsiveness to them.

For the doxastic gap between shield and greeting must be traversed by a mind that can see double and alternately, as the viewer of the trompe l'oeil is accustomed to do. It must be a mind capacious enough to see the motivation for divergent performances or distinct entitlements to the incommensurable commitments purveyed by oxymoron. The nominally self-sufficient "room" of the painter's studio is immediately represented as the prepositionally dependent "room" for a bullet in the chamber of a "gun." The gun in turn is looked at with the eye that might turn the muzzle on itself—perhaps the only escape from the room's enclosure—only to reveal the expansion of the universe, so to speak. For the same eye is prompted to see through the projectile convexity of the canvas as through the wrong end of a telescope. It has the effect of sending the figure of the painter into a distant orbit. The reversed trajectory of the projectile is a touchstone for the form of present-ness in which the motives for commitment (like the negation of Hegelian essence) hang in a deliberative balance. Thus the motive for knowing more is the necessary corollary of being motivated to assert any commitment at all.

Ashbery's "Self-Portrait in a Convex Mirror" follows through on this proposition by showing us how the poet is constantly intervening in his own motives. The conceptual *progressus* is driven by the realization that one has seen what there is to see by *seeing through* (ironically, this is Dürer's definition of perspective)[10] what is made manifest, to the devices of a concealment. It is tantamount to the assertion of a commitment whose attribution depends upon our seeing a further commitment, one that only the consequences of the first commitment can tease out. Neither the painting's "amazing" privileging of the subject's ego—painter and viewer—nor the poem's initial privileging of the object of the painting can suffice to know the "extraneous" as integral to the essential matter:

> A whispered phrase passed around the room
> Ends up as something completely different,
> It is the principle that makes works of art so unlike
> What the artist intended. Often he finds
> He has omitted the thing he started out to say
> In the first place.
>
> (Ashbery, 80)

The familiar parlor game of "telephone" evoked here is not just testimonial to the ambiguity of expression any more than the shield of a greeting is merely a well-wrought oxymoron. The original project of the painting, attributed as a commitment to "rule out the extraneous / Forever" (Ashbery, 72), belies its oversimplification by the punning, illusionistic effect of the word "rule." We might once again recall Brandom's "rules of *consequential commitment*" (Brandom, *Articulating Reasons,* 191) whereby every move in assertional gaming

---

10. In his well-known monograph *Anamorphic Art* Jurgis Baltrušaitis comments extensively on Dürer's *prospettiva*. His exposition emphasizes the transitivity of vision.

must make a difference or reveal consequences for what else it is appropriate to do according to the rules of the game. In the game of telephone, which for Ashbery seems to be hard-wired into the game of art, rule governance proves to be an orchestration of modified assertions that portend the necessity of new entitlements. It involves working with one's motives by observing the comparative effects of one's attributable reasons for possessing any such motives. It furthermore entails orchestrating the compatibility between present and future selves: instantiating a special mode of present-ness that does not await its outcome but determines it. What we contend with here is neither a token of immediacy nor the description of a simple dialectical motion with respect to past and future.[11] It is an increment, a kind of integer of action, in the way the manifestation of Hegel's Notion is more than the subject's blind self-possession. Rather, in its freedom, Hegel tells us, the substances of its [the Notion's] being and essence "now have essentially the status of an *illusory being,* of being moments of reflection, whereby each is no less immediately united with its other or its positedness and each contains its positedness *within itself,* and consequently in its other is posited as simply and solely identical with itself."[12]

Ashbery's poem concludes with a reluctance to yield to the illusionary temptation to plumb the interiority of self. Ultimately the poem denies what we previously understood as that "inner calm," which is the most metaphysical motive of the portraitist and quite explicitly animates the dramatic struggle embodied in the artifice of Parmigianino's painting. Ashbery articulates this reluctance with an admonition against the didactic hand of anyone who would sketch an explanatory diagram "on the wind," for

> The hand holds no chalk
> And each part of the whole falls off
> And cannot know it knew, except
> Here and there, in cold pockets
> Of remembrance, whispers out of time.
> (Ashbery, 83)

The part that knows the way of its relation to the whole, without knowing that it knew, like the Notional subject of Hegel's *Logic,* "falls off" in the sense

11. See the range of commentary on this point throughout Paul Ricoeur's *Time and Narrative* for this version of present-ness, especially vol. 1. *Time and Narrative,* 3 vols., trans. Kathleen McLaughlin and David Pellauer (Chicago: University of Chicago Press, 1984–1988).
12. See Hegel, *Logic,* 581–82, for the complete statement of this proposition—especially with respect to Hegel's assertion that "the Notion is the *individual."*

that it becomes a counter for higher-order motivations. We will remember that in book 2 of *Hegel's Science of Logic* "illusory being," manifested as *Schein* or appearance, was not the displacement of being by essence. It was instead essence's own positing (Hegel, *Logic,* 393). Hegel's thinking here is compatible with the idea of reflection as promoting higher-order motivations. Indeed motive, which I take to be the link to self-deception evident in any artwork where fallible or incoherent choices are presented, is also the conceptual topos that makes it possible to see something more than the motive denotes. It shows us how a philosophical project based on intersubjective practices becomes essential to understanding representational media, which ordinarily—and especially in the case of painting and lyric poetry—seem to presuppose an unproblematic autonomous subject. In Ashbery's poem these effects of self-deception give the lie to such feckless autonomism.

Caravaggio's Shield of a Greeting

I have wanted to see the "shield of a greeting" as the appropriately baroque touchstone of Ashbery's intuition about the subjective viewer—an intuition that eludes the stupefaction of Parmigianino's first viewer. Correlatively, I will also show how Caravaggio's "portrait" *Medusa,* executed on a convex shield of poplar wood in 1598, seems to be a prescient enactment of Ashbery's insight. It is one that portends an even richer ethical reward for the mind that can follow the painter's visual logic. Like Parmigianino's *Self-Portrait,* the *Medusa* was expressly designed to amaze: commissioned as it was by Cardinal Del Monte, to join the impressive collection of armor and armament amassed by Ferdinando I, the duke of Tuscany.[13] For the painter, and perhaps for us, the amazement seems designed to arrest the mythological thinking—out of Ovid—that too neatly resolves our struggle with the nemesis of vision. We have a portent of this nemesis in the gorgon image each of us faces in the mirror every day of our passing lives. Caravaggio is, of course, working well within an established tradition of decoration wherein Medusa was a veritable emblem of sixteenth-century shield-making.[14] But Caravaggio's blurring of the motivationally vexed defensive/aggressive character of this artifact of warfare with the compositional armature of an artwork reveals its own atavistic motives

---

13. See Leo Bersani and Ulysse Dutoit, *Caravaggio's Secrets* (Cambridge: MIT Press, 1998), and Catherine Puglisi, *Caravaggio* (London: Phaidon, 2000).

14. See Puglisi, *Caravaggio,* and Helen Langdon, *Caravaggio: A Life* (Boulder, Colo.: Westview Press, 2000).

Fig. 2 Michelangelo Merisi da Caravaggio, *Medusa*, c. 1596–98. Oil on canvas attached to wood. Galleria degli Uffizi, Florence, Italy/The Bridgeman Art Library.

and suspenseful drama. Unlike a shield, a painting is intended to *greet* the viewer. In this particular case, however, the painting evokes an aesthetic agency that is as provocatively challenged as any warrior struggling to preserve his human animus against the ultimate frozen spectacle of death.

As many critics have noted, the salient illusion of Caravaggio's painting is his technical negation of the convexity of the physical surface, extended in greeting but transcended by painterly artifice.[15] The artist creates the appearance

15. See both John T. Spike, *Caravaggio* (New York: Abbeville Press, 2001), 64–65, and Peter Robb, *M: The Man Who Became Caravaggio* (New York: Picador Press, 1998), 76.

of concavity or a recession that fights against the physical protuberance of the shield. Moreover, the concavity of recessive space would have been governed by the very rules of Albertian perspectivism that Caravaggio's career was otherwise staked against: for this master of the opaque backdrop, mathematical recession to a vanishing point is merely a narcissistic, spectatorial rationalization. Caravaggio was infinitely more interested in the incontrovertability of presence, incarnational immediacy: action not spectacle.[16] The shield of course is implicitly a token of the struggle between the roles of actor and spectator. The achievement of Caravaggio's painting then is that the spectacle of naturalism, achieved according to the rules of the rationalized picture plane, is trumped by Nature. Specifically, it is trumped by the nature of the shield. For the composition animates what would otherwise be a spectatorship frozen by our acculturation to a depth of field that the convex surface of the shield belies.

We might recall, once more, the stupefaction of those first viewers of Parmigianino's self-portrait. Their admiration was inspired by the finely wrought depth, the illusionary habitat of the soul. The visual habituations to Albertian vision are inevitably spiritualizing, by their inherent abstraction. This blinded Parmigianino's viewers to what was stirring on the surface of the canvas, where mirrors scintillate their most sparkling reality. Alternatively, Caravaggio's painting literalizes the shield of a greeting by denaturing the naturalizing efficacy of its artifice. The *Medusa* is indeed a painting wrought by rules applicable to a flat canvas. But the physical dimensionality (spatial recession) those rules ordain is defied by the curvature of the canvas upon which it is painted. Thus does the painting call upon the viewer to see through the physical means of convexity to the visible image or form of deep space, only to realize that its visibility returns us to the soulless form of convexity.

All of this of course dovetails in interesting ways with the mythological source of the painting. The mythological Medusa turns the object of vision to stone, an immobility already referred to as the stupefaction that refined painterly technique can induce by inhibiting the more worldly and pragmatic resourcefulness of human motivation. Projecting the image out of the picture plane, especially in scenes of dramatic action, had been a signature of Caravaggio's work ever since *Basket of Fruit* (1598), which depicts its eponymous subject precariously perched on a shelf. John Spike has speculated that the illusionism of the *Medusa* "scores points on behalf of painting at the expense of sculpture"[17]

---

16. See Bersani and Dutoit, *Caravaggio's Secrets,* chap. 2.
17. Spike, *Caravaggio,* 64.

if painting could move us into a space more rounded than the one in which the sculptural figure is available to us. Spike implies that Caravaggio is venturing beyond the canvas and pushing the viewer beyond a merely contemplative stance. Certainly, Caravaggio's canvas is more than his entry into a long-standing Renaissance debate about the relative value of distinct artistic media. He coerces the viewer's eye in two directions, inward to the optical resolution of the features of the horrifying "portrait" (a register of narcissism) and outward upon the architectural projectile of the wooden shield. This produces a circumstance where the hierarchy of motivation for visual adaptivity becomes the real issue for the attentive viewer. The imperative of adaptability is, after all, the crux of the Medusa myth inasmuch as Perseus's own mortifying trompe l'oeil (the mirrory shield) is an admonition to look the other way. The unique provocation of Caravaggio's painting is that the *other way* is bound to be a determinant of whatever way of seeing we already assert a commitment to. This would be according to the forms of account or motivation that hold the strongest sway over us in the first place. The imperative to break the hold of a singular form of account is what allows us to see the painting for what it is, or, more to the point, for the sake of what we *might become* as viewers of it.

Parmigianino's painting is a mirror to see into, but Caravaggio's is an admonition against seeing or at least against *seeing in*. After all, according to Ovid the gorgon's destruction is reflected in the mirrory shield as the most catastrophic of images: the frozen image. I think it is not too anachronistic to speculate about how Caravaggio's image evokes the antithesis of the frozen image. I am thinking of the film image, which works according to a principle of montage. It is a commonplace that montage complicates time in two ways. It creates the illusion of movement in the action of the cinematically represented protagonist or scene, and it manifests that illusion through the succession of a multiplicity of frozen frames. In order to make this point seem even less provocatively anachronistic, it could easily be said that Parmigianino sought to amaze by naturalistic imitation of the surface of the glass. By contrast, in Caravaggio there is no naturalistic valorization of the mirror surface itself, precisely because the mirror here is an admonition to avert our eyes, to disavow the frozen frame. Of course we cannot avoid the glass. But in it our eyes register the reflected image of the gorgon from a vantage point of temporality and its humanizing correlate, the mobility of the body. It is widely acknowledged by contemporary art theory that these aspects of seeing are habitually repressed by the coercive lucidity of Albertian vision, which reflects, so to speak, a timeless and therefore dead subjectivity.[18] So in Caravaggio, the glass is surpassed by the gaze.

Like the film image, everything in the face of the Medusa tells time—but it is the antithesis of the eternal time that her gaze inflicts. The veritable ropes of blood gushing from the Medusa's neck in Caravaggio's composition are long enough to confirm our suspicion that what we are seeing happened calculable moments before the camera eye captured it. The drop-jawed mouth, forever incapable of speech, and especially the downward cast of the eyes, all potentiate the impression that the head is seen, indeed fatally saw itself, from *above* the reflective surface. Did Perseus drop the shield in order to raise the head in his victorious grip? The hand raising the trophy above our heads of course is not present, or at least not apparent, however much its absence fails to inhibit our imagining the gesture. But the convexity of the shield and the painting of the eyes as downcast show us what we can see beyond the arrested gaze. We are prompted to wonder: has Perseus moved on—beyond the image in the mirror? If our sight is as belated as these effects imply, then it warrants some catching up.

Or to put things back in the perspective of the Notional dynamic of self-deception, and of Brandom's inferentialism, it might be fair to say that Caravaggio's painting involves us in the act of seeing the prospect of seeing more. It involves us in the act of determining more in the negation of our being able to see that we must avert our eyes. But there is an important caveat here. Our *catching up* with the mythic actor of the painting, with the logical trajectory of its compositional elements, depends on how we understand the motivational resources of our situation.

I hope that I have by now made it clear that Parmigianino, Ashbery, and Caravaggio all derive their unique powers from heightening our awareness that our motivational resources are the condition of our acting, not merely the vehicles for rationalizing our acting. Perhaps Caravaggio makes the point more unequivocally that such an awareness of motivational resources normativizes self-deception. For his *Medusa* renders us both subject and object as alternates of each other. They are distinguishable only in terms of what motivational impetus they provide, not in terms of any essentialist polarity. Our commitment to viewing the painting one way or another is therefore persistently driven by the evidence that we know more than we have just seen, that whatever attributions

---

18. See Martin Jay, *Downcast Eyes: The Denigration of Vision in Twentieth-Century French Thought* (Berkeley and Los Angeles: University of California Press, 1994), for a review of this judgmental consensus among theorists who see Albertian perspectivism as nothing more than a mask for the Enlightenment ego.

are current nonetheless reflect conditions of assertability, namely, norms that have not yet been attributed.

This is the case in several ways, not the least of which is that the image of the mirror image invites us to be both victim and victimizer of Medusa. This reversal of polarities is played out as a quandary about the respective places of painter and viewer. While Caravaggio's *Medusa* is not a self-portrait in a convex mirror per se, where the subjectivities of the painter and the viewer are clearly opposed and mutually exclusive, the face of the Medusa is nonetheless recognizable as a "signature" face for the artist. It is the face of a male model known as Mario,[19] who appears in other Caravaggio paintings, notably the erotically charged *Boy Bitten by a Lizard* (1594–96). For the viewer who recognizes Mario's visage to be a signature of Caravaggio's oeuvre at this point in his career, it constitutes both a recognition of the painter's ego (a kind of self-portrait) and a self-recognition of the viewer, without being a mirror reflection—hence no risk of the viewer being frozen in that recognition. It is in fact a head already severed, so to speak, from other canvases and superimposed here. Quite similarly, the gorgon's snaky hair casts a shadow into a deeper space, upon which she therefore seems to be superimposed, by the physical dimension of convexity that gives palpability to her shape. This mitigation of the polarity of surface and depth is as decisive as the mitigation of the polarity of subject and object previously noted. Just as the warring inferential trajectories of painterly technique and physical surface, imagistic arrest and physical mobility, male and female visages, prompt our recourse to more encompassing knowledge of the relevant motivational grounds of our viewing, they also sever us from familiar motivational grounds. They thus save us from the state of arrest that is the menace of the gorgon's power and the measure of the painter/slayer's power to overcome it. Caravaggio achieves this effect by discerning the bases for a viewer's deeper and deeper involvement with the motive for wishing to see one's self as one should not be seen, namely, in the fatal guise of one's own narcissism. The implicit self-deception that prompts us to higher-order motivations in Caravaggio's canvas, preempts the narcissistic self-loss that always menaces in the conventions of self-portraiture. As we have already noted, the desire to see one's reflection risks reflection upon its inadequacy to the heightened attentiveness of desire. Rather than succumb to disillusionment, we are prompted to fall back upon our ever more resilient powers of personal reflection. The displacements of self that Caravaggio's deceptions perpetrate

---

19. This is Peter Robb's contention in *M: The Man Who Became Caravaggio*, 76.

devolve to re-placements of the viewer with respect to newly arising motivational grounds.

I am aware that the logic of displacement emerging in my reading of these three artworks, as sites of a self-deceiving mind that destabilizes subjectivity, resembles the Deleuzian ethos/aesthesis of the "deterritorialized" self. I now wish to distance myself from some of the most radical implications of that Deleuzian stance. Clearly, in my appreciation of the benefits of the displacement of the self, I do not want to lose touch with the concept of the self altogether, as I believe Deleuze is prone to do. So I wish to distance myself from Deleuze, but without disowning a genuinely Deleuzian interest in the artwork as a staging ground for the modality of *event*,[20] where experimentation trumps judgment, where action radically qualifies knowledge. Deleuze characterizes this event as a "belief of the future, in the future,"[21] a trust in the becoming of a world beyond our immediate warrant for asserting it. This stance gains access to a certain mobility of subjectivity characterized by Deleuze sometimes as "nomadism" and sometimes as "cinema." I have specifically invited this wary comparison with Deleuze in my desire to see Caravaggio's painting as a kind of cinema. Deleuze's *Cinema I: The Movement Image* presents a view of the cinematic image that is compatible with my assertion of the beneficent knowledge that Caravaggio can show us to be inherent to self-deception. In many ways Deleuze's text is as much an epitome of Deleuze's philosophical ethos as cinema is an epitome of the experiential conditions that Deleuze thinks should compel us to embrace that ethos. But while it aims at the kind of enhancements of knowledge that I am claiming self-deception potentiates, Deleuze's text does so at the cost of the very identity that would benefit from such knowledge.

Deleuze's notion of the "movement image" articulates the conditions under which cinema can produce a new quality of experience, or as he puts it "carry out a qualitative leap."[22] For my purposes, this ought to be seen as a rough correlate of the illusionism that turns the static frame into a moving image. Making an, at least initially, invidious comparison between the close-up shots

---

20. The event, as Deleuze explains in *Pourparlers* (Paris: Minuit, 1990), is the logical "destitution" of the verb "to be." He means to privilege the connectedness of things over the concept of their classification as like things. He means to elevate the "and" over the "is" in a way that is compatible with cinematic montage. One thing gains its intelligibility by its connection with another thing without any presupposition of compatibility between the two.

21. See Gilles Deleuze, *Difference and Repetition*, trans. Paul Patton (New York: Columbia University Press, 1995), 122.

22. Gilles Deleuze, *Cinema I: The Movement Image*, trans. Hugh Tomlinson and Barbara Habberjam (Minneapolis: University of Minnesota Press, 1986), 89.

of Griffith and Eisenstein, Deleuze argues that Griffith can only give us an image "concerned with the spectator's conditions of vision" (Deleuze, *Cinema I*, 91), whereas Eisenstein strives for a more dialectical relation between the object and what it is not: Eisenstein juxtaposes particulars out of narrative or expositional sequence and ignores the terms of fit between objects and the world to which they are presumed to belong. The result, Deleuze says, is the production of a new quality, in the sense that the image and the perception are no longer identical with each other (63). In perception "we perceive the thing, minus that which does not interest us as a function of our needs.... But, conversely, the thing itself *must* then be presented in itself as a complete, immediate, diffuse perception. The thing is image and, in this respect, is perceived itself and perceives all other things inasmuch as it is subject to their action" (63). In other words, the qualitative leap occurs as a suspension of an attributable motivational framework in favor of a diffusion of associative topoi. Deleuze links this phenomenon with a Peircean "firstness," a quality that instantiates newness of experience without the longevity of reflective understanding. There is something of this in my account of Caravaggio's *Medusa*. Deleuze's clarion assertion that "cinema itself is a new practice of images and signs, whose theory philosophy must produce as conceptual practice" (280), gives further warrant to my thinking about visualization as a philosophical métier.

In part, the dynamism of Caravaggio's *Medusa* is captured by this Deleuzian perspective. The "cut" that separates the gorgon head also attaches the viewer to aspects of the world that our conceptual commitments otherwise remain oblivious to because of our conceptual commitments. It does so in the manner of that "minus" ("We perceive the thing, minus that which does not interest us") which Deleuze's "qualitative leap" overcomes. The effect is like the film "cut" that both separates and unites two moments by showing us their incommensurability. For Deleuze the incommensurability becomes the beneficent counter of a "singularity," a being without an identity and so *minus* the burdens of warranted assertability. Deleuze conflates warranted assertion with judgment taken at the expense of experience.

I want to point out, however, that Caravaggio's montage, so to speak, in no way makes judgment and experience mutually exclusive. This is in large part because however shocked we may be to realize that the action we are witnessing occurred before the time of our witness—it is equivalent to the horror of belatedness that would have befallen Medusa's victims—the knowledge of what it means for us is *of the moment*. There is a provocative present-ness to our realization that what we are seeing still remains to be attributed. In a manner of speaking it still remains to be seen. Everything depends upon our turning the knowledge of the belatedness of our commitments to what we see into the realization of new criteria of attribution for those commitments. The action of the beheading may have occurred without our seeing it. *But we are now seeing that fact.* Like the illusion conjured by Caravaggio—that we inhabit concavity while viewing his painting, when in fact convexity is the medium of vision—our realization that the action of the beheading must have occurred without our seeing it arises out of the resources of a new subjective motivational bias. This makes the knowledge of what should have been seen—either the decapitation or the visage of the gorgon before it cast its petrifying spell—no longer relevant. If, as I have suggested, Medusa's victims would have come to this realization too late, we might appreciate that in Caravaggio's canvas there is no *too late.* There is only later. In other words, the vital effect of Caravaggio's *Medusa* is its prompting the viewer to the assertion of new commitments with respect to the power of seeing. We are, after all, prompted over and over to see again.

The compunction of Amélie Rorty's "strong-minded" self-deceiver comes to mind again. For I am arguing that the strength of Caravaggio's composition is its inviting us to integrate what is not yet integrable, since we are always belated in choosing the terms of integrability. This integrability would be based on one's diachronic consideration of conflicts between desire and knowledge, for example, the play of convexity and concavity in Caravaggio's canvas. Needless to say, Rorty's view is compatible with Brandom's and Velleman's motivationally guided sense of a selfhood. It is predicated on the notion that the self-identification of the agent is always the identification with her motives. We are saved, in these approaches, from a Deleuzian dissolution of identity by the acknowledgment that motivations succumb to changing criteria of salience. Specifically, we know these criteria vis-à-vis the things whose notice warrants higher-order motivations and new criteria of commitment for taking up those motives.

Velleman goes so far as to say that where we see an apparently weak, that is to say, self-deceived motive triumphing over a self-evidently strong motive, we often miss something important. We fail to appreciate how there is an agent behind the weaker motive who is—weakness notwithstanding—involving himself in his motives. Or, as Velleman puts it, "The agent is another motive, functionally speaking" (*Practical Reason,* 143). If we can speak functionally here, we are obliged to recognize that even where one thing leads seemingly "nomadically" to another, motivation is ineluctable. Deleuze would prefer to see this as an occasion for celebrating the indeterminacy of *anything can happen*. In *Cinema I*, this state of affairs is figured as "any-space-whatevers" (Deleuze, 114).[23] But I think this is an abdication of narrative time. I prefer to see how the effects of artworks like Caravaggio's *Medusa* keep us responsive to Kent Bach's question: "What to do next?" We will recall that this question was prompted by the recognition that our lives are shaped by gaps between what we are in a single moment and what we are over time: e.g., Brandom's doxastic gaps. Like Perseus, for whom timing is everything, the viewer of Caravaggio's *Medusa* possesses a self *of the moment* and a self over time.

We understand, no less clearly, that this existence of a now self and a then self is an inescapable precondition of the ruse perpetrated by the mirror-shield which the painting itself tropes. So, standing before the painting, we are implicated in Bach's wish to put rationality on a diachronic basis. Likewise we are implicated in the diachronic autonomy that is sought in Velleman's notion of the agent as a motive (*Practical Reason*, 143). There is indeed a strongly episodic dimension to our experience of Caravaggio's *Medusa*. The painter induces our looking at the forbidden object, with full recognition that it is forbidden because it is so fatalistically objectifying, though here it has itself been as decisively objectified as any decapitated human visage. But there is also a sense that the act of viewing entails our own decapitation. For the objectification of the gorgon head is not merely the function of our subjectivity. It is also a function of what we make of our subjectivity in the further recognition that our eyes are moved to the periphery of an event: either to the unseen act of decapitation itself or to the act of seeing it belatedly. As I've already suggested, the effect is complicated by our realization that we are inoculated against the gorgon's spell by the downward cast of her eyes. For her angle of vision courts the illusion of our reciprocal ascent, on a line of sight that leads speculatively to the place where Perseus keeps his victorious grip on the monstrous trophy. But it also invites us to make eye contact from below where we might, everything else notwithstanding, risk sharing the fate of Medusa's victims.

If Velleman is right that our motivation is always a function of how we intervene in our motives, then Caravaggio's painting exemplifies the claim by

23. With the idiom of "any-space-whatevers" Deleuze is trying to obviate the chooser's choice about where to be in space. His premise is that we cannot choose if we are deliberating between already posited alternatives. As he puts it: "If I am conscious of choice, there are therefore already choices that I can no longer make, and modes of existence that I can no longer follow . . ." (*Cinema I*, 114). I would not quarrel with the superficial point about choices precluding other choices. But I do not succumb to the conclusion that the obviating of all choice is an access to freedom. Nor do I think that making a choice precludes the recognition that one has made a mistake, and must then make another choice.

averting our eyes from their own focalizing powers, by deflecting our gaze from any restful contemplation of the image, by prompting us to other vantage points of viewing it. As we have already observed, our ability to see the artistically contrived depth of the image, the shadows cast upon a background, deflects our gaze from the projective surface of the canvas, only to prompt our motive for counting it as a salient condition of viewing. In other words, motive determines motive. Our decapitation is, in this respect, and by contrast with Medusa and her victims, the métier of our endurance over time. Insofar as the mental action of directing one's attention, responding to new considerations, is joined with the physical action of the painting's subject matter, we know more convincingly how essential the capacity to do something next may be to the survival of our humanity.

As I have insisted from the start, Kent Bach's question "What to do next?" is both open-ended, as Deleuze might like to have it, and determinant—exhibiting human being as a maker of assertions, as commitive—as Hegel, Brandom, and Velleman might like to have it. Our consideration of Parmigianino's, Ashbery's, and especially Caravaggio's works shows us that there is no reason that these should be mutually exclusive propositions. The seeming discrepancies between open-endedness and determinativeness present again the prospect of negotiating something like Brandom's doxastic gaps. They simply presuppose the diachronic rationality—the reckoning of now selves with then selves—that I initially proposed might be the ethically beneficent work of self-deception. Each of the artworks engaged in this chapter figures the drama of now selves and then selves as a question about how one musters commitments to what one claims to know. Thus I can allege that the affinity of diachronic rationality with an inescapable narrative dimension of aesthetic experience—in both the verbal and the visual arts—intimates an ethical charge as well as a pragmatics for learning that ethic.

What may not be immediately apparent in this prospect is that, inasmuch as diachronic rationality entails a process of soliciting reasons in order to bridge doxastic gaps, it portends a human character that is both normative and self-superseding. It is an epitome of the *uncharacteristic character* I evoked in chapter 1 of this work. Now it remains to be seen how such character is sustainable across the threshold of intersubjectivity where our reasons matter most. They matter in proportion to our capacity to learn from the limits of our self-understanding, which the next moment in time relentlessly presents to us as a mandate to go on.

4

Being Out of Character / Normativizing Self-Deception

Reason-Giving and Normativity

We have been working so far on the assumption that reason-giving is a source of normativity for any character negotiating the competing motivational grounds of action. By this standard, diachronic rationality and the narrative emplotments it involves us in are normative. The relevant norms here are whatever reasons suffice to be self-explanatory as we face the self-differentiating moments of a dispassionately elapsing time. Accordingly, I have insisted that narrative plot is ineluctably a solicitation of reasons. As Beckett's *Unnamable* famously anticipates,[1] if we are forever in the thrall of the imperative to go on, we are forever tethered to the questions of what to go on to, and why. Given the reasons we have for being in one circumstance, what reasons must we summon to go on to another?

Normativity, of course, conflicts with the imperatives of personal desire. Desire or impulse is prompted as something independent of reasoning, threatening to skew our actions from rational purposiveness. In illusionism, when it is seen as a mechanism of self-deception, we are caused to mistake desires for reasons. We are inveigled to see what we think we desire to see. The philosophical imperative of normativity, which is most powerfully advocated by Kant, is in turn understood as a prompting in us to turn desires into reasons. It is, as he says, a tendency that is "natural and active in us even prior to the moral law."[2]

---

1. See Samuel Beckett, *Three Novels: Molloy, Malone Dies, The Unnamable* (New York: Grove Press, 2009).
2. See Kant's "The Metaphysics of Morals," in *Political Writings*, ed. H. S. Reiss, trans. H. B. Nisbet (Cambridge: Cambridge University Press, 1970). See also Christine M. Korsgaard, *The Sources of Normativity* (Cambridge: Cambridge University Press, 1996), 249, for rich commentary on this point. Korsgaard implicitly endorses the stress I wish to place upon "activity" in the remainder of this chapter.

And indeed the drift of recent thinking about self-deception by Bach, Mele, and Audi, among others, promotes the importance of understanding that there are no desires or beliefs without endorsing reasons. This is what makes desire a counter for rationalization and leads us to contemplate the reciprocity of rationalization and self-deception. One might say then that the interplay of reasons and desire bounds the discourse of normativity. It gives us further good reason, I think, to pursue a transition from an ethically judgmental notion of self-deception as irrationality to the ethically productive notion of self-deception that I proposed at the beginning of this enterprise: one whereby our errant selves and our active selves might be advantageously reconciled. For me this reconciliation is what diachronic rationality portends.

I therefore want to understand the warrant for this reconciliation to be the more general challenge of knowing when one is convincingly oneself. The self possessed of even the most self-indulgent habits of self-deception is nonetheless cognizant of the epistemic liabilities of not knowing what he or she is doing, not knowing what reasons would substantiate a claim upon his or her personal existence. I am not speaking merely of what Aristotle refers to as *enkrateia* or self-control.[3] Self-control presupposes the opposite of a standard notion of self-deception. It postulates an objectivity by which we can discount anything that doesn't constitute a presumptively best reason for acting. In an important way it begs the question of how we know what counts as the best reason. On the contrary, when the philosopher of norms and values Joseph Raz says, in *Engaging Reason*, "We are ourselves so long as, as we see it, we are responsive to reason,"[4] he couples identity with a process of reasoning that he calls "capacity rationality" (*Engaging Reason*, 69).

Capacity rationality is "a capacity to see the normative significance of the way things are, to comprehend what reasons they constitute, and the significance of that fact for itself" (Raz, *Engaging Reason*, 69). But Raz favors a test of normativity, rather than objectivity, precisely because it derives from our cultivating a responsiveness to reasons rather than our having recourse to any instrumental arsenal of reasons. By contrast with capacity rationality, irrationality can be understood as an exhibition of a lack of care about one's own epistemic conduct, one's inattentiveness to one's place in the world. Earlier I asserted that what counts for us as reasons is a function of our most fastidious noticings, that is to say, what we consider relevant to our worldly commitments.

---

3. See my *Aesthetic Reason*, 84–89.
4. See Joseph Raz, *Engaging Reason: On the Theory of Value and Action* (Oxford: Oxford University Press, 1999), 19.

Consequently, I see the kind of normativity implicit in "capacity rationality" as a de facto investment in the broadest possible range of responses to the world around us. The convergence of rationalist and aesthetic interests marked on this trajectory of thought mandates the normativizing of self-deception that I have embarked upon by challenging any characterization of the self-deceiving mind as merely pathological. Our disposition toward what I have called noticings, or seeing incrementally more, with incrementally more attention, makes us natural choosers. It is, after all, a disposition upon which any responsiveness to reasons would depend. We have seen this expressly to be the case in painting where illusionistic play and a proliferation of alternative perspectival vantage points are active.

Joseph Raz makes the point implicitly. He notes how the expressly "aspect-dependent" character of human wants aligns us perforce with a "classical," as opposed to what he terms a more contemporary "rationalist model," of choice-driven agency (*Engaging Reason*, 54). The aspect-dependent character of human wants is implicated in the discipline of noticings, since it de facto presupposes other things to notice. Accordingly, what Raz identifies as "classical agency" acknowledges how actions and objects that we desire may turn out to have countervailing liabilities that incite our desire to disown them *even as we want them*. Our ability to see aspects of wholes as relevant to our choices among wholes invites our deployment of comparative criteria for choosing among objects. By favoring the classical conception of agency over what he calls the "rational conception of agency," Raz is casting doubt on the efficacy of choosing a best reason for acting on the basis of the self-evidence of a desire to act—as if that desire is de facto a best reason. Raz is instead allowing for a model of choice based on understanding the active will to be an independent factor. He argues for a willingness to see reasons as making options for action "eligible" rather than concluding that one's choice of action is simply a function of there being no rational alternative—that is, no better reason for acting. The classical agent accordingly can tolerate the existence of widespread incommensurabilities among our reasons for choosing, especially where will is an independent factor in choosing options that seem reasonable (47).

Raz argues that a reliance on widespread incommensurabilities, which for the rationalist agent would be tantamount to simple irrationality, "gains support from ordinary human experience, which teaches us that quite commonly people do not survey all the options open to them before they choose what they do" (*Engaging Reason*, 66). Thus, as I have already suggested with respect to "capacity rationality," the real test of our rational agency requires our discovering ever more ingenious resources for broadening the scope of our responses to the world. In a way I am referencing nothing more than an aptly thick description of human character development, or a straightforward notion of character that presupposes its development. As I suggested in the first chapter of this book, such a view of character is curiously "uncharacteristic" with respect to the prevailing post-Enlightenment conventions of character representation, especially in the Western literary tradition. The expectation of a character's development too frequently takes the form of a genetic determinism based in the reputed nature of personality or in plot incident. This is the character presupposed by Raz's "rational agency." Such a character is, as Raz regrets, onerously encumbered by its strict eschewal of incommensurabilities. I prefer to contemplate character in terms congenial with Raz's classical agency, whereby deterministic elements are subordinated to deliberative métiers for making normative determinations.

Before taking an admittedly schematic view of the meaning of character in distinctly literary narrative, therefore, I wish to consider how my *uncharacteristic character* is very distinctly a creature of historical modernity in the West. This is to say that my "uncharacteristic character" should be understood, with a kind of prescient Hegelianism, to be an intersubjective entity before it is a duly subjective entity. My examination of this character will make a perhaps more compelling transition from my previous discussions of Parmigianino, Ashbery, and Caravaggio, if I begin by pegging its history to the notion of human being that is formulated in the early tradition of painterly portraiture.

The Reasons for Portraiture

According to many historical accounts of the emergence of portraiture as a legitimate genre of character representation, it might be said to have evolved in tandem with something like a discourse of motives for self-assertion. Those motives would be seen as determinative for the forms of representation themselves. As Harry Berger has convincingly argued in *Fictions of the Pose*,[5] the initial "old physiognomic formula" identified with the first half of the fifteenth century, whereby features of the face represented a natural index for interiority, gave way in the sixteenth century to an elaborate dialectic between the poser and the painter. This presupposed the subject's motive to be seen a

---

5. Harry Berger Jr., *Fictions of the Pose: Rembrandt Against the Italian Renaissance* (Stanford: Stanford University Press, 2000), 89–90.

Fig. 3   Lorenzo Lotto, *Portrait of Andrea Odoni*, 1527. The Royal Collection © 2009, Her Majesty Queen Elizabeth II.

certain way. Interiority, no longer nature-dependent, became a variable of the sitter's wish or motivation to be looked at by the painter in ways that were in turn dependent upon the normative cultural recognitions that were available for the painter-viewer and contingent upon the sitter's performance of them, or resistance to performing them.[6] Berger cites Lorenzo Lotto's *Portrait of Andrea Odoni* (1527) as a case in point. Berger typifies the practice of portraiture by treating it as a kind of exposition of the etymology of the Greek word

---

6. Berger commits himself to a significant hypothesis: "Whether or not the fictions of the pose mandated by these norms induce the 'ineradicable suspicions of dissimulation [quoting Joan Copjec],' they may be assumed to induce cognitive dissonance between the awareness of the unperformed self-representations and truth to the norms governing the performances inscribed in the portraits" (227). The cognitive dissonance he is responding to here mandates an assessment of which motives on the part of which party will suffice for the most viable viewpoint.

anecdota (things not given out): a form of secret knowledge purveyed as straightforward appearance.

But I would push the reading even further.[7] Lotto's portrait is most anecdotal in the sense that the sitter's solicitation of recognition is orchestrated as an anecdote of choices posed by the sitter for the painter-viewer. We might presume that the viewer's choosing is necessarily anxiety-ridden. It is, after all, a plausible mirror of the anxiety of the sitter who may not have chosen the attitude that will win the recognition he believes he deserves from his viewer. Nevertheless, in this case the sitter seems at first to have the advantage. Andrea Odoni, a Venetian antique collector whose choices are figured in the composition of the painting as a kind of circular frame, stares upon the viewer of the picture plane with all the presumption of a proven connoisseur. He seems to goad us: "Which of the items arranged before you reflects my connoisseurship best?" He is waiting for the naïf to choose badly, without taste, without discriminating knowledge. As if to abet the sitter, the painter has figured the viewer's anxiety as specifically a problem of knowing what to ignore, and of seeing that everything one notices requires ignorance of something else that is presenting itself with competitive urgency. But the real power of the portraiture in this case is the way that the painter has made the stakes of choosing badly as conspicuous a liability for the sitter as it is for the viewer: the compositional centrality of the collector exposes him to the risk of being upstaged by his collection. Are we to see the collector as the meaning of his collection or the collection as conferring the meaning of his person? Whether from the point of view of the sitter or the viewer, one realizes the fragmentariness of one's attention to be the necessary modality of one's understanding. The point is emphasized by the fragmentariness of the artifacts displayed. Raz's notion of the aspect-dependent nature of human wants is relevant here. For Lotto's composition dramatizes a reflective consciousness wherein the manifest motives for self-presentation necessarily relegate other motives to oblivion.[8]

The groundwork for the implicit discourse of motives that inheres in such

---

7. I am extrapolating very freely from Berger's discussion of the painting in *Fictions of the Pose*, 221–26. To be fair, Berger is less interested in the implications of aspectual identity. He is focused more on anxiety as an existential counter of the pose.

8. In this context it is worth considering J. David Velleman's idea that any workable concept of self is determined by an "aspectual autonomy." He means to consider the only sound basis for the self to be the capacity to present to one's consciousness one part of one's being as an object for reflection. As with Raz's aspect dependency, Velleman's reflective activity has a built-in narrative dimension like that entailed, I contend, by diachronic rationality. See especially Velleman's "Identification and Identity," in *Self to Self: Selected Essays* (Cambridge: Cambridge University Press, 2006), 357–59.

representational practices is tantamount to what I have previously characterized as a specific cognitive predisposition: one asserts a commitment to a self that can be valued under a certain description which is nonetheless subject to alteration. As I stipulated earlier, the validity of this commitment is borne out according to the coherence of its consequences with the values it otherwise claims to instantiate. In the annals of Western rationalism, the Enlightenment hero is often treated, as Nietzsche so snidely caricatured him in *On the Genealogy of Morals,* as nothing more than an animal bred with the right to make promises.[9] He would seem, in Nietzsche's skeptical view, to be bound to an eternal repetition of the reasons for holding any original commitments, without which his assertion of self-identity would be unimaginable. Within this view, the Enlightenment hero is a natural antagonist to the self-deceiver. The promise itself is a "device" of cultural agency whereby one's identity is ordained as a constraint to make experience cohere with first principles. But this familiar caricature of the rationalist self-realizer ignores the possibility that commitments to original motives can be made coherent with their consequences, insofar as they are themselves altered to accommodate what they did not seem to ordain. Nietzsche would no doubt argue that an encounter with the *ignis fatuus* is inescapable in the course of attempts at human self-realization. Indeed, on this assumption, the self to be realized should never be expected. Where expectations are defeated, illusionism is arguably assignable as the cause. We can easily imagine how this notion would be especially alarming in the Age of Reason when human consciousness of the expectations for self-realization are high, and when the possibility of self-deception takes on its most admonitory significance.

Robert Pippin prompts our equating the illusionism of self-deception, as I have described it here, with the inherent theatricality of the self: a vocation dependent on "the importance of role playing."[10] What is presupposed here is a difference between the public self and the private self like that which Proust dramatized so influentially in his *Recherché*. According to Pippin, one acknowledges a "kind of 'capacity' view of one's practical identity and unity, and the capacity in question is an ability to negotiate properly the relation of dependence and independence with respect to one's fellow agents, what to accept of

---

9. See Friedrich Nietzsche, *On the Genealogy of Morals and Ecce Homo*, trans. Walter Kaufmann and R. J. Hollingdale (New York: Vintage, 1989), 55, for Nietzsche's most scathing caricature of rationality as a fetishization of memory.

10. Robert Pippin, *The Persistence of Subjectivity: On the Kantian Aftermath* (Cambridge: Cambridge University Press, 2005), 327. Pippin's chapter on Proust, "On 'Becoming Who One Is' (and Failing): Proust's Problematic Selves," is especially instructive on this point.

how others take up and interpret and react to one's deeds, what to reject" (*Subjectivity*, 328). Berger's giving the name *fiction of the pose* to this inescapable "scenario," as he puts it (Berger, 175), conjures the narrative imperatives of human experience that I am suggesting might mitigate any overly rationalistic caricature of the self-deceiver. It might further intimate the complicity of the Enlightenment hero with this presumed nemesis. For such complicity of reason with self-deception is the hallmark of literary art. Literary plot-making in particular—since Aristotle, and much more persistently than in the world of painting—has rendered human activity, rather than human physiognomy, the most compelling register of meaning or value with respect to human character. Where characters act under the constraint of emplotment, they are predisposed to know themselves differently through the self-transformative baffles of their actions. Now I want to suggest that because they face the Beckettian/Bachean prospect of *going on,* they are more scrupulously obliged to know what they are doing. Within the arena of self-deception knowing and doing come together in a way that simple plot reversal does not permit.

So I will follow a more subtle implication of this commonplace about plot, especially novelistic plot, which gains enormous cultural currency under the auspices of Enlightenment philosophy. I want to propose that the novel is a form in which the Enlightenment hero is ineluctably a self-deceiver insofar as his rationality is subtended to a diachronic or narrative coherence that is in no way simply causal. It is rather normative. This is so with the understanding that where action occurs, rules for action are always the response to an explanatory exigency of the agent in question. Such normativity obtains whenever an action has compelling efficacy with respect to our situation of being in the world. I believe I have already intimated the stakes of this enterprise in my reading of Flaubert. But now I must explore their consequence more fully. The novel is a particularly lively stage for observing how the reasons one has for taking action depend upon what coherence they might lend to the story in which one's need to summon good reasons, or justifiable commitments, necessarily arises.[11] In this instance, self-deception is an integral condition of self-reflection over time, chiefly insofar as such reflective accountability is a de facto soliciting of hitherto inoperative and perhaps hitherto unimaginable reasons for action. What is portended here is a prospect for subjective autonomy

---

11. J. David Velleman's "The Self as Narrator" deploys Dennett's concept of a "center of narrative gravity." He thus grounds rational agency in a way that agrees with my own proposition, at the end of chapter 2, that the affinity between diachronic rationality and the narrative dimension of aesthetic experience in the verbal and visual arts anticipates the ethical work of self-deception. *Self to Self,* 208–9.

that is not epiphenomenal of Enlightenment principles, whereby autonomy is simply a measure of the coherence of past principles with the experiential variables of developing activity. Rather, it is an autonomy that is functionally legitimated. Specifically, it is legitimated in the activity of assimilating reasons to the mandate for new self-descriptions under which we can value ourselves in changing circumstances.[12]

In order to advance this thinking I wish to look at three novels that arguably limn the arc of post-Enlightenment modernity: Cervantes' *Don Quixote* (1605), Diderot's *Rameau's Nephew* (published 1805), and Nabokov's *Lolita* (1956). In many ways these texts are encyclopedic presentations of the self-deceiving character as it is represented in literary tradition. They are no less exhaustively exemplars of the unique transformability of novelistic form. Finally, each of these novels is a self-conscious attempt to epitomize a human character that is unimaginable without the precepts of Enlightenment idealism. I will argue that these overlapping topoi of human experience provide an apt laboratory for discovering how self-deception might be deemed normative for the ethical ambitions of human subjects aspiring to give rational accounts of themselves in a context of contested values occasioned by the narrative will. A substantial "self" is unquestionably at stake in the narratives of the characters that lend literary identity to my exemplary texts. These texts will therefore supply especially productive frameworks within which to defend the necessity of taking self-deception rather than mere error as the crux of the matter.

Error per se pertains to the objective validity of standards of judgment. As a value term it is a counter of universals. By contrast, selves are embodiments or enactments of standards of judgment. Insofar as they are subject to error, or something like *akratic* reasoning, they expose the dispositional foundations of belief. More emphatically, they intimate the warrant for subordinating judgment to the specificities of individualized subjective experience, which have been long and assiduously honored by Enlightenment idealism, notwithstanding the fealty of "Enlightened" character to the cause of the universal. The

---

12. Kantian autonomy is of course the touchstone of tradition here, though my argument breaks with any deontological predicates. I would obviously decouple my investment in this aspect of Kant from everything that intimates the privileging of a metaphysical self. As Christine Korsgaard has argued, the kind of autonomous identity that Kant is interested in need not be seen as strictly theoretical. That is, it needn't be a view about what we are scientifically. Rather, "It is better understood as a description under which you value your life to be worth living and your actions to be worth undertaking." Korsgaard, *Sources of Normativity*, 101. In other words, Korsgaard seeks to appropriate from Kant a version of practical identity not bounded by a universal ought.

self-deceiver, in this context, is a character whose nature is unknowable except through the vicissitudes of the most vexing activity.

Noticing Notice

In the simplest terms, I am proposing that self-deception is an indispensable crux of aesthetic form in the novel. I already intimated as much in my discussion of how motivational biases are affected by changing circumstances of action. My proposition is frankly antagonistic to a quite popular thematic view of self-deception: as the foil for the most banal sense of what it means to possess ethical character, to become the bearer of objective standards of judgment. I think that my proposal gains authority with the observation that in the novel the ethical dimension of character is the fulcrum of development. Here I will emphasize that development does not occur except as the dramatization of a capacity for "noticing" more. In a sense, the very conception that plot develops at all presumes upon the inevitability that a character will have to judge what counts for reality by finessing or noticing conditions which he could not already have imagined to be relevant to his or her identity. Without an acknowledgment of the validity of this presumption about novelistic protagonists, the abiding Aristotelian precept that plot-making is a métier of learning would have no meaningful or secure foundation. The technical ground of my reasoning here is of course indistinguishable from the "device" of *peripeteia,* so crucial to Aristotle's ranking of plot above character among the elements of tragic drama inventoried in *Poetics*.[13] If we take Aristotle seriously on this point, I believe that we must treat *peripeteia* itself, both elementally and strategically, as a métier of noticing. There is little controversy among ethicists that taking more astute account of the needs of others, or the situation in which one solicits the value of the self, is a sine qua non of what Hegel preferred to call *Sittlichkeit* in *The System of Ethical Life* (1801–2).[14] In fact, it might be argued

13. See especially section 11 in Aristotle, *The Basic Works of Aristotle,* trans. Richard McKeon (New York: Random House, 1941).

14. G. W. F. Hegel, *System of Ethical Life (1802/3) and First Philosophy of Spirit (Part III of the System of Speculative Philosophy (1803/4),* ed. and trans. T. M. Knox (Albany: State University of New York Press, 1979). I could put it in terms more communicative with the immediate context of my discussion of identity in the novel. I might say that noticing is an entailment of the "moments" of universality, particularity, and individuality. As with any dialectical motion, our responsiveness to new contingencies of existence is crucial.

that the whole project of recognition, without which no ethical institution is imaginable for Hegel, is a nod to the human capacity for noticing.

But before I proceed to develop this line of thought on the register of novelistic aesthetics I want to preempt some possible confusions. The aptness of the novel form for noticing this capacity, as a métier of the ethical work of self-deception, is not based on my belief that the novel is a unique domain of inquiry in this regard. I stated this in chapter 1. Rather, my focus on the novel here is a necessary complement to understanding how aesthetic works in general are involved in the essential narrativity of noticing. For similar reasons, it is also important to point out that that my choice of the three novels by Cervantes, Diderot, and Nabokov is in no way meant to be an attempt to represent the history of the genre, if any such gesture is even possible. This is especially the case given the novel's persistent blurring of its own formal boundaries with lyric/poetic, pictorial, emotive, and other topoi of human affective presence in the world.

Rather, something more pressing is at stake with respect to how the sources of human noticing and the dynamics of self-deception are revealed to be reciprocal with each other in novelistic practice. We have already recognized that *Don Quixote, Rameau's Nephew,* and *Lolita* represent a widely held belief in the genre's special affinity with Enlightenment reason and the affect of modernity. These fictional works are antagonists of a traditional culture that would otherwise dispose us to the agential inhibitions of doxa and ideology. Georg Lukács is the critic who has most starkly typified the novel as the art form that is unique in its comprehension of the "rift between 'inside' and 'outside,' a sign of the essential difference between the self and the world."[15] This rift is a cardinal warrant for noticing what is not coherent. So, the aptness of my choice of literary texts goes beyond their representations of Enlightenment self-deceivers. The adherence of the protagonists of these novels to subjective identity, as a locus of free agency, is precisely what inspires their self-deception in the modality of a "rift" between self and world. The irony is that, in the absence of such a rift, these protagonists would possess no narrative purchase on the world of human actions. So we might say that it is self-assertion per se that makes self-deception a métier of ethical conduct even in the guise of the seemingly most irresponsible and/or unethical personalities exemplified by Quixote, Rameau, and Humbert Humbert. As Lukács himself asserts, the rift possesses an ethical dimension in its very prompting for us to strive to produce

---

15. Georg Lukács, *Theory of the Novel*, trans. Anna Bostock (Cambridge: MIT Press, 1971), 29.

coherence between self and world: what in his earliest writings Lukács would have baldly countenanced as a Hegelian reconciliation. This explains Lukács's enthusiasm for realism (over naturalism and modernism) in the novel. What Lukács misses is precisely the motive for my desire to normativize self-deception as a métier of noticing: for this motive arises in acceptance of the proposition that the rift is an insuperable constraint of self-assertion. It is a commitment on account of which the endless mustering of self-explaining reasons must be acknowledged as an inescapable fact of human life.

Especially within the context of Lukács's theory of the novel, it might be worth observing that the mustering of self-explaining reasons, which I infer from the Lukácsian rift, invokes the spirit of bildungsroman. It does so in a way that suggests how fundamental insights about the novel bear upon the self-deceiving character. The meaning of the term "bildungsroman" might be most accurately glossed in the words of that seminal hermeneut Wilhelm Dilthey whose coinage it is: "the development of a human being in various stages, forms and periods of life."[16] Dilthey presupposes what I have claimed is key to the Notional logic of the self-deceiver. Indeed, Dilthey's assertion that in the bildungsroman there is a movement from error to truth, from confusion to clarity, from nature to spirit, has a distinctly Hegelian resonance. As I stated earlier, what matters most in the process of Notional self-realization is not the conformity of an act with a concept but an elaboration of the range of the applicability of the concept. I stipulated that this elaboration is bound by inferential determinants. Insofar as the bildungsroman features error, confusion, and confrontation with the antagonistic forces of nature, it focuses upon how the various stages, forms, or periods of a life cohere *without* a simple causality. The condition under which this is imaginable is, I would say, cognate with the self-deceiver's *development.* That development is ordained by a disposition to answer the question of what to do next without reductively assimilating the next moment to the past moment.

In the end, of course, Dilthey's Hegelianism embraces a goal of spiritual reconciliation, which my sense of the Notionalism of self-deception hedges against. For this reason, the bildungsroman, which in the parlance of literary study is the novel of education, or the pedagogical novel, is often reduced by literary critics to an assumption that learning is retrospective, that development

---

16. See Wilhelm Dilthey, *Leben Schleiermachers*, 2 vols., ed. M. Redeker (Berlin: Walter De Gruyter, 1870), 1:135; quoted in G. B. Tennyson's "The Bildungsroman in Nineteenth-Century English Literature," in *Medieval Epic to the "Epic Theater" of Brecht: Essays in Comparative Literature*, ed. Rosario P. Armato and John M. Spalek (Los Angeles: USC Press, 1968), 135–46.

is cumulative, that self-realization is its goal. Here I would depart from the Diltheyan path. But that does not deny the usefulness of Dilthey's original coinage in my present address to the novel form. As I indicated when postulating at the start of chapter 3 the pedagogical dimension of self-deception, the self-realization of the self-deceiver should not be comprehended as a unified personality, the product of his past. Rather, the past is a reference point for intuiting relations with what was not apprehensible within its horizon of notice. Against the grain of much scholarly oversimplification, I want to suggest that the kind of learning that is presaged in Dilthey's formulation, but which Dilthey himself ultimately rejects, invites provocative speculation. We might imagine that all novels, insofar as they exhibit the dynamics of self-deception on the thresholds of error, confusion, and conflict with nature, participate in the humanizing enterprise of the bildungsroman. We can take this a step further. If the bildungsroman is perforce a scene of error, confusion, and conflict with nature, where the discipline of notice would be crucial for character development, it is all the more urgent that we understand how self-deception is a motor of character in the novel. This is especially true if we treat all novels as implicated in the bildungsroman. By the same token, seeing the bildungsroman as a métier of self-deception guarantees the relevance of the art form of the novel to all other arts in which some development of the character of the audience (reading or viewing) is at stake.

Character and Compulsive Notice

What Cervantes, Diderot, and Nabokov have most conspicuously in common is their authorization of fictions that dramatize a confusion of the realms of the real and the illusionary. Such confusion is a widely acknowledged threshold of self-explanation generally speaking. The protagonistic selves featured in *Don Quixote, Rameau's Nephew,* and *Lolita* are, at first glance, easily judged to be deceived about their grasp of "reality": one that we would otherwise sanction as an unproblematic norm. As such, they are especially vivid specimens of human abnormality. They are accordingly highly unlikely props for a reader's ability to meet what I have alleged to be the specifically ethical demand imposed upon readers. Readers who vicariously identify with the agency of fictional characters, or who recognize the apparently incorrigible fallibility of that agency, must reckon with the agential challenges of the reading experience to answer the question "What should I do next?" In this context thinking and doing must be considered indistinguishable.

The conflation of thinking and doing by the protagonists of these three novels is indicative of how problematic the question "What should I do next?" can be. For each of the characters—Quixote, Rameau, and Humbert—thinking and doing are vexingly intertwined because these protagonists are unusually responsive to the texture of their social worlds. What amounts to a virtually pathological responsiveness is exhibited as an enhanced capacity for noticing what "normal" people would not. Quixote's impulse toward idealizations of the world is a function of the acute particularization of his observations. He is a slave of his perceptions insofar as their proliferation, in the most mundane events of life, demands ever more attentive commitments to imaginative transformation: "Our hero's imagination converted whatsoever he saw, heard, considered into something of which he had read in books of chivalry."[17] Rameau is stigmatized by his interlocutor (Diderot's persona) as "one of the weirdest characters in this land of ours."[18] Because, as the narrator tells us, "Nothing is less like him than himself" (Diderot, 34), Rameau's self-assertions are indistinguishable from the prospect of seizing upon some aspect of his experience that alienates, either voluntarily or involuntarily, his self-recognition. Every new theater of experience elicits from him a more nuanced performance of his existence. Finally, Humbert Humbert is the self-admitted avatar of a human perversity. It is a quality of mind that is, however, unimaginable without appreciating how his powers of discriminating the so-called nymphet from a real girl presuppose a preternatural disposition toward the particulars of experience. What's more, the significance of these particulars is inversely proportional to the ever tinier minutiae that capture his notice.

And yet there something even more important than my adducing these characters as an occasion for thinking about the specific quality of noticing that I associate with self-deception. It is the task of showing how the acumen for noticing, epitomized by the protagonists of each of my exemplary literary texts, becomes in turn a stake of reading those texts well. I would say that reading these texts correctly depends on *our* noticing that the corollary of Quixote's, Rameau's, and Humbert Humbert's unusual attentiveness is a not uncommon trait of the lively imagination: paranoia. The nagging fear of incomplete knowledge is indeed the nemesis of one's asking the question "What should

---

17. Miguel de Cervantes, *Don Quixote*, trans. Tobias Smollett (New York: Modern Library, 2004), 52.
18. Denis Diderot, *Rameau's Nephew / Alembert's Dream,* trans. Leonard Tancock (New York: Penguin, 1966), 33.

I do next?" It threatens paralysis and the loss of narrative meaning, without which characters in novels especially, but all agents possessed of some sense of destiny, would face a crude dehumanization.

In her *Seeing Through Self-Deception* Annette Barnes concedes that self-deception is animated by a desire to reduce anxiety.[19] This anxiety arises as cognizance of the possibility that what I do next may turn out to undermine my desires. I would suggest that it is precisely such anxiety that fuels the Enlightenment rationalist's prejudice against self-deception. Accordingly, Quixote, Rameau, and Humbert Humbert present the perfect foils for this caricature of rationality: each knows himself at least well enough to know that he needs to know more before he can decide what to do next. This is, as Herbert Fingarette maintains, a recognition on the part of each of these protagonists that one needs to *spell things out.* The compensatory anxiety exhibited by each personality denotes a desire to accommodate a wider purview of knowledge, not in subservience to some deontological stricture of reason, but out of the desire for a rational self-possession that is more fully humanizing. In this respect, we can equate anxiety-driven self-deception with self-preservation, or what Annette C. Baier has called a "life-preserving skill."[20]

I will have more to say about Barnes's and Baier's arguments in the final chapter of this book. For the moment, it will suffice to say that the life-preserving skill of the paranoid noticer is strategically significant in contexts of indeterminacy such as perennially menace the protagonists of narrative plots. This is particularly conspicuous when characters are anxious about the potential meaningfulness of their actions, or the potential devastation of their personalities by a meaningless flow of events. The notion of self-deception as self-preservation mitigates the more chastening characterization of self-deception by thinkers like David Pears and Donald Davidson as a blameworthy irrationality.[21] The self-preservative modality of self-deception opens a critical prospect: the capacity for noticing may be as important to a reader with rationalistic pretensions as it is to a fictional character whose reasoning is manifestly

---

19. Annette Barnes, *Seeing Through Self-Deception* (Cambridge: Cambridge University Press, 1997), 31–32. For Barnes, the self-deceiver is specifically anxious to believe that *P* because he or she is afraid that not-*P* really is the case. Anxiety reduction depends upon the self-deceiver's censorship of evidence against *P*.

20. Annette C. Baier, "The Vital But Dangerous Art of Ignoring: Selective Attention and Self-Deception," in *Self and Deception: A Cross-Cultural Philosophical Enquiry*, ed. Roger T. Ames and Wimal Dissanayake (Albany: State University of New York Press, 1996), 53–72.

21. See Donald Davidson, "Two Paradoxes of Irrationality," in *Philosophical Essays on Freud*, ed. Richard Wollheim and James Hopkins (Cambridge: Cambridge University Press, 1982), 289–305, and David Pears, *Motivated Irrationality* (Oxford: Clarendon Press, 1984).

a pretense of reality. In both cases the operative principle of survival is a variable of one's ability to give reasons to oneself for sustaining beliefs over time and for sustaining activity such that one's reason-giving powers do not succumb to the power of any self-excluding belief.

Don Quixote

The necessary brevity of my readings of *Quixote, Rameau,* and *Lolita* will, I hope, be justified by my desire to show how each reveals a distinct aspect of the problem of survival understood as a discipline of noticing. I have anticipated that what these texts have most in common is the insight that noticing is a métier of reading and that reading is a métier of noticing. On the basis of this reciprocity, the discipline of notice implicates readers in the normativity of self-deception. The question about what to do next is the motor of that reciprocity. I believe that these points are generalizable to a view of the novel in its broadest historical and theoretical reaches.

To begin we must understand how Don Quixote is the epitome of self-deception, at least insofar as self-deception may be thought of as a métier of noticing. Specifically, the vocation of knight-errantry, for which the character of Quixote is emblematic, presupposes what the capacity for noticing demands of human attentiveness—time or duration. Errantry is a form of wandering that incurs the errors of experience. Cervantes' protagonist is notoriously modeled on Amadis de Gaula, a fourteenth-century mythic prototype of the knight errant. De Gaula epitomizes errantry both as the activity of wandering and as the temporal openness without which such wandering is inconceivable. Indeed, Amadis de Gaula was also known as Amadis sin Tiemp.[22] Amadis is deemed to be born out of time (without time) because he is born out of wedlock. In other words, he is not out of time in the sense of being timeless, but in the sense of being off the clock, so to speak, of a teleologically bound or closed narrative, such as that which the sacrament of marriage itself makes paradigmatic. His time is not yet recorded in the registry of permanent identity, which the sacrament of marriage would confer. Rameau, the homeless ego, and Humbert Humbert, the man of the open road, because they are the vehicles or producers of narratives that are quite rigorously respectful of the persistence of

---

22. See Vasco Lobeira, *Amadis of Gaul,* trans. Robert Southey from the Spanish version of Garciodonez De Montalvo (London: John Russell Smith, 1872), 11.

time, are such knights-errant themselves. But, as I hope I have anticipated by already distinguishing mere error from self-deception, errantry transcends error. It is a function of the embodiment of human commitments under the duress of those temporally accruing differences of human perspective that give us a unique purchase on the project of self-preservation. No single perspective, however harshly ironized by time, will succumb to fetishization because there is literally no time to distract us from the ensuing moments of experience, the ensuing demands upon our attentiveness.

Cervantes famously signals the stakes of the reader's own adventure in this novel by dramatizing the authorial anxiety that motivates the narrator's composition of a preface. In "The Preface to the Reader," Cervantes invokes the reader's natural idleness as the anti-mask of the narrator's motivating anxiety: "Idle reader, without an oath thou mayest believe, that I wish this book, as the child of my understanding, were the most beautiful sprightly and discreet production that was ever conceived" (Cervantes, 35). The author immediately confesses his fear that he is not equal to the task of writing the preface. With this the author makes the protocol of reading *Quixote* roughly coterminous with the fate of the book's protagonists—author and character. The specter of terminus itself is revealed to be the common nemesis of the proposed errantry. In the midst of his struggle to compose a sufficiently self-authorizing preface, the author's anxiety is answered by a "friendly" interlocutor whose own origin and authority remain significantly obscure. The "friend" of "The Preface" intends to help the enterprise of the book by recommending writerly means to authorial ends. The interlocutor's remedy for authorial self-doubt, a beneficent harbinger of self-deception, is the perfect counterpoint to his own mysterious identity: he urges the author to deploy tediously conventional forms, linguistic clichés, scholarly agit-propery, epigraphic and epigrammatic adornments, and the pageantry of citation to fill out the dimensions of the conventional preface. Presumably such tinkering will finesse the task of *prefacing* the work. These editorial suggestions are all candidly proposed as stratagems of deception. Of course, the "friend" licenses the anxious author to make up poems and poets, to recall texts from memory, or from his own mis-remembering of Latin phrases and scholarly references. These devices, he assures the author, will produce the illusion of a preface and give the author confidence in the legitimacy of the book it prefaces.

Aptly enough, the susceptibility to, or weakness for, the ploys proposed by the author's "friend" are revealed to be already manifest in the ironic embarrassment of Cervantes' reader. For we quickly understand that the reasons which buttress the friend's advice apply to ourselves precisely insofar as we are presumed to be gullible and inattentive. The author's own confession that he has allowed the friend's remarks to supplant or stand in for the authentic performance of a preface ("I admitted them without hesitation or dispute, and resolved that they should appear instead of a preface") (Cervantes, 39) further confirms our dependency upon reasons we do not yet possess but which we are now cued to anticipate. What are displayed above all in Cervantes' "Preface to the Reader" are the reasons for a preface that must be adduced before it can be a bona fide preface. More to the point, however, is our growing realization that the preface is indistinguishable from the book that ensues, as the friend astutely observes: "If I am not mistaken, your book needs none of those embellishments in which you say it is defective, for, it is one continued satire upon books of chivalry; a subject which Aristotle never investigated" (Cervantes, 38). This preface specifically is a testimonial to a process that the novel itself sustains. The point is even more explicit if we recognize that the modality of the fiction that ensues from the preface is reminiscent of the device of "heroic hypocrisy" or "double truth," a rhetorical métier that was exploited by Renaissance and Counter-Reformation European artists. I warrant these artists knew something about self-deception that they couldn't admit in my terms.

The practitioners of "heroic hypocrisy" and "double truth" sought something like a repertoire of higher-order motivations in their tolerating seemingly irreconcilable propositions—like the proposition of the preface with respect to the book it pretends to encompass. They entertained beliefs that would otherwise have lent themselves to mutually exclusive pretexts of argumentation and experience. This required their negotiating the incommensurability of grounds upon which any of these beliefs could be equally well predicated, depending on which aspects of the beliefs were attended to by the one who asserted them. Fredrick de Armas has documented Cervantes' enthusiasm for these practices as ordained by the Aristotelian philosopher Pietro di Pomponazzi (1462–1525).[23] There is a kind of aspect-dependency at work here, not unlike Joseph Raz's basis for distinguishing rational and classical agency. The double truth, after all, presupposes the possibility of seeing the comparative relevance of the elements of a belief as part of the task of knowing what prospects for their applicability might present themselves as premises of action. It is a prompting to know that all beliefs possess hidden aspects. A certain errantry is entailed.

---

23. See Fredrick A. De Armas, "Cervantes and the Italian Renaissance," in *The Cambridge Companion to Cervantes*, ed. Anthony J. Cascardi (Cambridge: Cambridge University Press, 2002), especially 35–37.

For example, Pomponazzi frequently espouses the simultaneous endorsement of religious dogma and philosophical precepts that are diametrically opposed but opposed nonetheless on alternative grounds. These grounds are traversed within the purview of some other attentiveness to aspects. So, making sense is a variable of choosing to recognize one set of motivational biases over another. One's choice within this framework involves an ever more complex enterprise of aspectual attentiveness to the world.

In giving his account of the travail of writing a preface, the author of *Quixote* himself confesses that he preferred the book to be "performance, clean, neat and naked without the ornament of a preface" (Cervantes, 35). For what is a preface, especially in this instance, except an insecure second thought purveyed as a primary thought intended to give secure ground to what follows? Between performance and thought, whether it is forethought or compensatory reflection in the wake of erroneous forethought, there opens a speculative field. This is very much the field upon which Quixote does battle—throughout Cervantes' novel—with the foes of his own best belief in himself. The terms of the contest invariably turn on what the operative motivational contexts might be. Such is the case in Quixote's preface when we realize that we are in the process of seeing how the reasons that justify writing the book may also be the reasons for doubting its explicability, that is to say, for doubting the relevance of any preface.

The "double truth" is at work in this novel everywhere that the intelligibility of Quixote's actions is seen to depend upon motivational imperatives that are hidden vis-à-vis the most apparent motivational biases governing the act of reading. When these motivational biases are revealed to be inappropriate or inoperative, the reader is prompted to identify with new possibilities of motivated agency. Implicitly, Quixote's lack of a self that could be grasped as a set of essential properties reflects upon the character of the reader. For he is enticed to accept the proposition that identity is nothing more than a threshold of motivational necessity per se. While I believe this claim undergirds the entire structure of Cervantes' narrative, I will take an instance of Quixote's forced collusion of deception and self-deception in chapter 11, volume 1, book 3, to exemplify it. Fittingly, this is a quintessential episode in the "plot" of answering the question "What do I do next?"—a plot that persists vividly throughout both volumes of *Don Quixote*. We have already appreciated that it is a plot which always originates in a scene of anxiety or self-doubt.

In the episode I wish to discuss, Quixote proposes to address his doubt about Dulcinea's fidelity by following the example of his idol Amadis in "acting the desperado, the lunatic, the madman" (Cervantes, 244). Quixote reasons as follows. If it turns out that his beloved is indeed unfaithful, his madness will anesthetize the grief. If she is faithful, he will enjoy the truth in his "right senses" (Cervantes, 245). In this case he would possess the volition which licensed his belief that he could be mad in the first place. Quixote's entire enterprise in this episode is shaped by his aspiration to reconcile a now self with a then self. I have alleged this to be the abiding ethical work of self-deception generally. Accordingly, Quixote does not know that Dulcinea is unfaithful. He merely assumes that any imaginary beloved could be unfaithful to her lover's self-sustaining belief in her fidelity. So we must reckon with the fact that his "now self," troubled by what he does not yet know of Dulcinea's disposition, is already committed to the belief in his own madness. He thus finds motive to render that madness instrumental to armoring an imaginable "then self" against the eventuality of discovering either the beloved's faithfulness or faithlessness. The "now self" is a hedge against the hazards of irony to which a "then self" would otherwise be helplessly exposed. Indeed, Quixote couches the stratagem in terms of a professional (at least for the knight-errant) dictate: that he know everything relevant to his situation, especially what the constraints of his situation bar him from knowing. He therefore writes a letter to Dulcinea that seems to anticipate what is not overtly solicited: knowledge of her capacity for infidelity (Cervantes, 253). The letter purveys to Dulcinea the knowledge of his madness as a counter for the motivational bias to which her betrayal would be duly proportionate. In other words, the self-deceiving self is conjured in the service of Quixote's anxiety that he does not know enough. In response to Sancho's flattery at the artfulness of Quixote's letter, "I verily believe your worship is the devil himself, and knows everything," Quixote replies, "All that knowledge . . . is necessary for the employment I profess" (Cervantes, 254).

That is to say, Quixote deceives himself by orchestrating the motivational biases for thinking himself mad, in order to protect himself against the possibility of his being outflanked by maddening knowledge that he has, as yet, no reasons to countenance. His madness is thus rationally fortified. It may not be dismissively diagnosed as a descent into the abyss of the irrational, even if that is the appearance that Quixote mightily struggles to purvey as the relevant counter of reality. Madness will be an occasion for heightening attentiveness to the warrant for motivational biases and consequently a pretext for their proliferation. The more he manifests his "mad" behaviors, the more occasion Quixote has for reflecting on the warrantedness of the madness—such that he can know himself to be ever more adequate to the task of knowing himself. Because such knowledge is inherently aspect-dependent, it is densely situational with respect to the protagonist's actions.

This aspect-dependency is perfectly congruent with the episodic frequency of the *picaresque* mode, which *Quixote* famously endows to novelistic tradition. The errantry of the *picaro* dovetails succinctly with Quixote's métier of self-deception. For Quixote not only denies himself the epistemic excuse for a belief in "fixed" truths, such as the real name of Dulcinea del Toboso, or her brute physical and vocational incompatibility with his chivalric ideal, but he wanders ever more attentively to the most peripheral parts of the world. There his actions might substitute for motivational biases that the world occupied by Dulcinea's real person could not warrant. It is no small irony that Dulcinea is sustained in Quixote's mind as a chivalric ideal in proportion to the spectacular lack of notice she has paid him. Cervantes makes the point almost too didactically by having Quixote relate to Sancho the tale of a young noblewoman who falls in love with an unsightly and stupid lay brother.

This tale is as follows. The noblewoman answers the amazement of the lay brother's superior, who astutely notices the incompatibility of love and looks with this: "'Signor, you are very much deceived . . . if you think I have made a bad choice in that fellow, who seems so simple . . . for, in that particular which I admire, he is as much of a philosopher, nay more than Aristotle himself'" (Cervantes, 252). If one's grasp of reality depends upon the part to which one attends, one's attention is inherently irreconcilable with any simple standard of totality. Totality inhibits notice by its all too manifest lucidity. More to the point, if the noblewoman is herself deceived, she could only be described as being self-deceived insofar as she sustains commitments to no essential properties of herself. Rather, her identity is a feature of her detotalizing attentiveness. Accordingly, her own presumption of the superior's self-deception is inversely proportionate to that man's nonaspectual grasp of his "brother's" person, namely, his lack of a capacity to notice what he doesn't already see in its totality.

I have already observed that *notice* is the crux of what Joseph Raz calls "classical agency." I have invoked classical agency over against the rationalist model of agency and in service to the cause of diachronic rationality. It is supple enough to accommodate the incommensurabilities that arise among reasons for choosing an object of desire or a path of action within an ever more attentive purview of the reality at hand. As I have indicated, this accommodation does not succumb to the pathos of irrationality. Indeed, such pathos is smartly dismissed by Cervantes when he closes this chapter of the novel with Sancho's uncomfortable notice of Quixote's naked "particulars," as the errant knight strips off his breeches to commence the carefully planned scene of madness (Cervantes, 256). The unwanted spectacle of Quixote's private (not to be noticed) parts is what gives, albeit comically, Sancho's warrant for taking Quixote's madness seriously. Sancho is seriously chagrined. And so we are reminded that the accommodation of the incommensurabilities that arise among reasons for acting is effectively a high sensitivity to the aspect-dependency of our nature.

Rameau

In *Rameau's Nephew* Diderot makes our reckoning with the aspect-dependency of human agency out to be an even more proactive proposition than Cervantes does. In Diderot's text the self-deception entailed by this reckoning is manifestly generative for character, rather than merely symptomatic of character. Moreover, it is strikingly conducive to the dynamics of diachronic rationality. The point is most starkly articulated in Rameau's complaint that his own identity is superseded by his uncle's famous persona. He explicitly harbors this knowledge as his own wish to be or to become someone else. Rameau's capacity for self-preservation is, like Quixote's, duly commensurable with his capacity to discern alternative dimensions of his persona. This is apparent when he retails the episodes of his life, in a manner that proves unintelligible to his interlocutor, "I." "I," dubbed "the philosopher," is the counter for the act of noticing that is occasioned by the performance of Rameau's manifold self-differings in the course of the narrative. We see immediately, however, that Rameau relentlessly catches himself in acts of hypocrisy, cowardice, and discreditable conduct, which undermine the idea of a unified character. In other words, his desire to win recognition of the capacity to notice his own incoherencies or inconsistencies is the salient motivational bias sustaining his performance of an elusive identity. It trumps any investment in character as a touchstone of identity.

It is crucial that Diderot provides an audience for this performance. For the first-person interlocutor, who is a placeholder for the reader's own motivational biases as an interpreter, serves as a conspicuous staging ground for noticing noticings. We see exactly what is at stake when Rameau challenges "I" with the superiority of his own powers of notice: "Nobody knows me better than I do myself, and I haven't said it all" (Diderot, 45). The reader is put on notice both that he is in a competitive relation with Diderot's protagonist, and that he will be no match for the protagonist's talent. After all, this talent portends an open-ended narrative, a perforce diachronic rationality for which the reader is unprepared. The protagonist's power of notice is beyond the reach of any one who would pretend simply to know the reason for Rameau's fallibility as a character. I want to see how Diderot deploys such a flawed personality—against which rational judgment could be rendered by the Enlightenment "I," the philosophical judge, or the heroic antagonist of irrational self-deception—as a touchstone of surprising ethical growth.

The episodes of this growth are not developmental in any maturational sense, however. But precisely because they are dialogic with respect to the "I," they challenge the self-limitation of the readerly mind for which I have alleged Rameau's philosophical interlocutor is a placeholder. Another way of putting this is to say that the episodic growth dramatized in Diderot's narrative is, like Quixote's, inflected by the métier of errantry. But in this case errantry arises from Rameau's and the philosophical "I"'s predispositions toward ventriloquism. Rameau plays to the audience of the "I" so that the former's every gesture is a solicitation of recognition. Recognition, however, depends upon a variety of clues to the "nature" Rameau purveys. Furthermore, and more important, Rameau persistently theatricalizes that nature by taking on the voices of other others with whom the "I" cannot help identifying. The philosophical I is himself being addressed by Rameau as nothing but an other. The "I"'s own susceptibility to this apparently infectious theatricalism prompts his own presumption to speak for other versions or dimensions of Rameau's character by assuming Rameau's voice or the voices of Rameau's antagonists, in incidents of social life where Rameau claims to have suffered injustice. These ventriloquisms portend a learning process that bears not on character as entity, but on character as a limit case of reasoning that will inevitably be reflected upon and rationalized further. They promote a broadening range of responsiveness to the world that I have identified with the most edifying motives of self-deception. Insofar as self-deception is implicated in "capacity rationality," it is a touchstone of our disposition to be choosers of better reasons for our self-characterizations. The variations of characterization, or topoi of assignable motives that proliferate through the ventriloquist antics of Rameau and his interlocutor, promote an intensifying anxiety on the reader's part. The reader never sees enough to secure the kind of warrant for judgment that the caricature rationalist, otherwise figured in the philosophical "I," would certainly presume upon.

The subordination of character to proliferating topoi for reasoning follows decisively upon the heels of Rameau's boast that "nobody knows me better than I do myself" (Diderot, 45). As I have indicated, this statement precipitates the dispersal of self into the arena of competing motivational biases. In one typical instance, Rameau explains that he has caused his eviction from the domicile of his patrons by confessing that the persona he has purveyed to them as a "lunatic, impertinent, ignorant, lazy, greedy old fool" (Diderot, 46) was a ruse. He means for us to understand that the former deception of his patrons enabled their self-deception in turn. By virtue of the invidious contrast he invited them to draw between themselves and himself, they were inveigled to believe that they were in possession of the qualities of Enlightenment mind—sense and reason—which Rameau lacked. When his patrons are subsequently compelled to reckon with Rameau as a man possessed of sense and reason, they prefer to oust him from their midst rather than confront themselves in the guise of their own folly. Rameau's explanation of the predicament necessitates his assuming the voice of their indignation: "Be off with you, and don't show your face here again—the fellow has pretensions to sense and reason it seems! Clear off! We've got those qualities ourselves" (Diderot, 47). In the voice of his patrons Rameau concedes his own self-deception: that he could make himself known to them as himself without their knowing it. The very fact that self-deception is linked to the assuming of "other" motivational biases, and that the self-sustaining intelligence of Rameau's social enterprise here requires a taking up of new cues to reconcile itself with shifting motivational grounds, promotes a revision of our attitude toward self-deception.

Rameau's indefatigable rationality, in the midst of seeming irrational behavior, is made counterintuitively apparent by his interlocutors. In response to Rameau's lamenting his self-inflicted homelessness, the "philosopher" recommends a stratagem for Rameau's reconciliation with his patrons. The philosopher then ventriloquizes the necessary groveling to which Rameau must submit himself: "Forgive me, Madame, forgive me, I am an unspeakable wretch" (Diderot, 48). We are thus made deeply cognizant that better reasons for acting are unimaginable without a reimagining of the motivational determinants of the elements of scene. This entails Rameau's choosing new props for whatever action can ensue. As if to emphasize my point, Rameau subsequently flings himself into a pantomime of the "philosopher's" ventriloquized abjection. What is manifested here is a subjective homelessness that is nonetheless agentially committed. These ventriloquistic acts dramatize Diderot's locating of character in active commitments rather than in the qualities of an "essential" personality.

The reasons for actions are thereby rendered virtually experimental topoi of deliberation. On the one hand, the ventriloquizing subject (Rameau and/or "I") exhibits a willful incompatibility or incommensurability between his words/actions and the motivational biases or the operant reasons for them. To ventriloquize is to speak for oneself otherwise and to speak for another out of personal motives. The ventriloquizer therefore seems to enact self-deception in the most self-reductive way as an evading of identity altogether. But to read *Rameau* this way would be to miss an insight that dovetails with J. David Velleman's notion: that knowing who you are is always a matter of knowing what you are doing. I do indeed think Velleman is right that our "considerations" or noticings of the world count as reasons for acting and knowing what we are doing (see Velleman, *Practical Reason*, 23–24). Thus we might see how the ventriloquisms that propel Diderot's "dialogue" exemplify how any picking out of aspects of the world is a mode of reasoning. Ventriloquism is nothing but a picking out of salient traits to represent to oneself and to others irrespective of what beliefs those representations otherwise embody. We might therefore conclude that ventriloquism is an elaborate staging of the occasion for choosing reasons to believe in what one is doing.

Ventriloquism, in this respect, is an analogue for what Rameau struggles with in his social relations generally. He is forever confronting the necessity to discern new motives for the actions he is already enmeshed in. By implication, this is what all of us who come to share the philosophical "I"'s regard for Rameau as a worthy interlocutor must come to understand in the act of reading itself. We must permit our actions to challenge our beliefs, or we will succumb to the dogma of the self at the expense of any viable—in Velleman's terms—self-understanding. What can be learned from intercourse with Rameau would be preempted by our taking up the pretense of the monovocal first person: the philosopher's self-blinding paranoia. Despite his self-incriminating indulgence of Rameauean ventriloquism, the philosopher boasts an invidious comparison with the former's endless role-playing or pantomiming: "And yet there is one person free to do without pantomime, and that is the philosopher who has nothing and asks for nothing" (Diderot, 122). His obvious hypocrisy notwithstanding here, the philosopher is a caricature of disinterestedness, which invites us to ascribe to him a feckless aestheticism. Such aestheticism contrasts with Rameau's human artistry. To have nothing and to ask for nothing is to be exempt from the powers of notice and to be oblivious of the shifting ground of motivational bias that they denote. On the other hand, such powers of notice are richly potentiated by pantomime and ventriloquistic performance.

The fact is, virtually everything that is said in *Rameau's Nephew* is a performance. In *Rameau's Nephew* performance itself is revealed to be preeminently the pretext for another "saying" of belief that, in turn, proffers a new stage for performance. The words spoken before they are mimed in performance call us to account for the necessity of noticing what had not formerly been counted as a reason for believing those words. The consequence of this notice that something was not noticed endows the peripeteic torque of irony. It does so, however, without granting that release from the burdens of rationalization that conventional irony too glibly licenses. For example, at the conclusion of *Rameau's Nephew* Rameau gives a retort to the philosopher's judgment that he (Rameau) is "an idler, greedy, cowardly and with a soul of dirt" (Diderot, 123). Rameau reminds the philosopher that this judgment corroborates what "I believe I've told you already." Rameau thus incriminates the putative judge in the litany of crimes to be judged. Rameau's mocking of the philosopher's lack of notice—that Rameau has already rendered this judgment against himself—is of course a performance of an act of self-understanding. It exemplifies the mobility of the self that drives Diderot's narrative throughout. Here self is a counter for subjective reflexivity that entails recognition of reasons it has not yet counted as dispositive for the beliefs one is prompted to act upon. This is a self that subsists upon its commitments to mutable aspects of its experience. It is distinguished by a revisionary disposition that goes along with the diachrony of that experience.

Aristotle, in *Ethics,* interestingly confirms the rightness of these speculations with his too little examined assertion that "reason, more than anything else, *is* man" (par. 1178a, 1105). That is to say, each person seems to be reducible to his faculty of understanding or to the activity of adducing reasons occasioned by variables of circumstance that demand our notice or consideration. Aristotle grasps the fact that one's sense of one's own protagonistic identity is a function of a critical distance from one's self that is at the same time effectively constitutive of the self.[24] It is quite true that we implicitly alienate or negate

24. It is also worth emphasizing again how Velleman's diachronic rationality is derived from this Aristotelian insight. This is what authorizes Velleman's idea that the reasons we give for actions are elements of a story that we make up as we go along. In *Self to Self,* Velleman takes up the Aristotelian point in support of his own concept of an aspectual self. He is imagining a self that is coordinate with the situational particulars that promote reflecting upon one's own presence. Velleman is quite parsimonious in the definition of self that arises from these meditations: "In my view, 'self' is just a word used to express reflexivity." See *Self to Self,* 354.

ourselves in taking up a critically reflective vantage point with respect to the actions that hitherto grounded our identity. But Aristotle seems to make the further point that one's capacity to reason or to understand follows one across the episodic threshold of one experience after another that is the material substrate of agential being. Aristotle seems to presuppose a continuity of understanding through the episodic vagaries of experiences that qualify or revise the self we seek to understand. If "reason, more than anything else *is* man," his personhood is a continuous inquiry into the springs of whatever action one takes that occasions one's knowing better than to have taken it. This amounts to something like a Kantian apperceptive I, rendered as a métier of learning instead of as an exclusively ontological ground of knowledge.

I believe that this is both a fair description of the only self that Rameau stakes a claim to and of Diderot's métier as a narrative artist. It furthermore epitomizes how the narrative dimension of aesthetic experience serves what I called, at the end of chapter 3, the "ethically beneficent work of self-deception": the reconciling of now selves with then selves. We can now see how self and self-deception are mutually dependent aspects of narrative experience. When, at the close of *Rameau's Nephew*, Rameau laments the loss of his wife, the philosophical "I" speculates that Rameau's self-avowed taking to "bands and a skull cap" was motivated by grief. His interlocutor wryly replies: "If you like, but the real reason is so as to wear my basin on my head" (Diderot, 125). Rameau's evocation of Quixote here is subtended to a larger conceit. He immediately informs the philosophical "I" that he's heard the bells that signal the opera is about to commence in the nearby theater. He is late. We readers are, I would argue, shockingly apprised of the fact that the entire narrative has been an interlude between the summons of the audience to the theater and the commencement of the music—a way for Rameau to pass the time. In effect, Diderot assimilates Rameau's allusion to Quixote's basin—a form of Quixotic errantry in itself—to the reader's realization that the theatricality of the narrative that has just unfolded is itself only a pretext for passing the time until the pleasures of the theater can be resumed.

Diderot thus establishes a prospect for seeing that one always countenances a self whose deception is entailed in knowing oneself to be anticipating something else: another condition of noticing. Furthermore, this noticing is a marker for our disposition to answer the question of what to do next, without which—so I have been arguing—the question whether or not one is self-deceived ceases to be interesting. Quixote's basin is the token of such notice. Upon departing for the opera, Rameau taunts the philosopher with the farewell, "Isn't it true that I am always the same?" (Diderot, 125). He poses the question in the instance of a conspicuous self-differentiation—revealing himself to have used "I," and the reader, as a distracting interlude. Thus we are prompted to observe that the philosophical "I," in replying "Alas, yes, unfortunately" (Diderot, 125), has missed the point.

Rameau's "sameness" in word and deed is not iterable except on the condition that he is always disposed to welcome an accretion of self in the informative misprisions of reasoning: where what is not immediately apparent counts as the relevant prospect for knowing ourselves. Perhaps this is the Beckettian modality of going on with presumably other reasons than we already possess. All of the reshapings of Rameau's character, through ventriloquism or through the simple role reversals entailed by the theatrics of dialogue, are determined by restagings of the frame of reference for self-assertion.

It may be that the most explicit articulation of this "gist" of *Rameau's Nephew* is Rameau's famous retailing of the story of the Rogue of Avignon. It is the tale of a Jew betrayed to the Inquisition by a duplicitous servant. This narration of a quintessential other-deception inveigles the reader (in the guise of the philosophical "I") to suffer the sensationalistic pleasure we take in the most vile actions of the story as a burden of moral anxiety. The tale forces our notice that the storyteller's relish in telling it—its preening artfulness—mirrors our culpability in relishing the story so thoughtlessly. It thus reveals the story to be a locus of motivational biases other than what counted initially as our dramatic interest in the most depraved motives of the renegade. Because the vivacity of Rameau's retailing of the story is overtly seductive, the philosophical "I" must decide which is more horrible: the villainy of the renegade or the tone of voice in which Rameau purveys it. Notice of this would be especially incriminating for the interlocutor/reader who thinks he already knows who he is in the act of "reading" the flaws of Rameau's character. In other words, the philosophical acumen of the reader is revealed to be accountable for not having already noticed a more relevant register of wickedness than that represented by the renegade. The one who would tell the story with such self-serving delight may be worse than the villainous protagonist. More menacing yet, we must think that the reader who indulges such delight vicariously may be worse than the teller of the tale. If we recognize our inattentiveness to our own vicarious pleasure in judging the renegade with ruthlessly invidious self-regard, we appreciate the risks of our own renegade status with respect to the morality we are otherwise so confidently possessed of.

Humbert Humbert

The stakes of our noticing self-deception as a scruple of notice are dramatically escalated in *Lolita*. This is apparent in the conspicuous moral admonition that is purveyed as the occasion of Nabokov's notoriously deceptive "Preface," credited to the eponymous John Ray Jr., Ph.D. Ray shines his "ray" of insight equivocally upon the text reputed to be authored by Humbert Humbert. Our anxiety that we might be held culpable, as puerility-inspired readers, for the very lasciviousness that the preface purports to purge in the exhibition of Humbert Humbert's character, is of course exacerbated by the deceptions we have seen to be latent in the conventionality of the form of the preface itself. Such notice was primed by our reading of Cervantes' "Preface to the Reader." In other words, we cannot fail to notice the peril we put ourselves in by following the logic of the preface, which advises us to treat the content of *Lolita* as the form of a self-deception. Or it might be more accurate to say that this is the peril portended by Ray's "Preface" if we do not heed the moral lesson of Humbert's narrative. But I want to be clear. The moral stakes here have more to do with the forms of attention Humbert's narrative elicits than with the pedophiliac acts of the protagonist. I will argue that Humbert's physicality diminishes in proportion to the reader's ever more multidimensional notice of the conditions for making commitments to belief in the meaningfulness of his deeds. Nabokov's feat is to put Sense and sense (sensation) on a continuum of deliberative activity. This is in no way to deny the moral culpability of the pedophile. It is rather to put our stance toward the immorality of the pedophile onto a new agenda of agential duties.

The crux of the matter, I think, is signaled in Ray's erstwhile proof of his editorial and ethical bona fides. He cites his previous success with a publication entitled "Do the Senses Make Sense?" wherein, as he "modestly" attests, "certain morbid states and perversions had been discussed."[25] At first glance the scholarly benchmark seems to possess evidentiary authority. But sense deceives "Sense" ineluctably within the purview of the pun that self-consciously blurs the line between physical and cognitive registers of experience in Ray's title. Ray of course recommends the diagnostic efficacy of the work that bears the symptomatic title without equivocation. With this moral didacticism, Ray instantiates the rationalist model of agency, which we saw, at the beginning

---

25. Vladimir Nabokov, *The Annotated Lolita: Revised and Updated*, ed. Alfred Appel Jr. (New York: Vintage, 1991), 3.

of this chapter, can be contrasted with the classical agential stance toward a realm of incommensurabilities. Ray would appear to be on the side of the rationalist agential stance with its unequivocal intolerance of incommensurables. And yet, in closing his address to the reader, Ray purveys the text of *Lolita, or the Confession of a White Widowed Male* as both a "case history" *and* a "work of art."

Within the canon of classical aesthetics there may be no more obstinate incommensurability. What's more, rationalist Ray concludes with an admonition that seems to ignore the rationalist's problem as Raz describes it: to recognize incommensurabilities among reasons is to render actions licensed by those reasons irrational (Raz, *Engaging Reason*, 49). Furthermore, Ray's admonition that reading "Lolita" "should make all of us . . . apply ourselves with still greater *vigilance* [my emphasis] and vision to the task of bringing up a better generation" (Nabokov, 6) dovetails paradoxically with the capacity for choosing among incommensurable reasons. I have been arguing, along with Raz, that only a classical rationalist account of agency can accommodate this capacity.[26] Ray's "Preface" unwittingly warrants a rational "vigilance" conducive to noticing reasons other than those an agent ostensibly desires. This is tantamount to a choosing among incommensurabilities, as opposed to a rational elimination of incommensurabilities. Nabokov's rhetoric might be on the side of the rationalist agential stance, but his artfulness in drawing out the self-contradictoriness of that rhetoric puts him on the side of the classical agential stance.

The warrant for tolerating incommensurabilities entertained here is the crux of Nabokov's challenge to the reader of *Lolita*. In the crudest terms, Nabokov invites us to choose between an aestheticization of pedophilia—which would be Humbert's self-deceiving idea that the production of a work of art about pedophilia forgives the act—and a pedophile's abuse of the category of the aesthetic—which would be Humbert's self-deceiving idea that he knows what art is by invidious contrast with the moral disgust aroused by the spectacle of life. Here the pedophile is one with the normal man of taste. The choice is even more difficult than that portended by John Ray between a "case history" and a "work of art." For Nabokov shows us how the work of art is no less subject to the kinds of analysis we might associate with a "case history" than the

---

26. No doubt Ray couldn't challenge Raz's contention that "since desires are reason-dependent, their persistence depends on persistence of belief in the reason and that necessarily those who have them want the strength of their desires to reflect the weight of the reasons for them, and accept criticism if it does not." See Raz, *Engaging Reason*, 62.

"protagonist" of the case history is subject to "artistic" license taken by the analyst. Even more pointedly, the abuse of the aesthetic is presented as no less deserving of the therapeutic remediations we might otherwise reserve for the abuses perpetrated upon the "child" by the pedophile.

Humbert Humbert's own aesthetic disposition as a hypertrophic noticer is of course determined by the loss of his childhood beloved, Annabel Leigh. This event transpired upon the threshold of his own sexual initiation. We are led to believe that Humbert's "normal" identity would have been formed completely if the consummation of this act of coitus had not been intruded upon by "two bearded bathers." Their appearance is coupled, so to speak, with the more lengthy incursion of four months' time that elapses between this incident and Annabel's death from typhus in Corfu. Simultaneity and duration meet in loss, here understood as a métier of self-knowledge and as a prospect for self-realization. The deprivation of the moment of self-realization puts the childhood Humbert on *notice*, insofar as he is impelled, in fetishistically Proustian terms, toward recapturing the moment. Recapturing the past requires at least the kind of vigilance that John Ray's "Preface" admonishes the reader to submit to. In this case, one's vigilance or powers of notice must rise to the challenge of the proliferation of differences that time occasions through change. Accordingly, Humbert succumbs to a tropological obsession. He pursues bearded resemblances between the original Annabel, idealized on her island of time—a figurative Corfu that is no less commensurable with its referent than is Humbert's longing for the deceased—and the succession of childish beauties that mark the progress of his life as a sequence of lost moments.

Thus Humbert's theory of the nymphet presupposes a temporal gap between the nympholept and the nymphet, "man and maiden": "It is a question of focal adjustment of a certain distance that the inner eye thrills to surmount and a certain contrast that the mind perceives with a gasp of perverse delight" (Nabokov, 17). In other words, incommensurability is the ineliminable condition of noticing or discerning the self as a necessarily self-deceiving proposition. The apprehension of the authentic nymphet eludes the powers of self to ascertain self-recognition, except perversely, as the compulsion to notice more, to become, as Humbert himself acknowledges, an "artist *and* [my emphasis] a madman" (17). The conflation of artist and madman adduced by Humbert here—like John Ray's conflation of the case study and the work of art—marks incommensurability as an occasion for self-consciousness about the aspect-dependency of self-recognition underlying the "perverse" self.

At this juncture, it is worth noting that the aesthetic disposition and dubious aesthetic alibi that Humbert confers upon himself in this passage is oddly congruent with the Humean idea of connoisseurship famously articulated in *Of the Standard of Taste*.[27] I believe that it intimates the degree to which Nabokov is fostering a better theory of art than either Ray or Humbert himself can muster. In Hume's account incommensurability and aesthetic taste are gloriously compatible: "A thousand different sentiments, excited by the same object, are all right," Hume says, "because no sentiment represents what is really in the object. It only marks a certain conformity or relation between the object and the organs . . . of the mind" (Hume, 6). Not coincidentally, the occasion of Hume's thinking about what constitutes the "delicacy" of the power of notice is an episode from *Quixote*. As Hume reminds us, Sancho boasts of his family's extraordinary judgment with respect to the constituent elements of wine. He then recounts the story of two relatives who discern incommensurable qualities from their sampling of a common hogshead. Both declare the wine to be tasty, but one discerns the taste of the leather, the other the taste of iron. The discovery of a key tethered to a leather thong at the bottom of the drained vessel confirms the necessity to honor the incommensurable judgments. These incommensurables are otherwise ridiculed by all who would, Sancho says, wish to cast doubt on the rationality of the experiment. We, by contrast, are invited to see them as different aspects of a common actuality for which different reasons could be called to account.

I want to consider the possibility that Nabokov's *Lolita* disciplines its reader to the same tolerance of incommensurables. It thereby prompts our seeing the aspect-dependency of our responsiveness to the world as preferable to the rational certitudes that preclude the possibility of self-deception. It is emphatically the recognition of competing motivational biases that gives *Lolita* its unique narrative coherence. Self-deception, in this respect, is continuous with the rationality of an experience that can only be justified on the basis of anticipating what mistakes are embodied in it. It furthermore warrants our accepting the anxiety that accompanies the knowledge of our not knowing enough. Such anxiety, I have already argued, is the animus of heightened notice. It is, not surprisingly, indistinguishable from the linguistic paranoia that we shall see is the métier of Humbert's narration. I want to show then, how the tolerance of incommensurables in these instances is coordinate with a sense of

---

27. First published as part of Hume's *Four Dissertations* (1757). See *Of the Standard of Taste and Other Essays* (New York: Bobbs-Merrill, 1965).

self as agent. I mean to highlight a capacity for self-understanding whereby the self sees a motive for doing things otherwise.

Humbert's prose is ceaselessly doing things as if in paranoid compensation for precisely the kind of gaps of knowledge upon which his notorious theory of the nymphet is predicated: as a fundamentally temporal phenomenon. The incontinent punning, the syntactical and semantic patternings and interpolations of pattern, the endless lexical transfiguration of characters, places, and abstract nominatives, all recall us to a cognizance of time lost and of temporal prospects we cannot fully anticipate. In this way, they constitute the aesthetic density upon which both Humbert's claim to being an artist and the reader's ability or inability to sort artwork from case study—if such sorting matters—depend. Indeed, I think I have already anticipated that it is precisely the narrative's potentiating of a tolerance for incommensurables that obviates any such hard and fast distinctions.

Now we might better appreciate how the anxious predisposition that seems to animate the linguistic overdetermination of Humbert's narrative gives warrant for his claim to an aesthetic alibi. Furthermore, we might better understand what counts as the aesthetic here if we see this disposition as a form of "pseudorationality." Adrian M. S. Piper has proffered the term "pseudorationality" to explain how self-deceivers are driven by what she calls *"our highest order disposition to literal self-preservation."*[28] Self-deceivers will notice what lends integrity to a most favored self-understanding, which they anxiously seek to protect in the course of their doing things. It is important to realize that, for Piper, self-deceiving pseudorationalists identify their theory of self with their agential experience, rather than subordinating their experience to a theory of self (Piper, 309). Piper allows no distinction between rationally integrated agency and what she calls "literal self-preservation" (303). Accordingly, I would argue that the preservation of the rational intelligibility of the self is the general phenomenon to which any pragmatic understanding of self-deception must be subordinated.

In *Lolita* Humbert Humbert's self-preservation is in fact rationalized by the artifactuality of the work that he produces. It is proffered in the end of his narration as nothing less than a timeless aesthetic object. Humbert makes the point explicitly when he taunts the reader's affective involvement in the narrative on the final page of the novel. The reader's complicity with Humbert's

---

28. See Adrian M. Piper, "Pseudorationality," in *Perspectives on Self-Deception,* ed. Amélie Oksenberg Rorty and Brian P. McLaughlin (Berkeley and Los Angeles: University of California Press, 1988), 297–323.

self-preservation is rendered inescapable. After all, the warrant for that self-preservation is asserted at precisely the moment when the reader is about to consummate his own experience/identity as the reader of this text: "And one wanted H. H. to exist at least a couple of months longer [than the murdered Quilty], so as to make you [Lolita] live in the mind of later generations" (Nabokov, 309). If we are reading this, we have finished the book in a way that confirms the truth of the statement. It follows then that the pseudorationality of Humbert's narrative inheres in what the reader has already grasped. There is a perfect complementarity between Humbert's self-preservation and the linguistic métier by which the reader has preserved his or her identity as a reader to this point. The idea is perhaps best epitomized by the linguistic effect that was observed in the punning title of John Ray's "Do the Senses Make Sense?": a proffering of incommensurable meanings that nonetheless excites our vigilance—as per Hume's key and thong—for yet unobserved conditions that would forestall our capitulation to irrationality. The conditions of reading are orchestrated in such a way that memory and the urgency of the imagination to compensate for its losses are, like the controlling elements of Humbert Humbert's mind, the controlling elements of Nabokov's prose.

In order to appreciate the most salient quality of experience exhibited by the mind of the self-deceiver in Nabokov's novel we need only sample a representative instance of Humbertian perception. It is the moment of Humbert's reckoning with the absolute loss of phantasmic Lolita to the dreary fact of Dolly Schiller. Humbert sits passively in the grip of the scene before him. He has parked his car on the street corner of one of those "dead-of-night towns" he laments he has already seen too much of: "Rubinov's Jewelry Company had a display of artificial diamonds reflected in a red mirror. A lighted green clock swam in the linenish depths of Jiffy Jeff Laundry. On the other side of the street a garage said in its sleep—genuflexion, lubricity; and corrected itself to Gulflex Lubrication. An airplane, also gemmed by Rubinov, passed droning, in the velvet heavens" (Nabokov, 282). The passage exhibits what all of Humbert's narrative subsists on: relentless notice that what one remembers of a presentational pattern is incipiently a reordering of the pattern. This reordering is based upon the necessity to assure oneself of the coherence of the moment of active recall with its original. Such knowledge of course includes what no recall could confirm precisely. For the recollecting mind knows that it is doing something else, something other than recalling what it is recollecting. The lights of the airplane are "gemmed by Rubinov" because there are twinkling aspects of ruby redness that need to be reflected in the air where movement is the relevant métier. The reflective medium is inexorable. The gems are, after all, already reflected in a ruby mirror. Likewise, genuflexion and lubricity are plausibly the motions of the mind that Gulflex Lubrication cannot release to fluid movement because it lacks the reasons that Humbert's overactive mentality instantiates.

The vantage point of this knowledge might be best characterized as the special disposition to worry about the inadequacy of the reasons why things appear the way they do. Without that worry, one might say, the self figured here would lack the quality of perseverance altogether. Humbert's entire relationship with Lolita exhibits this mustering of new reasons for perceptions by registering their permutation. This is the motion of the mind moved by its own need to know itself better simply insofar as it endures duration. Lolita's mere presence at Humbert's side involves his perceptual attunements to that presence in an ever more self-complicating relation with the world.

From the moment when Lolita is only a permutation of alliterative, consonant sounds on the tip of Humbert's tongue, "light of my life, my sin, my soul . . . Lo Lee Ta" (Nabokov, 9), the reader is encouraged to reckon with her presence as a conative activity. The activity proceeds according to a kind of anticipatory logic. As the passage "illuminating" Rubinov's Jewelry Company exemplifies it, the activity is effectively an intimation of contexts in which the mind can sustain its attentiveness under different descriptions. As we have noted often, these are perforce the constraint of any persistence in time. So, not surprisingly, Humbert's first descriptive embrace of Annabel Leigh encompasses an ensemble of physical attributes: the dark brown mole, the indrawn abdomen, the crenulated imprint left by the band of her shorts. But none of these particulars coalesce into Annabel's image. They instantiate Lolita's person. Annabel's image eludes Humbert and the reader both, except in the ever more various counters of imagination he adduces for recognition of his reasons to continue the pursuit of the original girl. Similarly, the lexical items that animate Humbert's wish to consummate an embrace of the past, in all of the episodes of the narrative, proliferate features of a body of experience which it otherwise would presumably capture as a strict finitude. I believe that such capture, had Humbert experienced consummation with his original Annabel Leigh, would be starkly recognizable to Nabokov's readers as precisely the failure of imagination that I have posed self-deception against.

Indeed, I want to emphasize that capture is not an ambition of Humbert's enterprise, especially if we treat it as a superveningly aesthetic one. Humbert is "authoring" and "authorizing" Nabokov's novel. But I would not suggest for a moment that the enterprise is aesthetic in the terms that seem to be courted by Humbert himself: "aurochs and angels, the secret of durable pigments, prophetic sonnets" (Nabokov, 309). That would be a fetishistic aestheticism. It would indeed dictate only the most effete capture of the object.

Over and over we see that Nabokov works in a precisely contrary fashion. For example, when evoking Lolita's antics as a tennis player, in the void left by Quilty's "kidnapping" of the nymphet, Humbert once again does so syllabically. He pronounces "Lo, Lola, Lolita" (Nabokov, 236) as if putting her into some aspectual relation with herself. In the reverie that ensues, Nabokov reveals that Humbert is no more capable of permanence (the secret of durable pigments) in conjuring the absent Lolita than he was in conjuring Lolita as a substitute for the absent Annabel Leigh. We shall see that permanence in this context is distinct from persistence, as temporal unity is distinct from agential integrity. Fixing his attention on Lolita's lithe athletic feats, Humbert is compulsive in his notice of all of the conditions of his perception that bode for more comprehensive and self-complicating knowledge of the scene of witness. Lolita, watched by Humbert, prompts his further notice of another bystanding male:

> And as I looked as his oval nut-brown face, it dawned upon me that what I had recognized him by was the reflection of my daughter's countenance—the same beatitude and grimace but made hideous by his maleness. And I also knew that the child, my child, knew he was looking, enjoyed the lechery of his look and was putting on a show of gambol and glee, the vile and beloved slut. As she made for the ball and missed it, she fell on her back, with her obscene young legs madly pedaling in the air; I could sense the musk of her excitement from where I stood, and then I saw (petrified with a kind of sacred disgust) the man close his eyes and bare his small, horribly small and even, teeth as he leaned against a tree in which a multitude of dappled Priaps shivered. Immediately afterwards a marvelous transformation took place. He was no longer the satyr but a very good-natured and foolish Swiss cousin, the Gustave Trapp I have mentioned more than once, who used to counteract his "sprees" (he drank beer with milk, the good swine) by feats of weight lifting—tottering and grunting on a lake beach with his otherwise very complete bathing suit jauntily stripped from one shoulder. *This* Trapp noticed me from afar and working the towel on his nape walked back with false insouciance to the pool. (Nabokov, 237–38)

What plays out here are the incommensurable but reasonable—in the sense that different aspects of notice warrant different reasons—states of mind that give Humbert's attentiveness a pseudorationalistic trajectory. It thickens his account of himself as a self-knower. It likewise intimates that self-deception is a sine qua non of such knowledge, insofar as we are aware that the incommensurability of the objects of his attention are supersessions of the original perspectives in which they are initially taken to make sense. As in the syllabic annunciation of this scene, each thing Humbert observes is the occasion for realizing there is something more to be taken account of, until there is so much to digest that Humbert himself is stricken with a spectacular bout of regurgitation: the ultimate incommensurability. Literally, the episode concludes with Humbert vomiting "a torrent of browns and greens that I had never remembered eating" (Nabokov, 238). The loss of memory, as we know from his theory of the nymphet, is correlative with a heightening of the powers of focus/notice—"a focal adjustment of a certain distance that the inner eye thrills to surmount." The scene of Humbert's regurgitation is nothing but a bringing of those powers to the point of surmounting the identity that already knows what it wishes to know. The regurgitative crescendo instantiates an agential identity that is emphatically untethered to the past, one that is persistent not permanent.

In a way, Humbert's language constitutes a proliferation of aspects of the scene that highlight his regard for the incompleteness of his own self-possession and/or self-understanding. The act of vomiting succinctly figures this notion. Humbert's notice of the "nut-brown" male's look is an occasion to recognize the otherwise undetectable licentiousness of Lolita's unseen (except as it is reflected in the face of the observed observer) countenance as sluttish rather than childish. This, in turn, occasions Humbert's discernment of the spectacle of her leg-pedaling reaction to the "missed" tennis ball as an occasion for noticing the physical excitement of the moment. It is a premise for anxiety about the sexual motive that now lurks in the shadow of the act. This in turn occasions Humbert's notice of the now easily inferable deliberateness of the "miss." For it conspicuously hits its mark in the facial orgasm that Humbert discerns as the closed eyes and bared teeth of the other observer. This in turn renders the "dappled Priaps" noticeable as a warrant for Humbert's sexual paranoia.

At this point, however, we realize that we are deceived if we have forgotten that the entire account of this scene commenced with Humbert's deeply menaced "recognition" of the mystery man in the shadow. We easily imagined that it was a sexual predator whom we were meant to recognize. But because we are drawn into the intricate web of Humbert's aspectual notice and are keyed to the details of Humbert's account, we may therefore fall into a trap. We may find ourselves thinking that Humbert's "transformation" of the priapic nut-brown observer into the benign Swiss cousin, Gustave Trapp (whom Humbert tauntingly reminds us he has "mentioned more than once") (Nabokov, 237) is unwarranted and irrational. On the other hand, our return to the initial recognition of this figure might obviate the apparent contradiction. This might be the case if we understand that the recognition is not applicable to all the perceptions which obtrude between the word "recognized" and the invocation of the "good natured and foolish Swiss cousin" (237). In other words, we might be prompted to forgive the seemingly unwarranted transformation of the "satyr" into the "Swiss cousin," by reasoning that the apparent incommensurability of Gustave Trapp and the figure in whom we have invested considerable sexual menace is in fact commensurable on another register of value. We might remember the physical fitness that Humbert had earlier attributed to Cousin Gustave. Then we could recognize "this Trapp" to be the trap that it is. For his physique may be revealed to be only another, more benign, aspect of the same physicality that, in our more paranoid view of things, cast a shadow over Lolita's athleticism. Perhaps the main point here, however, is the near athletic exercise of our own powers of notice as readers. Perhaps we are even primed to see the missed ball on the tennis court as a touchstone for the missed aspects that insistently prey upon the mind of the uniquely attuned self-deceiver, whose experience we are now quite profoundly implicated in.

Our complicity is torqued by Nabokov's penchant for forcing us to notice things in a way that compares with what Humbert calls the "ever alert periscope of my vice," impelling him to see what is not there on the basis of what is there. He indulges the most ironic examples. The "half-naked nymphet" he espies in a "jewel-bright window" one night is revealed in a subsequent instant to be a spectral aspect of an "obese partly clad man reading the paper" (Nabokov, 264). Such perception portends a gradation of "infinite perfections," imaginable enhancements of the man reading the paper, or his myriad counterparts. Such perceiving is sustained as a ratio of what Humbert calls the "little given and the great promised" (Nabokov, 264). In its asymptotic way, the gradient of "infinite perfections" gives us a duly *perverse* feeling of security that the anxiety of never seeing enough will persist.

We need only take up one instance of this phenomenon to bring my argument to its conclusion. Nabokov stages an opportunity for the reader, almost reflexively, to mime Humbert's syndrome of compulsive notice: determined as it is by lost time and the open-endedness of time in which what is lost is known on a continuum with what is yet to be known. Humbert emerges from a swim with Charlotte Haze, whom he has just homicidally fantasized committing to the bottom of Hourglass Lake. In this falling grain of time Humbert occasions our notice that everything in view, in such imaginatively drawn scenes as he now populates for the reader, exists upon the gradient of "infinite perfections." For on that epistemic incline, we who aspire to a complete vision of things possess complete knowledge of what incompleteness must be borne. We take the point dispositively when Humbert's and Charlotte's appearance is remarked upon by their shore-perched friend Jean Farlow. Jean challengingly announces that she has almost painted them into her own picture. She is composing the scene that Humbert and Charlotte were about to enter when she "noticed" as she says "something you [Humbert] overlooked" (Nabokov, 89). Jean points out that Humbert was drowning his wristwatch in the depths of Hourglass Lake, a detail presumably missed by the wearer of the watch. But Charlotte trumps this notice with another: "'Waterproof,' said Charlotte softly, making a fish mouth" (Nabokov, 89). Who would have noticed the aptness of the fish mouth analogy but Humbert's most attentive reader? Jean Farlow parries then with a memory of two children whose shadows are necessarily unnoticed in the high noon of the present moment. But they once made love in the same place where Humbert and Charlotte are standing. The reader must notice that they are the shadows of childhood Humbert and Annabel, an insight prompted perhaps by Jean's further notice that "their [the children's'] shadows were giants." Then, apropos of almost nothing but the occasion for noticing what is not explicit, Jean Farlow evokes Quilty by punning mention of his Uncle Ivor. The inference of Quilty's presence in the mention of Ivor would be all but unimaginable except for the most retrospective reader. This is the reader who can perceive the growth of shadows in the succession of pages that move like a passing sun.

And indeed, the point becomes clear 183 pages later when married Lolita confides the name of her abductor to Humbert, who curiously declines to report the word to the reader. Instead, Humbert echoes the word "Waterproof" (Nabokov, 272). This conspicuously belated repetition of "Waterproof" appears to denote a loss of memory on the reader's part inasmuch as it appears to be a non sequitur. We are nonetheless invited to read it as a perfect sequitur since it fills the space where we expected to discover the proper name Clare Quilty anyway. But, as was the case in the instance of the first utterance of "Waterproof," the word is here a marker for missed notice. It is perhaps the marker for a reader's specific anxiety about not remembering when it first occurred in the text. Indeed, we may in time remember that the occasion of the word's first utterance was also the moment when Quilty was "mentioned," without Jean Farlow actually spelling it out,[29] except by her deceptive reference to Uncle Ivor. We will realize that that moment was, no less than the present moment, an incitement of the reader's self-deceiving pretense to understand, to know more than the context really allows. The reader will not submit to the ignorance entailed by Jean's elusive anecdote: "Ivor in the ivories. . . . Last time he told me a completely indecent story about his nephew. It appears—" (Nabokov, 89).

Aptly, in the moment when "Waterproof" is repeated—in lieu of Humbert spelling out Quilty's latency in it—the roughly adjacent word "quietly" serves to tease out Quilty's presence for the reader who is appropriately attuned to Nabokov's prose: "Waterproof. Why did a flash from Hourglass Lake cross my consciousness? I, too, had known, it, without knowing it, all along. There was no shock, no surprise. *Quietly* the fusion took place, and everything fell into order" (Nabokov, 272, my emphasis).

The word "Waterproof," reprised here, poses the problem of the reader's lack of knowledge of Quilty's ever relevant whereabouts in this book. On this basis, we might indulge the thought that *quietly* teases out the self-deceiver's impulse to seize upon lexical aspects that support whatever reasons might allay our anxiety about that lack of knowledge. On this view, "Waterproof" is a de facto cue for us to read "quietly" in a way that rationalizes, or *locates*, Quilty. It will not be lost on the reader who succumbs to this temptation, that "cue" is Quilty's nickname. With these self-sustaining cues to further reasons—reasons for what is already imaginable, but with respect to other ends—the problem of incommensurables becomes a narrative of possibles, a duly diachronic rationality.

Nabokov is inviting our self-deception. But, as I have insisted, his concern is with the powers of notice latent in self-deception that too often go unperceived. I want to suggest that when they are perceived, their normativizing effect may be apparent: reason-giving and self-deception subsist upon each other. With this knowledge, in this text, we might therefore be inclined to reason further. We might reason that Lolita, a character who is persistently shown to exist beyond the bounds of Humbert's characterization of her, a character fugitive from characterization, who is perpetually *out of character* in a

---

29. We will recall that self-deception is understood by Fingarette as a métier of "spelling out."

manner of speaking, exists preeminently for the sake of Nabokov's book. This claim of course is starkly incommensurable with Humbert's own: that the book *Lolita* exists to make Lolita's character "live in the minds of later generations" (Nabokov, 300). This sentiment, as I have already intimated, is a relic of an aesthetic that *Lolita* the book dispenses with.

Thus the idea of the novel as a vehicle for moralizing self-deception—self-deception taken to be a belligerent irrationality—is displaced by the idea of a novel constitutively bound by the terms of self-deception. *Out of character character,* so to speak, is a counter for the imaginative agency that I have been asserting self-deception can potentiate. This notion of the novel is alternative to the Enlightenment-inspired, self-heroizing aestheticism that we might otherwise discount as little more than a caricature of German Romanticism. That ethos encourages us—in a stridently anti-Aristotelian manner—to take character as an unshakable premise of any narrative art. This would vitiate the peripeteia-driven character development that we have seen the self-deceiving rationalizer—in the guises of Quixote, Rameau, and Humbert—maintain as a vital activity of mind. It should be clear by now that, at the beginning of this chapter, I identified Aristotelian peripetiea with the discipline of noticing in large part because it presupposes a tolerance of incommensurables: it epitomizes the recognition that objects we desire, in the course of our realizing those desires, may reveal aspects that inspire countervailing desires.[30] In other words, the very aspect-dependency that instantiates Raz's "classical agency" in Quixote, Rameau, and Humbert allows me to characterize their shared rationality as grounded in an unstinting responsiveness to the duration of our experience in the world. This is alternative to a conceptually inspired preemption of the world and all of its seemingly unimaginable possibilities.

---

30. In this case I would equate tolerance for incommensurables with Gombrich's account of how seeing (with respect to the illusionism discussed in chapter 2) requires a critical parity between making and matching. Every recognition of a schema entails the accommodation of a "correction." Though this correction is technically incommensurable with the schema, the intelligibility of the schema—as grasping a circumstance subject to change—is inconceivable without the correction. I would argue that this circumstance is epiphenomenal to the game of giving and receiving reasons: every schema gives reasons and every correction solicits reasons. See *Art and Illusion,* 307.

5

Picturing Self-Deception

Perception and Agency

I have maintained that the self-deceiver is more intensely a creature of temporality than the standard rationalist. So the register of visuality might at first seem a less promising threshold upon which to examine self-deceptive behavior than the narrative arts and their essentially linguistic means. But visuality does not, of course, preclude narrative sense-making. The visual image is perhaps even more immediately connected to the forms of self-deceptive behavior. Its narrative imperatives may be more immediately felt by the viewer than by the reader of a literary text because the sensuous contiguity of things is less easy to abstract oneself from. As I have already observed, the basis for this claim is strikingly apparent in the phenomenon of visual illusion. In *Art and Illusion* Gombrich makes the point that imagistic illusionism makes it seem as if the eye knows a meaning of which the mind is ignorant. The relevant knowledge here cannot be adequately characterized as an autonomous intuition—as if pictures and pictorial content were fully determined and intractably specific.[1] It can, however, be usefully grasped as an element of the densely inferential activity of *spelling out*. This is a narrative enterprise by virtue of the mandate to go on that I have alleged to be always inscribed within such enterprises.

In other words, on the register of visuality we presuppose a special tolerance for the incompleteness of experience. Here is a rough equivalent to the tolerance for incommensurables, which authorized the rational self-deceptions exemplified in the previous chapter. Linguistic texts, at least on the declarative

---

1. Here I am in agreement with Dominic Lopes's observation that Gombrich is exceptional in his proposition that "pictures are by necessity selective in how they represent their subjects." See Lopes, *Understanding Pictures* (Oxford: Oxford University Press, 1996), 112.

level of the sentence, seem to be more reluctant to indulge such ongoing contingency. Kendall Walton has surmised that this is because words perform an essentially assertoric function by providing reasons for beliefs.[2] The assumption here is that belief preempts or inhibits any self-revising animus. By contrast, and as Gombrich reminds us, our disposition to accept the ineluctability of a self-revising perception on the register of visuality goes all the way back to the tradition of Roman wall painting. Roman wall painting seems to be wrought of a penchant for self-complicating illusionism (Gombrich, 140–41). Gombrich understands August Mau's "four Pompeian styles" of wall painting as testifying to a persistence of the desire to make things more explicit, to spell out more perspicuously the motives behind representation, especially as representational forms invite illusionistic transformations.

One must constantly be looking for further information about the conditions of visibility where illusionist play is narratively afoot, as it is in the full account of Mau's four styles.[3] The first style begins as a painterly imitation of masonry. The second style projects space through the impenetrably "real" masonry of the wall. The baroque stylization of the lines of perspectively situated architectural structures in the third style reminds us of the real masonry, which is revealed to be their only plausible physical support, and which the second style urged the viewer to forget. The knowledge of illusion and the knowledge of its dissolution subsist together in the fourth style. In a sense, the fourth style displays their incommensurability as a condition of viewing. Thus the succession of styles can be read as a "spelling out" of the conditions of viewing that prompts a more capacious viewpoint: one that nonetheless does not depend upon its own self-limitation. It is one that carries a burden of self-consciousness with a decidedly narrative trajectory. For the viewer is bound to switch from one system of viewing to another simply by virtue of their perceptual propinquity.

On the basis of the ensemble of practices summarized here, Roman wall painting epitomizes for Gombrich the unique degree to which appearances on

---

2. The point of view that I have presented so far is ultimately at odds with Walton's position. I have spoken of how images give us reasons for pursuing more apt beliefs. I nonetheless agree with Walton about how reasons and beliefs go together in verbal acts. See Walton's discussion in *Mimesis as Make-Believe: On the Foundations of the Representational Arts* (Cambridge: Harvard University Press, 1990).

3. Norman Bryson discusses Mau's "system" at length in *Looking at the Overlooked: Four Essays on Still Life Painting* (Cambridge: Harvard University Press, 1990). Bryson relies upon a more recent redaction of Mau, *La peinture murale romaine: les styles décoratifs pompéiens* (Paris: Picard, 1985). Bryson wants his reader to be mindful of the challenges to the strictness of Mau's taxonomy. But the dialectical dynamism I have identified here is not in doubt.

the visual register entail a necessary collaboration between the image and the seeing subject. Likewise they underscore the interdependency between the conceptual schema that make perception intelligible and the adaptive intelligence that corrects for the changing particulars of perceptual experience. Gombrich maintains that this enterprise is continuous throughout the history of painting. It amounts to acknowledging a persistent lack of fit between perceiver and perceived. As Gombrich explains it, perceptual expectation, embodied in visual schemata, inexorably succumb to the corrections of the viewer, who must contend with the incommensurability of what she knows and what she is meant to know.[4] Particularly in the context of visual illusionism, Gombrich makes the important point that "ambiguity as such cannot be perceived" (Gombrich, 259). We can only register its effect in the act of switching from one visual reading to another. Gombrich suggests that the collaborative activity implicit in this "switching" is occasioned by any desire to image the world. Once again, I point out that the willingness to contend with incommensurability is a rationalistic project concordant with the Razian notion of classical reason. I articulated this in the previous chapter as one in which incommensurable values do not preclude a productive collaboration among discrepant viewpoints.

In this chapter I will go further to say that the collaborative activity Gombrich invokes is a token of the existential state of present-ness. I have consistently linked this state to the possibility of intuiting self-deception as a condition for entering the ethical domain of rational agency. Modes of visual representation that reveal the collaboration of discrepant and contrasting viewpoints force us to conceive visuality as preeminently an activity rather than a constative proposition. In this way they set the stage for our thinking about how the instance of seeing is necessarily in tension with the possibility of *seeing again*. I wish to call this notion of seeing, which entails an empirically manifest, and temporally inflected, *seeing again*, "second sight." Second sight will serve as a controlling conceit for my attempts to argue how seeing and self-deception are integral to the modes of rational agency that have been at stake in this discussion from the beginning.

Gombrich's point about the unrepresentability of ambiguity—except by virtue of the switching from one reading to another—is speculatively linked

---

4. In *Art and Illusion*, this motif of schema and correction pervades Gombrich's account of the proximity of illusionism to all visual representational practices. I would suggest that the logic here is consistent with my earlier discussions, following Raz, about the aspect-dependency of classical rationality. See especially *Art and Illusion*, 100, 116, 108–9, 147–48, and 271–72.

to the perceptual experiments of Adelbert Ames. I might therefore begin my progress toward a view of self-deception as a modality of second sight with a brief summary of Ames's discoveries. We shall see that Ames's thinking bears out several previously stated hypotheses about self-deceiving behavior, specifically with respect to the dependency of beliefs upon reasons and the fungibility of reasons with respect to the beliefs they support. We need only recall David Sanford's account of the "reversibility" of the dependency between reasons and beliefs in self-deception. Typically, a belief depends upon the evidentiary reasons for holding it. But if one prefers an alternative belief, warrantable reasons may be suborned to the cause of the desire to hold that belief.[5] This understanding of human behavior is cognate with the dynamics of ambiguity in perception illuminated by Ames's famous *chair* and *room*. I want to suggest that in those experimental contexts the illusion is actualized by an implicit manipulation of reasons for beliefs and thereby fosters a compelling self-consciousness of one's participation in an ongoing present.

The Ames chair is, in effect, a peep show. Three peepholes purvey distinct views of a tubular chair. But when the objects are viewed outside the constructed viewpoint they reveal diverse shapes. Only one of the chairs is a fully constructed chair. Our belief that we see a chair in each instance of perceiving through the peephole depends upon what reason is construable in the perspective imposed by distinct viewpoints. Likewise, the Ames's room presents its viewer with a frame that appears to open upon a perfect Albertian view of space. This illusion is created by the familiar perceptual cues to which we are conditioned by the geometries of spatial design that are coordinate with all rectangular enclosures: such as a floor of parallelograms receding in Albertian perspective. Albertian perspective prompts us to see things diminish in size as they approach the horizon. However, a figure that traverses the space of the Ames's room from front to back will appear to become larger rather than smaller. Correlatively, a figure that moves across the back wall of the room seems to grow larger and smaller, without reason, until the viewer observes the room from outside the constructed viewpoint; that is, from above. What is revealed from above is a trapezoidal structure with the walls leaning outward and the floor projecting on an incline. Through the peephole the perceivable figures appear to be "impossible." This is the so-called *Ames transformation*. All apparent distance cues are incommensurable with the retinal size of the

---

5. See my discussion of the relativity of "anticipating and ostensible reasons" in chapter 1 and especially Sanford's "Self-Deception as Rationalization," 159–60.

image. To the knowing viewer, however, the illusion discloses the dependency of beliefs upon an implicit and necessary switching between systems of viewing or reasoning. Here is an implicit warrant for choosing among discrepant reasons to believe. At first glance, and assuming our passive reliance on the register of the retinal image, that is to say, what reasons endorse it, we cannot believe what we're seeing. The reasons ordaining the experience appear to be divorced from the process of reasoning altogether.[6] But just as the retinal image *hides* the truth of the contingency of the peephole perspective, I would argue that there is a hidden assumption in Ames's demonstration that all too frequently remains unacknowledged: that all viewpoints are inherently reasons for belief. Even more urgently, we must face the fact that our commitment to further reasoning is irreducible in the unrepresentable ambiguity of the visual field that otherwise appears to defy reason.

In other words, Ames's illusions might convince us that we perceive according to our implicit commitments to *see again.* We take a second sighting for granted as a condition for seeing at all. Furthermore, we are bound to second sight by the very self-consciousness of the aspectual nature of seeing that the Ames experiments highlight. In this chapter I want to imagine that visual artists who are especially attuned to this knowledge are, in their aesthetic practices, more perspicuous spellers out than the rest of us. I have previously characterized this disposition as an unusual degree of responsiveness to the duration of human experience. There is a Hegelian dimension to this fact that I intimated in my discussion of Notional knowledge at the beginning of chapter 2. So I now want to explore how several visual artists, in a variety of visual media, exhibit this Hegelianism. In this way I will suggest that they potentiate what I have called the ethical work of self-deception: the reckoning of now selves and then selves.

Before I get to specific cases, however, I should note that Dominic Lopes has picked out a feature of pictorial experience that justifies the kind of investigation I embark upon here. In *Understanding Pictures,* he combines a Hegelian Notional intuition with an agential disposition. Picking up on Gombrich's point about the essential "selectivity" of pictorial presentation/experience, Lopes disputes the abiding prejudice that says the body in space is dispositive for understanding pictures as static embodiments of perceptual viewpoints. Rather, he argues that pictures "make a combination of commitments and

---

6. For a fuller account of the Ames experiments, see R. L. Gregory, "Analogue Transactions with Adelbert Ames," *Perception* 16 (1963): 277–82.

non-commitments that cannot be made by any visual experience.... Aspects should not be regarded as purely spatial" (Lopes, 121). For example, curvilinearism instantiates commitments to properties that are seen by an unfixed eye. This comes, however, at the cost, so to speak, of noncommitments about the degree of curvature of represented edges and the relevant size of objects so represented (129). Commitment with respect to one dimension is a noncommitment with respect to other dimensions that might otherwise be prioritized if one's motivational biases were different. It is possible to say on this basis that the taking up of commitments is a self-avowal, in Fingarette's sense of the term, and a reminder of the degree to which ethical selves require some improvisational facility. The artists I wish to engage here will specifically fortify this assertion. But more significantly, they will make it possible to generalize from it. They will show us how what I have alleged to be the normativity of self-deception can be shown to be a consequence of that second sight wherein the now self and the then self are conspicuously poised to come to terms with each other. I think it should already be clear that now selves and then selves are always aspectually intuited and comprehended.

We therefore must not ignore the fact that second sight, as I use the term, locates our *readings* of experience within a contextualist framework of reasoning. There what matters most is our prospect for improvising richer contexts of commitment. What commitments govern a situation are less important than the capacity for altering and replacing them. This capacity guarantees the intelligibility of our commitments in time and presupposes our attentiveness to the manner of our making commitments in the first place. Not surprisingly, the artists I discuss assiduously conflate perception and commitment. Furthermore, they do so in a way that assures our self-consciousness of ourselves as reasoners for whom incommensurability is a métier of self-assertion. Even more important, they do so in a way that makes self-deception ever more plausibly a sine qua non of responsible selfhood. The ethical imperative here is of course a narrative practice insofar as we believe, with Gombrich, that switching from one system of reading visual aspects to another is a foundational ambiguity of visual experience and one that presupposes the collaboration between image and observant subject. This ethical imperative likewise coheres with Sanford's account of the interdependence of reason and belief, which we can now see as a substrate of self-deceiving reason. All of this is to say that there is ample warrant to search out visual practices in which possessing the speculative reach of self-deception is an operative condition of viewing. As I have said before, such practices augur an enhancement of the viewer's self-reflective capacity. Or I should say that this is the case precisely to the degree that such self-reflection is not reducible to a purely instrumental concept of the self.

I began this chapter with the assumption that all visual experience ought to be understood in terms that Gombrich stipulates are determinative for illusionist projection. My purpose is not to confuse categories, to blur the line between what is perceptible and what tricks perception. Rather, I presuppose that such categorization elides the fact that there are always suppressed motives in any intuition of an imagistically represented world. It is perhaps for related reasons that John Elster in *Sour Grapes* has insisted upon a strictly delimited notion of purpose with respect to something like the representational act.[7] Elster's notion of purpose has, as its prerequisite, the entailment of a feedback mechanism. He explains that any activity that would be deemed purpose*ful* or even merely purposive, must be modifiable according to the changing conditions under which any purpose is taken up.

In the analysis that follows we will see that such a feedback mechanism has been implicit in my account of self-deception as a self-preserving rationalization. More to the point, in the course of this discussion I have been intimating that perception and purpose are symbiotic. Or this is the case if we accept that every perception has intelligibility because some motive is assignable to it and hence some commitment is entailed by it. In any event, the underlying point is that perception, in this case visual perception, carries a strong inferential charge, a warrant for further *spelling out*. This warrant is arguably even more urgent than it would be in cases of linguistic representation where the *spelling out* is presumed to be already accomplished in the grammatical paradigm. If, as Gombrich characterizes it, visual perception prompts us to imagine that there is something the body/eye knows that the mind does not, then the visual field is effectively less closed off than the grammatically articulated linguistic representation. So illusionism is not so reductively a trick of perception. It is more a trajectory of perception that, because it is inflected by the relative incompleteness of the visual field, proffers a rationalistic prospect for other ways of making sense than our immediate sensory rapport gives us a purchase on. The visual figuring of incompleteness, like the worry of the literary protagonists whom we have become acquainted with as self-deceivers compulsively

---

7. See Jon Elster, *Sour Grapes: Studies in the Subversion of Rationality* (Cambridge: Cambridge University Press, 1983), 105–7.

needing to know more, invests the specter of indeterminacy with a motive for rational determination.

The link intimated here—between illusionism in the visual field and self-deception as it bears on self-realization—highlights the most specific relevance of the work of the visual artists whom I now wish to engage at some length. I deliberately choose visual artists whose practice encourages us to grasp visuality as an ongoing activity more than as a historically determinative gesture within a unique métier or medium. I have selected artists from diverse visual media because I want to displace the analytical frames—the *history* of painting, the *technologies* of film, photography, and video, and so on—that have imposed themselves upon the various aspects of visual experience so as to hide the very aspectual dimension of visuality itself. For my purposes it is this dimension that makes illusionism so rich a site for speculating upon self-deception as a scene of rational production. It is therefore all the more helpful to focus upon it without the distractions thrown up by the formal taxonomies of visual art criticism.

James Elkins has recently noted that "there is no intrinsic connection between formalism and attention to visual detail," or what I am treating as the dynamics of notice and of diachronic rationality. Elkins seems to say that, in some cases, our attunement with visuality requires a suspension of the paradigms of vision.[8] I should note, however, that I am not, by deploying the term "visuality," claiming that the perceptual ground I mean to traverse is independent of aesthetic making. The works to be grappled with here are unapologetically works of art, deeply implicated in the historical value of aesthetic making and the relevance of aesthetic making to human actions in general. Finally, because I wish to elude the formalist paradigms that distinguish visual media from one another, I choose artworks that incorporate what we often deem to be incommensurable visual technologies within a single compositional matrix.

Jacopo Tintoretto, Jeff Wall, Gerhard Richter, Bill Viola, and Peter Greenaway make up the eclectic quintet of exemplars that serves the purposes I have just prioritized. Over the course of this chapter and the next, my aim will not simply be to mount a close reading of specific works that proves the exemplarity of the respective artists. Rather, I want to see these artists as collaborators of sorts. As an ensemble, they explore the limits of reason that the aesthetic registers of self-deception are capable of disclosing.

---

8. See James Elkins, *Visual Studies: A Skeptical Introduction* (New York: Routledge, 2003), 109.

Switching Visual Registers in Tintoretto

Jacopo Tintoretto's *The Discovery of the Body of St. Mark* (1565) is a good point of departure because it dramatizes a conflict of rationalistic dictates. The painterly composition hinges on the most infamous *dispositif* of rationalistic visual projection,[9] the Albertian geometrical grid. Single-point perspectivalism is worked here in such a way that the substrate of illusionism inherent to it, and usually disguised by it, is revealed to be incommensurable with rational representation. But it is simultaneously seen to be coordinate with an awareness of the possibility of rationalized representation. I will show that Tintoretto, Wall, Richter, Viola, and Greenaway are artists for whom it might be said that such a tolerance of incommensurables is the sine qua non of their aesthetic effects. All deploy practices that challenge the zero sum game that philosophical theories of incommensurability typically enjoin us to play when the fate of Enlightenment rationality hangs in the balance. I will point out that the opportunities for rational *spelling out*—whether we designate it in terms of enhanced notice, second sight, or diachronic rationality—can only be recognized by dispelling the specter of incommensurability as a terminus of rational conversation. So my challenge in reading the work of Tintoretto, and his methodological artistic kin, will be to spell out their means of sustaining a tolerance of incommensurables that guarantees the perseverance of Enlightenment rationality, even in the course of contesting it.

I have argued from the beginning of this book that all such contestations involve us in unusually intense dramatizations of present-ness, in a reassessment of the ethical scope of character, and in an assertion of the normativity of self-deception. It is therefore apt to begin a discussion of Tintoretto's *Discovery* by making a strictly formalist observation. The painting's protagonist, St. Mark, stands on an orthogonal line with the vanishing point of the composition, as if to describe the privileged vantage point of viewing. His gesturing hand marks the convergence of all the orthogonal lines of the composition upon which the rationality of the Albertian perspectival scheme, which we saw undergirding the experiments of Adelbert Ames, depends. Furthermore, the self-abstracting timelessness of Albertian character instantiated here, as opposed to the timely present-ness I have ascribed to self-deceiving character, would appear to be reified in the compositional empowerment of the saint's

---

9. Here Louis Althusser's use of the term *dispositif* is most relevant. The term plays a significant role in his argument in "Ideology and Ideological State Apparatuses" and in his lesser-known aesthetic treatise "A Letter on Art," in *Lenin and Philosophy*, trans. Ben Brewster (New York: Monthly Review Press, 1971).

Fig. 4 Jacopo Robusti Tintoretto, *The Discovery of the Body of St. Mark* (*The Finding of the Body of St. Mark*), 1565. Pinacoteca di Brera, Milan, Italy/The Bridgeman Art Library.

denotative vantage point. The saint's placement at this vantage point thus seems to flaunt a representational logic that has been exhaustively excoriated by critics of this visual regime,[10] whether one calls it Albertian, Cartesian, or simply rationalist. Those critics construe it as a valorization of a defensive, authoritarian subjectivity.

By contrast, Rudolph Arnheim has observed that the possibility of "crossing" apparently incommensurable viewing systems is the chief source of our

---

10. See Martin Jay's "Scopic Regimes of Modernity, " in *Vision and Visuality*, ed. Hal Foster (Seattle: Bay Press, Dia Art Foundation, 1988), 3–23.

interest in this composition.[11] This is a line of thought that buttresses my notion that viewpoints are inherently reasons for beliefs. Such a possibility is revealed in Tintoretto's compositional scheme as a warrant for believing differently about the conceptually authorized perceptions purveyed in the painting. Arnheim convincingly demonstrates that we may not take refuge in the saint's privileged viewing position. Rather, we are encouraged by Tintoretto to see from a viewing point that denotes a world seen inferentially. Inasmuch as it requires a rotation of our gaze, Tintoretto's composition presents a world that is seen "as if" by another person (Arnheim, 288). Arnheim characterizes it as the instantiation of another perceptual situation denoted by a vanishing point with which the viewer, who is keyed to the saint's denotative gesture, has no rapport. The viewer is therefore predisposed to take no consequential notice of it.

But before we can appreciate Arnheim's usefulness in taking this painting as a dramatization of powers of notice or second sight, we must take a full view of what Tintoretto has accomplished on the picture plane. This is a painting about "discovery," a momentous act of notice, in more ways than one. The saint is of course witnessing the discovery of his own body, secretly entombed in Alexandria at the time of his martyrdom. The body is to be removed to Mark's city, Venice. The body at his feet is a doubling of his standing self and intended to be a double for the corpse to be retrieved from its secret tomb. But more to the point, the saint's gesture, which Arnheim noted was most pointedly a discovery of the Albertian vanishing point, does not occasion a rationalization of space in the usual way. The infinity of that distance is blocked. Furthermore, at the point of blockage we discover a scene of action that almost too didactically mimics the dimensions of the picture plane upon which the Albertian artist can make space recede. The scene is a *seeing again* of the act of grave-robbing. It is an other's grave. But it is likewise a seeing again of the viewer of the painting, insofar as the raised lid of the sarcophagus opened here strikingly reflects the aspect ratio of the Albertian picture plane. Bright as it is, the luminous panel illuminates a path (along the right wall of the church nave) for the rotation of the viewer's gaze away from the "official" vanishing point, rather than attracting the moth-like eye of the Albertian viewer into the light itself.

And indeed there is something to discover if one moves one's eyes horizontally across the picture plane, instead of into the luminously occluded distance.

---

11. Arnheim's article "Perception of Perspective, Pictorial Space from Different Viewing Points" gives me a useful technical base from which to reassert the initial premises of this chapter. See "Perception of Perspective, Pictorial Space from Different Viewing Points," *Leonardo* 10 (1977): 283–88.

Our gaze is brought first to a view of the body of Mark being lowered from the tomb. When we arrive at the far right margin of the composition we confront the spectacle of figures who are supplicating the saint. These objects of our notice both exist on an orthogonal line of sight that would skew the architecture of the nave of the church in which the entire scenario of the painting unfolds. Quite literally we discover our viewing selves differently than we would recognize if we were bound by an identification with the spatial orientation of the saint. In effect, the architectural frame is denied us by the framing viewpoints. As Arnheim makes clear, perception doesn't conform to the spatial system in a picture: "Viewers are not captives of the perspective system presented to them by a painting. They are free to view the world in the picture not as their own but as someone else's—a perceptual world whose vanishing point is not determined by their own viewing point but by that of another person, whose presence consists in nothing but the world that person sees" (Arnheim, 288). Perception is alive to the possibilities of discovering other vantage points of notice that do not so much *round out* the picture of reality, but make us cognizant of the obstacles to picturing per se. Perception trumps picturing.

Certainly a Gombrichean "switching" between registers of visualization is occurring here. It makes the painting a token of unrepresentable illusionism. But it might be even more precise to say that a kind of self-deception is entailed in the switching between picture systems or perspectival vantage points. This switching challenges the idea of picturing, as Nelson Goodman wants us to understand it, as a merely denotative framework that harbors a variety of predications within it.[12] For example, a painting of the discovery of Saint Mark denotes the saint's life story, the church architecture, the cultural practice of grave robbing, the architectural dimensionality of the tombs, the protagonists of the action displayed. The denotations are also knowable as the predicates of specific architectural styles that apply to churches and tombs, the historical fashions of the protagonists' attire, and the social places to which they are assignable on that basis. But it is important to notice that the pictorial system, in this regard, is more self-enclosing for the viewer than Tintoretto's composition itself. On Goodman's account, pictorial systems presuppose a boundedness of notice, and of the commitments available within those boundaries, that perception does not. Within the dynamics of perception per se the range of beliefs that one is prompted to make commitments to is broader than

---

12. See Nelson Goodman, *Languages of Art* (New York: Bobbs-Merrill, 1968), 127–73 and 225–32.

the protocol of commitments dictated by the pictorial system itself. Similarly, motivational biases for belief are not self-preemptively articulated by perception. The very necessity of Gombrichean "switching" between manifestly incommensurable systems, that is to say, of countenancing incommensurable systems as intrinsic to the experience of taking notice, allows for the possibility that a now self and a then self are in contention with each other.

In other words, the rotation of the gaze incites a perceptually driven crossing of picturing systems. This is manifested as the viewer's awareness of an incommensurability that compels him or her to reason differently, and to acknowledge motivational biases for different beliefs. It furthermore supports my view that self-deception might profitably be seen to be a correlate of learning. Tintoretto's compositional scheme in *The Discovery of the Body of St. Mark* might therefore be characterized as a kind of restaging of the action of discovery based on highlighting different noticings or aspects. But the most relevant noticings will pertain not so much to the story of the discovery of the saint per se. Rather they will bear most directly on the viewer's resources for noticing aspects of painterly composition that might otherwise simply become redundant for a single predicate of picturing, specifically, the discovery of the body and the story of the saint's martyrdom.

Tintoretto presents a different story than we might think is depictable according to the title of the painting. The most relevant noticings in this case are aspects of the viewer's capacity for notice: or the recognition that the viewer is most fundamentally present to herself in the exercise of that capacity for notice. When we see the grave robbers from the right margin of the picture plane, a view that is at odds with the discovering eye of the saint, not to mention the focal point of the architectural space which supports that world, our own worldliness is informed by a kind of secret knowledge. The discovery of the saint of course depends upon the original secrecy of the burial. But we are here self-conscious that what is secreted in the painting is the knowledge that there is more to see in a Gombrichian, illusionist way (e.g., the dynamic of schema and correction) than the spectacle of discovery itself can disclose. With respect to this point, it is important to note the supplicants in the right foreground of the canvas: a plague victim, a possessed man, and a woman. Their visual significance depends upon the discovery of the orthogonal that supports the figure of the grave robber above them. It is conspicuously divergent from the dominant lines of the church architecture. In more ways than one, the supplicants are begging for their own bodies. After all, the specter of mortal robbery is upon them. Like the other doublings or mirrorings (the illusionist sarcophagus lid, the foreshortened body of the replacement saint at Mark's feet, and so on) that lead us to contemplate what is not directly before our eyes, the figures of the supplicants might be best understood as aspectually inferential trajectories of thought. They are, in that respect, on the trajectory of thought that leads mortal fear from the fact of the body to the imagination of the soul.

This is an acknowledgment that the secret contingencies of any single point of view augur for a capacity to spell them out. Quite clearly, the supplicants in the painting can lead us to think about the faithlessness of the body with respect to the afterlife. The dichotomous realms of body and spirit are displayed incommensurably. We are, after all, witnessing the unfolding episodes of an afterlife from which the consciousness of the saint's body is seemingly exempted. This is the case notwithstanding the fact that the observational authority of the saint, embodied at the viewing point of the Albertian paradigm, belies the loss of consciousness otherwise attributable to his corpse and reanimates the body of the viewer. All of this is therefore strong testimonial to the necessity of our keeping faith with the continuity of perceptual experience beyond the ideational frames of picturing. The commitments that instantiate the self—deceived, so to speak, by the inadequacy of reasons for belief that any one set of perceptual constraints would promote—are thus revealed to be mutable within the framework of some protocol for taking up new commitments.

As was the case in all of my previous accounts of self-deception, there is a normative knowledge afoot in the provocations of Tintoretto's canvas. This normative knowledge is operative, not in the sense that there is some prior rule of intelligibility that would motivate a viewer to take up commitments. It is apparent rather in the viewer's accruing new motivational biases that changing perceptual imperatives occasion as reasons for belief. Or, more specifically, one could say that the viewer's changing perceptual imperatives are an occasion for reasoning beyond the bounds of beliefs to which we are committed independent of the viewer's temporally mutable experience. I am attempting to articulate here how the force of Tintoretto's painting might be attributable to its way of setting us up to look to see again. This is very much analogous to how the Ames illusions convince us that perceptions are reasoned according our accepting commitments to a kind of second sight. Such second sight, as we have seen, is coherent with the narrativity of action. Whatever normative knowledge is at stake here is beholden to the viewer's engagement with the temporal variables that action—and the inferentialism induced by treating norms as inherent to activity—mandates. Even if the relevant action is only a rotation of the gaze or a longitudinal transit across the picture plane, the devices of Tintoretto's composition attune us to the drama of a self-surpassing knowledge. This "transcendence" may appear to mock the passage of the soul from the body, especially as the painting is a rendition of the passage of the body through an inescapable and seemingly expandable space. We may count the relevant body to be that of the saint and its representational counterparts, or that of the viewer in countenancing the multiple dimensions within which the body can be contemplated. Either way there is a sobering piety in knowing that *every body counts* as a significant aspect of the contemplative enterprise.

What is most important to take account of, then, is that the self-surpassing knowledge dramatized in Tintoretto presupposes self-deception. After all, changing perceptions supplant operative beliefs and the commitments undertaken in them. It must be said that self-deception in this capacity promotes a normative knowledge that would otherwise, under standard definitions, be pegged to faith in an a priori rule or to some other deterministic causality. To the contrary, self-deception here is a topos on which we can map a learning curve. Or, even more explicitly, it is a topos for understanding how the whole problem of norms arises, as Talcott Parsons famously asserted in *The Structure of Social Action* (1937),[13] from the problem of explaining action. I am suggesting that compositions like Tintoretto's actualize as well as represent the dynamics of this problem. From the start of this work, I have contended that the phenomenon of self-deception situates us, more responsibly than we might otherwise be disposed to be, within the problem of explaining action. The explanation of action is after all what gives gravity and urgency to the important question: what to do next? If self-deception can indeed be instrumental to answering this question, then it has the kind of moral claim on us that I have maintained works of art will tend to potentiate when they reveal our undeniable complicity in self-deception.

It might seem counterintuitive, risking a category mistake, to assert that visuality and visual experiences generally are implicated in the explanation of actions. But this is surely not the case once we grant that visual experience is as temporally urgent, as time sensitive, as strongly warranting human responsiveness in time, as any other cognitive engagement with the world. When I

---

13. Stephen P. Turner usefully elaborates on Parsons's stance in *Brains/Practices/Relativism* (Chicago: University of Chicago Press, 2002), 140–41. Turner deduces that where we observe the apparent effect of normative rules, we often overlook the fact that rules can be read back into a set of actions that originates more fortuitously through habituation.

stated at the end of chapter 4 that unstinting responsiveness to the duration of our experience was an ethical burden that the experience of self-deception might help us take up, I was counting on my reader's ability to see the self-impoverishment entailed by the most obvious alternative: lack of response abdicates the duties of spelling out, of diachronic rationality. It vitiates the keener notice upon which our human purposiveness otherwise subsists. Lack of response renders moot the question of what to do next and is counter to the rational subject's anxiety about the fullness of knowledge that we have seen animates the self-deceiving mind in a fundamental way. Clearly, I do not think that there is much difference between visual and verbal artistic media on this point. But I should note that in both realms of aesthetic experience we can tell the difference between well-executed and poorly executed aesthetic performances on the basis of how efficiently our powers of notice are recruited to the cause of action. The agent of response to the presentational elements of the aesthetic experience is a party to every class of artworks. To the degree that this is the case, I am maintaining that the dynamics of self-deception inhere as a vicissitude of the responsiveness of the viewer or the reader. We might say that our recruitment to this activity is inextricable from our being present to the scene of action.

If Tintoretto, a painter renown for the quickness of his gestures on the canvas tells us anything, it is that seeing is an act as much as painting is an act. In this regard it is worth remembering Roland Barthes's prescient consideration of the status of the visual image in *Camera Lucida*.[14] It is specifically worth noting that Barthes favors the *punctum* image over the *studium* image. The *punctum* image animates. The *studium* image is cerebrated. The former's exhibition of the qualities of personal embodiment and unpredictability is more compelling for Barthes because of the strong inference of its involvement in the temporality of act. Barthes, of course, is a visual thinker who insists on the primacy of divining the intentions that establish and animate images in some dialectical relation with what belies their animus. Ultimately, *punctum* and *studium* are characterized by Barthes as copresent in their incompatibilities (Barthes, 42). But I think it is fair to say that the subtle privilege Barthes gives to the *punctum* image suggests that the question of what we are capable of seeing might subtend the question of what we are capable of doing.[15]

---

14. See the opening sections of Roland Barthes, *Camera Lucida*, trans. Richard Howard (New York: Hill and Wang, 1982).

15. Indeed, Barthes says that the *punctum* image makes apparent otherwise unnoticed details of a view that can't be taken in, but "fill[s] the whole picture." Ibid., 26.

Unfortunately, what I read as Barthes's scruple, vis-à-vis the agency of the visual thinker, has been diluted these days by a rising rhetoric of visuality and visual literacy that has fetishized the mere artifactuality of the visual object at the expense of the temporality that occasions our most perspicuous notice of it.[16] But this trend need not prevail.

The Temporality of Jeff Wall's Liquid Intelligence

In the spirit of Barthes's investigations, Jeff Wall and Gerhard Richter, a photographer and a painter respectively, are both formally preoccupied with the relation between the photographic/film image, taken to be more alive to temporal change, and the painted image, taken to be a mere residue of temporal change. Their work orchestrates reciprocities between what appear to be incommensurable epistemic stances and technologies. They therefore provide a resource for seeing how the explanation of actions supervenes aesthetic practices and attitudes that might otherwise seem to obviate the realm of action in favor of a more detached and contemplative ethos.

It might seem a counterintuitive proposition to say that visual experience is implicated in the explanation of action. But, as was vividly the case with Tintoretto, the vitality of the visual experience in Wall and Richter is quite conspicuously bound up with the comparative stakes of the commitments a viewer is invited to take up. The drama is intensified by the artist's insistence that we choose our commitments vis-à-vis the shifting motivational biases that the perceptual continuum (in this case the visual field), in its essential instability, unfolds for us. We are, in the context of this knowledge, invited to see how dependent we might be on inference rather than evidence, in order to inhabit those biases with any degree of rational cogency/agency. We might even agree, inasmuch as logical integrity always depends upon some protocol of *spelling out,* that evidence is de facto inference. I have claimed that we can only know what we believe normatively by accepting the fact that we are perceptually

---

16. I am thinking here of a tendency among scholars working in the fields of visual studies or visual culture to imagine ways of severing perceptual experience from the matrices of cultural self-understanding, i.e., the intentionality of interpretation. Interpretation is deemed to be incurably contaminated by subjectivity. I am thinking especially of the influence of Benjamin, Foucault, and Deleuze upon visual studies. These are all quite brilliant theorists who nonetheless stymie investigation of how visuality might be integral to the cognitive dimensions of agential experience. Paradoxically enough, they treat the perceptual datum as beneficently irrational. Perception is characterized as instrumentally irrational with respect to the goals of doing justice to otherness and honoring an indeterminate will.

bound to see again—that seeing is always inferentially charged. On this basis we might emphasize the aspects of artistic work that dramatize this fact.

I take Jeff Wall's 1984 photograph *Milk* to be an eloquent dramatization of how the urgency for an explanation of action is inferentially impacted in the act itself. In my next chapter I will juxtapose Wall's practice with Gerhard Richter's series of photorealist blur paintings, the suite entitled *October 18, 1977*. By this means, I think it may be possible to understand how an artistic practice that makes the dramatization of inferential knowing a condition of seeing dovetails with the project of Enlightenment learning—without succumbing either to nostalgic or cynical retrospection.

Both Wall and Richter start from the document, an evidentiary as opposed to an inferential premise. In his catalogue essay for Wall's 2007 retrospective at MoMA, Peter Galassi specifically locates *Milk* among the group of Wall's works that can be called "near documentary."[17] In these photographs the artist self-consciously restages an event he claims to have witnessed himself. I emphasize the act of witness for its obvious kinship with the métier of notice. This nominally static "memory" of an event nonetheless occasions a presentness for the viewer that makes the time of viewing an emphatically active proposition.

Milk itself is a large-scale transparency illuminated within light box framing. It displays the still, seemingly immobilized, figure of a man holding a box of milk sheathed in a paper bag. The immobilization of an otherwise active physique takes on a paradoxically gestural character insofar as the milk is caught unglassed, so to speak, in the air. A glass of milk within the painterly and photorealist traditions would be an apt subject matter for depiction, under glass, rendered specimen-like, purely artifactual. But here we are dealing with spilled milk, an unintended consequence not to be wept over, one that eludes the act of conceptual framing, that eludes artifactuality altogether. In this case however, the speed of the camera shutter has captured the otherwise uncontainable liquid. More provocatively, the milk captured, as if frozen in air, thereby becomes an index of the motion of the body grasping the box. The almost sculptural imaging of the milk registers the wake of a previous violence. In a complementary way, the motion of the milk in air becomes an index of the power of the camera to still the action. The face of the figure, like the milky wake that is compositionally his counterpart, is set or *frozen* with an expression of rage. It is conspicuously reactive to some cause that we are only

---

17. See Peter Galassi, *Jeff Wall* (New York: MoMA, 2007), 35.

Fig. 5   Jeff Wall, *Milk*, 1984. Reproduced by permission of Jeff Wall Studio.

cognizant of with respect to the extraordinary visibility of the milk. It is important to emphasize that without the device of the camera the motion of the milk would be beyond our capacities of vision or intellection.

Despite our knowledge of the work as imbricated in the temporality of the artist's experience, Peter Galassi reads the image of *Milk* as "a timeless, self-sufficient image—a world in itself" (Galassi, 36). Galassi is content to call it "tableau." But this would seem to concede that the value of photography is too strictly epiphenomenal of its formal means, as if photography generically represents the technical limits of shutter and aperture. Though Wall himself touts the usefulness of the conventions of the tableau, there is much in the history of the genre that seems to be challenged by the cognitive demands *Milk* makes on a viewer, and by Wall's own remarks in an important essay entitled "Photography and Liquid Intelligence" (1989).[18] In this essay Wall observes

---

18. Jeff Wall, "Photography and Liquid Intelligence," in *Jeff Wall: Selected Essays and Interviews* (New York: MoMA, 2007), 109–10.

that photography is "perfectly adapted for representing" the complicated shape of splashing milk. By his own account, the stop-action effect achieved by the camera occasions a meditation on the contrast between what he calls the "glassed-in" or "dry" dimension of the institution of photography and "the sense of immersion in the incalculable which I associate with 'liquid intelligence'" (Wall, 109). By contrast with the "dry part," which Wall identifies with optics and mechanics (shutter and aperture), I want to argue that liquid intelligence denotes an inferentialist modality of knowledge. Wall's thinking along these lines is epitomized in *Milk*. The photograph occasions the inference of an invisible action that the concretized spill does not so much represent as mandate our notice of. Moreover, it does so by perceptual means that do not succumb to the comparatively facile conceptualization of cause and effect.

This reading I think goes hand in hand with Wall's self-professed intuition that digital technology gains importance for the photographer proportionate to his ability to make montages: "The essence of photomontage is that you don't need to have everything you envisage in your picture captured on one piece of film or one frame. Elements can be gotten separately, on different frames at different moments and combined afterward."[19] The effect Wall is getting at here is, in one sense, invisible in the manner of cinematic montage. It presents something that photographs per se cannot capture. This is why Wall observes that though montages might be photographic, they are not photographs proper. They make "visible things that couldn't be made visible through photography—imaginary occurrences, fantastic creatures, special effects" (Rondeau, 154). Wall is speaking here of the digital joining or splicing of discrepant images, distinct times and spaces. He is shrewdly attuned to the fact that the connectedness of discrepant images is not an appearance represented but the coaxing of inferences that appearances otherwise belie. That is to say, the apparent representation contains contradictions—perceptual contiguities rather than conceptual continuities—that are only explicable from outside the viewing point. The effect Wall aspires to is not so different from what is achieved in Tintoretto's crossing of picturing systems. When Wall elaborates his understanding of liquid intelligence as "the sense of immersion in the incalculable . . . [that which] appears with a vengeance in the remote consequences of even the most controlled releases of energy" (Wall, 110), I think he is speaking in terms that are congruent with the self-surpassing knowledge I ascribed to Tintoretto's dynamic mise-en-scène. "Remote consequences"

---

19. James Rondeau, interview with Jeff Wall, in Wall, 154.

are dispositive for the self-deception that is entailed in recognition of that which is undetermined. This self-deception is specifically entailed by the commitments one takes up in a presumption to know what one's own motivational biases prompt as reasonable action. It is not the case that "remote consequences" constitute what is unthinkable. Rather, they constitute what is provisionally unthought, given certain constraints of knowledge. They thus constitute potentialities of thought that are realizable only in proportion to one's more scrupulous notice of the otherwise unnoticed contingencies of what one is perceiving and thinking.

The question then is: what does realizing those potentialities mean to the viewer/thinker? Wall intimates a somewhat fanciful, and perhaps too strictly metaphorical answer. He suggests that we might be studied by what we study in nature, depending on how carefully we look at what we're doing. Wall cites the Tarkovsky film *Solaris,* in which scientists studying an oceanic planet find that a kind of intelligence inheres in the object of their inquiry that, in a manner of speaking, studies them back. The scientists suffer hallucinations in which their own past experiences are reproduced in compelling detail, warranting a new response that we could imagine is very simply a function of new aspectual orientations (Wall, 110). The trauma of self-surpassing knowledge endured by Tarkovsky's characters is what the viewer of *Milk* both registers and surpasses when caught up in the flow of Wall's liquid intelligence. Potentialities of thought, in this case, must be reconciled with volatile inferences. Such inferences are occasioned by what stands outside the perspective of thought about something that is already personalized in memory or in perceptual habit, or in one's habitation of more impersonal picturing systems. Again, we might think about how Tintoretto's crossing of picturing systems occasioned something like the experience of seeing a world that makes us feel the alienated determinateness of our own existence. It is as though we ourselves are objectified by our experience of dislocation, but without a loss of lucidity about that predicament. Wall is even more emphatically Hegelian about this possibility in a way that reflects the Notional proposition discussed in chapter 2. He seems to subscribe to the Hegelian claim that illusory being is not external to essence.

In an essay entitled "Unity and Fragmentation in Manet" (Wall, 78–83) on Manet's struggle to dislocate the body from the visual mechanisms of perspective without conceding its disintegration, Wall is quick to quote directly from Hegel's *Phenomenology of Mind.* He notes that for Hegel the seemingly "distraught soul," the dislocated or disintegrated self, is an appearance of Spirit in the guise of "'a universal deception of itself and of others'" (81).[20] The shamelessness manifested in stating this deceit, Hegel boasts, is just on that account "the greatest truth" (Wall, 81).[21] Self-deception is embraced by Wall for its power to reveal the inappropriateness of judging a picture as either a thought about an object or a virtually timeless perceptual intensity. There are, to echo his own words, incalculably "remote consequences" which nonetheless count for us as reasons for our own persistence in time. In the final chapter of this book we will see that this state of mind is kindred to the anxious desire for self-preservation that Annette Barnes takes as her cue for redefining self-deception.

Within the present framework, however, it might be said that *Milk* simultaneously animates this anxiety and depicts it. The "spilled" milk is both abstract and concrete. I think the apparent duality is meant to be misleading in its neatness. It poses something like the problem that Wall says Manet faced with respect to the "ersatz unity" of the French Salon. Wall contends that the misleading choices to oppose that unity with mere fragmentation, or with a primitivized harmony "constructed from archetypal bodies which alone can occupy the perfect space of unalienated perspective" (Wall, 84), were eschewed by Manet. He chose, instead, a project of "memorializing unification of the image around a ruined, or even dead, concept of the picture" (84). As if following Manet's example, Wall in *Milk* will not capitulate to the incommensurability of movement and stillness. He will rather insist upon what he calls "a labor of relation" (85). No doubt Wall is thinking of Hegel again and of Hegel's insistence in the *Logic* upon thinking conscientiously through contrastive effects.[22]

Consequently, we might focus upon how our own rapport with Wall's protagonist in *Milk* is conflicted. The gesture of seeming rage or stressfulness, frozen in the high-resolution mapping of the milk in space, cannot be read simply as a Rorschach of the human figure's mental state. This would be an unself-deceived perspective. I say that in part because the milk is as fully embodied as the sitting figure. But it is also because the entire picture plane exhibits the same degree of focus. Even the conceptually deeper space of the interior stairwell, seen through glass on the left margin of the composition, exhibits a

---

20. Wall is using the Baillie translation of the *Phenomenology* here. See Georg Wilhelm Friedrich Hegel, *The Phenomenology of Mind*, trans. J. B. Baillie (New York: Harper and Row, 1967), 543.
21. Ibid.
22. See my own discussion of Hegelian thinking through contrastive effects in chapter 3. I have noted that contrastive thinking proceeds by dint of a syllogistic reasoning that does not succumb to a "spurious infinite."

crystalline resolution. This is to say that the relations among the elements of the photograph cannot be reduced to an allegory of time and space, however tempting Wall has made it. Conceptually, as I have already suggested, we are caught up in the click of the camera's shutter. We fall under the spell of the stop-action miracle of the milk. Nevertheless, the availability of the image out of time surprisingly takes up our time. We consequently succumb to a more elastic, contemplative order of temporality. It is time that we might not otherwise *waste* on the naturally stilled elements of the composition that are themselves too well suited to the *still life* of the photographic métier. In effect then, everything comes to life as an inferentially rich aspect of a present-ness thereby fraught with attentional anxieties. Such anxieties are ostensibly a function of the mandate to switch from one orientation to another, since nothing in the visual field falls into the background.

Indeed, the figure/ground conceit is a familiar rationalistic cue to hierarchy and comparison, which like the representation of the shutter speed in the stop-action image, prompts a contrastive play that is too easily reducible to a conceptual ratio of differences. It inhibits forms of attention or notice like those "remote consequences" that *liquefy* intelligence in Wall's terms. Liquid intelligence makes contrastive thinking into an activity whereby the necessity of one set of perceptual coordinates compels a deliberation upon the commitments that another set of perceptual coordinates would invite us to take up. Our taking them up is an imperative of our heightened responsiveness to new perceptual coordinates. The greater intensity of the new motivational biases that arise out of our cognizance of inadequate notice ("remote consequences") succumbs in turn to the skepticism of our countenancing further unintended consequences of our notice.

I now want to suggest that Wall's rejection of the more punctual rationalizations licensed by the figure/ground ratio is an invitation to something like tragedy. It thus links his project to the rationalistic ideals of Enlightenment: self-determining agency and self-authorizing freedoms. As Horkheimer and Adorno remind us, the price of these ideals is always tragedy. And, in a way, Wall's photograph *Milk*—taken in the terms with which I have sought to find rapport with it—submits to the tragic constraints of reconciling one's self-knowledge with the frailties of the self that claims to know. To know the significance of the emotional spasm evinced by the facial expression of Wall's protagonist and the splayed physicality of the spilled milk demands submission to a matrix of inferential witness. Wall's photograph can perhaps be summarized in that statement. The point is most dauntingly represented in the brickwork across which the image of the milk is splayed. The wall presents an endlessly distinctive repetition of the form of an individual brick. The high resolution of the brickwork will not be relegated to background or backdrop. Nor will any single brick stand as representative of the others. Consequently, the answer to the question about how to take it all in entails a mandate to stretch out the time figured in the almost calligraphic materiality of the milk. The hypertrophic lucidity of the milk, after all, is already emblematic of our capacity for sustaining the greater attentiveness that makes such time readable, so to say, as experience. The self that reads this way knows itself to be beholden to what remains to be rendered knowable. This circumstance epitomizes the self-deceiver's embeddedness in temporal process, in the work of diurnal existence.

The fact that Wall, in almost the entirety of his photographic output, starts from document, and from the evidence and artifacts of the diurnal, of everydayness, suggests that he counts the readability of time as integral to the integrity of our experiencing it. The readability of time subsumes the less liquid, more glassed-in, embodiment of time that we encounter in the theatrical gesture of the posed action. Wall seeks to impose a protocol of accountability for what the gestural script does not make legible.[23] Thus, in the case of *Milk*, we are recruited to an explicitly contrastive work.[24] In making this point, I am suggesting that Wall does not lightly invoke the Hegelian mandate for a self-consciousness that realizes its de facto illusory essence with respect to what it negates. Such a relation is made apparent in the way the scene of Wall's photograph resists the desire of the viewer to see it from his own point of view. As was the case in Tintoretto's *Discovery*, the viewer of Wall's composition is bound to the predicament of seeing himself seeing again. For he must reckon with fact that the emerging registers of notice instantiate something like the world viewed by another person. This is, no doubt, the truth of the emotional state of the figure whose self-contradictory stillness, visually speaking, is ominously, perhaps frighteningly, out of control. The tragedy that grounds Enlightenment

---

23. Wall has written a brief essay on gesture, "Gestus," in which he states: "The contracted little actions, the involuntarily expressive body movements which lend themselves so well to photography, are what remain in everyday life of the older idea of gesture as the bodily, pictorial form of historical consciousness." He thinks this magnification of what was not seen, because it was too small, is what photography can, so to speak, *enlarge* with respect to our powers of notice. See *Jeff Wall: Selected Essays and Interviews*, 85.

24. I have already observed that Hegel's eschewal of the "spurious infinite" expressly inveigles such contrastive work. This is a presupposition of everything else that I wish to say on the ethical stakes of self-deception.

agency, à la Horkheimer and Adorno, entails just such a displacement of the self in its pursuit of self-realization.

Accordingly, we might say that Wall's composition encourages the "distraught and disintegrated soul" to come to grips with itself in Hegelian fashion. The photograph does so not by representing the soul as a protagonistic figure, but by coercing the viewer to *go on*—perceptually, attentively—beyond the specular arrest of the photo's protagonist. Wall presents a prospect for respecting Hegel's "universal deception of itself and others" by honoring the reasons that accrue to one's sense of oneself, *as another person,* in the persistence of perception. Once again, we might say that the persistence of perception in Wall's photograph may be a demonstration of the photographer's endorsement of the Hegelian presumption that illusory being is not external to Hegelian Spirit or essence. The persistence of perception is, after all, the touchstone of everydayness, of the near documentary that is figured throughout Wall's oeuvre and which he identifies with the small unnoticeable aspects of everyday life.

These relative minutiae, rendered virtually invisible by the misleading lucidity of more specifically characterized viewpoint, might become beneficent incitements to the laboring eye (Wall, 85). It gains more astute attunement with them through the constitutive enlargements of photography. So we might be expected to find in the persistence of perception the unique rapport with reasoning that Wall's work can cultivate as a mode of tragedy. The "shamelessness" of Hegel's self-deceiving, "distraught soul," which Wall identifies with Manet's struggle with the Salon, resonates in *Milk*. It is apparent in how the absolute quotidiana of the scene is in tension with the *seen*. Or I might say the scene is in tension with an activity of seeing that may not rest in the familiar ceremoniousness of the gesture on display. In other words, we may not see the off-center protagonist of the photograph merely affectively, as a distraught soul. As I have characterized it, *Milk* makes it clear that the tragedy of vision inherent to Wall's everydayness inhibits our seeing the "distraught soul" as a counter for pathos. Such pathos is certainly something that Hegel instructs us to eschew. Correlatively, its eschewal is something that Horkheimer and Adorno understand as a prerequisite of their desire to save tragedy from liquidation at the hands of the culture industry. Tragedy, in this view, remains a discipline of thought by means of something like a tolerance for incommensurables. Indeed, the density of everydayness purveyed by artists like Wall obtains for us as an admonition not to essentialize our perceptions in the manner of classical pathos. Pathos invites a melodramatic purgative that would put whatever does not fit within our vision of the beautiful soul safely outside the bounds of our notice. The alternative, as we will see in the next chapter, is to remain resourcefully within the conflictual space of *peripeteia*. There the self-deceiver feels the pressure of notice as the condition of being present in a world where something still remains to be done. When we look to what comes at the cost of our not seeing perspicuously enough, we earn a new form of self-respect.

6

Spelling Out the Viewer

Carrying on Enlightenment

Before I get to Gerhard Richter's self-respecting purgation of pathos and his own bid to save tragedy for representation, it is necessary to situate these gestures historically. I want to place Richter's project within the perspectives of modern and postmodern aesthetic theorizing, especially as they bear upon the prospect for keeping faith with tragic experience. While it is not uncommon to characterize both the modern and the postmodern as inherently tragic eras, our standard accounts of modernism and postmodernism rarely acknowledge that honoring the stakes of tragic knowledge entails resisting the temptation to make a fetish of human suffering. I eschew both the modern eternalizing of suffering in the continuous revelation of human self-deception and the postmodern ironizing of suffering into a vengeful playfulness.

A more rigorous alternative would be to acknowledge that tragedy is more than an affective legacy of our past actions. It has real cognitive bearing on our future actions as well. It consequently warrants real cognitive stratagems to thwart the fatalism it courts. I believe we can come most productively to this recognition by respecting a purely conventional Greek stricture on the concept of the tragic. Greek tragedy is predicated on *accepting* self-deception as a crux of self-realization. It acknowledges a modality of self-deception that is inescapable in our way of living in time. The Greek polis, the scene of the Dionysian festivals, figures this temporality by emphasizing the individual's accountability to the knowledge of others.[1] The Greeks stipulate that we are

---

1. See Jean-Pierre Vernant and Pierre Vidal-Naquet, *Myth and Tragedy in Ancient Greece,* trans. Janet Lloyd (Cambridge: MIT Press, 1988), for an extensive treatment of how tragedy holds individuals accountable to the civil collective.

creatures of *hamartia:* the expectation that there is always an element of the context of our actions that we lack knowledge of. In tragic emplotment the protagonist is most dispositively him- or herself in a moment of *peripeteia* or reversal. In other words, *hamartia* is the condition of that reversal and grounds it. This lack of knowledge has consequences for us that fundamentally challenge our self-understanding in some ensuing moment of action. It is the Oedipal curse of belatedness that even Oedipus endures. The fact that he thinks he knows more than he does makes him a classic self-deceiver. The fact that Oedipus knows that he thinks this, at the conclusion of the drama, makes him a good counter for the revisions of the concept of self-deception that underwrite this discussion. I hardly need to point out that Oedipus recognizes his inextricability from the ensuing moment of his most self-destructive action, even when self-annihilation seems to be the cost of recognition. The dispositive fact of Sophocles' plot is that Oedipus, like some prescient Beckett character, unable to go on, goes on. Where we must sustain the continuity of self across these shifting contextual boundaries of temporality, self-deception is de rigueur for self-conscious agency.

What we need, in order to capitalize on this insight, is a resource of rationalist agency that Horkheimer and Adorno—who are inspired by a vivid sense of the historical continuity of Greek tragic experience with modernity—rightfully identify with the power of Enlightenment mind. But they know, even better than the postmodern critics and artists they inspire, that Enlightenment mind risks betraying itself when it turns this rationalism into an absolute principle of will. On the contrary, they argue that "Enlightenment is realized . . . when the nearest practical ends reveal themselves as the most distant goal now attained," when it can "transcend the false absolute, the principle of blind domination" (Horkheimer and Adorno, 42). We are asked to accept the persistence of reason beyond the bounds of its own principles. The kind of Enlightenment that Horkheimer and Adorno would like us to carry on, by resisting the seductions of the false absolute, would seem to depend on our accepting the tragic inevitability of self-deception in modern subjectivity in tandem with protocols of self-consciousness about that self-deception. I want to argue that this pairing makes the ends of postmodern subjectivity coherent with the means of modern formalism. It saves us from sacrificing ends to means, or means to ends, from recourse to the zero-sum games that Enlightenment rationalism otherwise seems addicted to.

While Horkheimer and Adorno do not discuss self-deception per se, they clearly identify the failure of modern Enlightenment with the "wholesale deception of the masses." This they count as the signal political tragedy of the twentieth century. The deception of the masses is, of course, comparable to personal self-deception. From the point of view of critique, it invites the human subjects to accept the challenge of knowing better than what their own experience tells them. And yet I believe that a full understanding of what this might entail requires contexts of argument that Horkheimer and Adorno did not have access to.

We have seen in some detail how, in contemporary philosophical circles where self-deception is a subject of some analytical urgency, the trend is to see self-deception in terms of the subject's weakness for anticipating erroneous action. Error indexes the subject's insufficient contextual knowledge of the options for action. This thinking has given rise to theories of self-deception that attempt to understand how diverse contexts of desire or need constitute diverse motivational biases in action: these motivational biases can be rationally assessed and induce strategies of "error detection and minimization."[2] In other words, self-deception has come to be viewed as a form of hypothesis testing, whereby one's sense of oneself depends upon assessing and, if need be, revising the repertoire of reasons that support one's acting according to any desirable instrumental belief. One is self-deceived or not only insofar as one's motivational biases are taken up as commitments in relation to other biases that, if entertained, might entail less costly errors of judgment.

One could say then that these analyses of self-deception, though contextually remote from the Frankfurt school, are linked to it. For they share the intuition that the Enlightenment self knows its experience all too preemptively as its own, as a set of motivational biases that is misrepresented to itself as a spontaneous truth. In a manner of speaking, the structure of the self, as Horkheimer and Adorno see it, sows the seeds of self-deception by its inflexibility with respect to what it does not know about itself. That is, the Enlightenment self knows itself too exclusively by dint of something like its resistance to otherness. Horkheimer and Adorno trace this phenomenon to the fact that the Enlightenment subject is so presumptively predicated on a Cartesian methodology. This methodology inculcates in the subject a denial of differences that would threaten to divide the subject from itself by precipitating crises of self-contradiction. These are of course the very differences and warrants for change that mutable experience in time compels us to recognize. They do

---

2. See Mele, *Self-Deception Unmasked*, especially 31 and 53.

indeed expose us to the primal inevitability of tragedy. Consequently, for the Enlightenment subject who eschews this tragedy, the enterprise of self-knowledge, like the knowledge of what is "other" generally, comes to be subordinated to, and confused with, a modality of self-domination. This amounts to the subordination of everything, in its natural differentiation, to the "unnatural" unity that is man. Of course Vico, Nietzsche, and Freud had all articulated the paradox of knowing, as Horkheimer and Adorno observe: "Men had to do fearful things to themselves before the self, the identical, purposive, and virile nature of man, was formed" (Horkheimer and Adorno, 33). That self-formation is a form of self-repression has become a truism of our critical times. But what is worse, for Horkheimer and Adorno, is that this logic sufficiently blurs the line between self-discipline and political violence against others to promote tragedies like the Holocaust. Such observations, however well founded in their original contexts of argument, go awry when they invite an all too easy conflation of aesthetic modernism with historical-political oblivion: the much-vaunted incommensurability of art and politics.

Modern formalism, which exhibits this problematic self-discipline of Enlightenment mind, particularly in its claims of autonomy, its valorization of present-ness, and its eschewal of historical time, is thus an all too easy target for postmodern critics. They would, on these bases, implicate aesthetic values in the manifold injustices of twentieth-century political history. Even more problematically, postmodern critique is licensed by such logic to demand a redress of these injustices on a specious assumption: that the solution to the self-deceived subject of modernism is the self-dissolution of subjectivity altogether. The acknowledged weakness for self-deception justifies the purgation of selfhood, as if self-deception were a fatal *hamartia* rather than a resource for the life-furthering rationalizations inspired by the Greek tragedians. Postmodernism proposes its own political urgency on the basis of the understanding that modernist subjectivity is insufficiently skeptical of itself. So it proliferates more and more radical protocols of self-skepticism. The problem is that this radical effacement of the rationalist ego risks precisely the depersonalization that we identify with mass deception in advertising culture, politics, and in the elitist academies of artistic taste. We thus come full circle with the ills of modernism.

So the question posed for those of us still pondering the problem, out of the guilty resources of our troubled Enlightenment mind, is, How will art be productive in the twenty-first century without merely producing or reproducing its epistemic nemesis? I have been suggesting that it will be productive by exploiting its complicity in self-deception as an expressive resource, rather than a masochistic guilty conscience. I will add that self-deception is distinguishable from and preferable to mass deception as an analytical topos for inhibiting the ills of Enlightenment mind. For self-deception, by my account, sustains our rapport with the cognitive agency that such a mind needs for its own diagnostic aptitude—not to mention its hoped for critical efficacy.

Richter's Blur

Like Jeff Wall, Gerhard Richter acutely situates us in relation to the issues I have raised here. He points us toward an aesthetic practice that keeps faith with the intellectual stakes of modernist formalism without succumbing to the postmodern *j'accuse*. As I have intimated, this would be an aesthetic practice that engages tragic self-deception, accommodates the experience of time/history entailed by self-deception, and thereby promotes the possibility of carrying Enlightenment incrementally forward in a manner that the authors of *Dialectic of Enlightenment* themselves might have approved of.

Richter is a particularly apt subject since he is a postmodern avant-gardist whose work is notoriously difficult to pigeonhole as postmodern. Richter's career thus mocks the manner in which postmodernism's eschewal of formalist pigeonholes has become an all too well feathered nest of academic critical expertise. The bulk of the work that has won Richter international recognition was produced during the "postmodern" 1970s, 1980s, and 1990s. But Richter's work is simultaneously deeply engaged with the practices of high modernist painting, particularly from the 1940s through the early 1960s. Moreover, Richter is both a photorealist and an abstractionist, a fashioner of seemingly frivolous pop-art conceits and of sobering history paintings. His own diametrically opposed statements about the relative priority of form and content in aesthetic practices highlight what seems to be the practical indeterminacy of his aesthetic. One finds such antithetical poses throughout his chronicle of his career, *The Daily Practice of Painting*.

> Formalism stands for something negative: contrived stuff, games played with color, form empty aesthetics. When I say that I take form as my starting point and that I would like content to arise out of form (and not the reverse, whereby a form is found to fit a literary idea), then this

reflects my conviction that form, the cohesion of formal elements . . . generates content.³

What shall I paint? How shall I paint? "What" is the hardest thing, because it is the essence. "How" is easy by comparison. To start off with the "how" is frivolous, but legitimate. . . . The intention: to invent Nothing— no idea no composition, no object, no form—and to receive everything; composition, object, form, idea, picture. (Richter, *Daily Practice,* 127)

Robert Storr has called attention to the seeming irreconcilability of these stances in his catalogue essay for the relatively recent MoMA show *Gerhard Richter October 18, 1977*.⁴ For Storr these statements epitomize Richter's accomplishment as a painter: one who illuminates the future of painting by refusing to imagine it in the terms by which it has been anticipated. For this reason I would like to focus on Richter's accomplishment in the fifteen remarkable canvases that make up the *October 18, 1977* cycle of paintings. I will put particular emphasis on how the seeming incommensurability of Richter's comments on form and content portend, in the formal practice of his painting, a notion that Enlightenment might go on by the *redeployment of form as content.* In Richter's work we come to understand form as the vantage point from which we know the self-deceptions embodied in content. If this sounds like the dogged modernist dialecticism favored by Horkheimer and Adorno, generally out of favor with contemporary critics, I will accept the affiliation with a caveat. Richter's resistance to what Horkheimer and Adorno so famously dubbed "the culture industry" seeks no reconciliation of cultural contradictions in the critical prosecution of its self-deceiving practices.

Aptly enough, the form and the content of Richter's *October 18, 1977* paintings are provocatively at odds with each other. Thematically the paintings document a contemporary historical-political tragedy that was widely broadcast by the international media: the suspicious prison deaths of the leaders of the notorious Baader-Meinhoff terrorist gang at Stammheim Prison in 1977. It is a historical tragedy on multiple registers. The event exposes the self-destructive naïveté of the terrorists' political idealism, their *hamartia,* so to speak. As well-publicized victims of the power of the state against which they

---

3. Gerhard Richter, *The Daily Practice of Painting,* ed. Hans-Ulrich Obrist, trans. David Britt (Cambridge: MIT Press, 1998), 127.
4. The show ran from November 5, 2000, through January 30, 2001. See Robert Storr, "Chapter III: The Paintings," in *Gerhard Richter: October 18, 1977* (New York: MoMA/Abrams, 2000), especially 97.

had struggled, they became perverse emblems of state power. Their own complicity in the sacrifice of innocent lives for "higher" political ideals implicated them in the injustice of the fate they suffered in Stammheim prison. The social urgency of the content Richter has chosen for the paintings, in its sheer publicity, would seem to make form altogether irrelevant to expression. It invites a postmodern rhetoric of anti-aestheticism, a sublating of aesthetic values to headline politics. Aptly, with respect to this appearance, the sources for these works, as is the case for so many of Richter's paintings, are an atlas of the most unartistic images that can be culled from the popular press: from *Stern, Der Spiegel, Paris Match,* the tabloids.[5]

But the superficial appearance is false. Formally, the paintings of the *October 18* cycle belong to the subgenre of Richter's work that might be called photo-blur paintings. The particular strength of these canvases derives from their refusal to be either abstract or concrete, thus putting these categories of experience into provocative relation with each other. The *October 18, 1977* paintings vitiate the conceptual content that otherwise guarantees the terms "abstract" and "concrete" their standing as key analytical topoi of high modernist art criticism.

Richter's photo-blurs are produced from slide projections of the newsprint photographs that are their source. These images are then worked up by illusionistic photorealistic, painterly technique—that at first seems to hide the brushstroke—into representations of camera work. The lucid photo-images are subsequently blurred by squeegees and fastidious brushwork designed to bring the blur surprisingly into focus. In other words, Richter ironically trumps the modern co-option of painting by photography. The blur in the photographic painting is subsequently resolved as a plane of focus by detailed brushwork, reproducing the appearance of the blur in ever more heightened sensuous specificity. Indeed, the viewer who approaches the picture plane of the photo-blur paintings, as if to adjust the focal length of the viewpoint, discovers the enhanced resolution in the brushstrokes of the blur as an inverse proportion of what would otherwise be the blurring distance from the picture plane. That is to say, the *techne* of the camera, which historically testified to painting's more fallible relation to the object, becomes the salient object of attention here. After all, the blur is just that aspect of photographic process that marks its unique susceptibility to error. Looking at a range of paintings executed in this

---

5. For a clear view of Richter's sources and their reciprocal impact upon his use of them, see Gerhard Richter, *Atlas*, ed. Helmut Friedel (New York: D.A.P., 2006).

photo-blur modality, we can say that Richter has used a photorealist technique to reproduce that which reveals photography to be subject to the very weaknesses formerly ascribed to painting by photography. The blur, which purveys the focal plane as an armature of composition, now becomes the fulcrum for the reversibility of the perspectives governing our intuition of form and content.

Richter's métier in the photo-blur paintings generally sustains a rich, albeit abstract, reflection on how form and content depend on each other. And yet, the *October 18, 1977* series in particular concretizes the issue of how knowledge of the reciprocal dependency of form and content constrains the self-knowledge of the viewer of the artwork. Even more important, such knowledge equips the viewer to confront the tragedy of history with cognitive resources that bridge the distance between modernist rhetorics of form and postmodern rhetorics of form and politics respectively.

For the purposes of my argument in relation to Tintoretto and Wall, it is only necessary to consider a few of the paintings that make up Richter's *October 18, 1977* series: *Arrest I*, which depicts the arrest of Holger Meins, Andreas Baader, and Jan-Carl Raspe in Frankfurt on June 1, 1972; *Confrontation 2*, one of a series of three pictures of Gudrun Ensslin engaging the camera of a German journalist as she is led to a police lineup; *Hanged*, which shows Ensslin hanged from the grill in the window of her cell; and the triptych *Dead*, which shows Ulrike Meinhof's body in telephoto close-up.

What we see in all of these canvases—in their framing, their composition, and their pervasive monochromism—is conspicuously indistinguishable from the newspaper/magazine photo record of the headline news story from which each derives. The document is present here, as it is in Jeff Wall's work, as a token of everydayness. As I have already noted, Richter's documentary sources are always the most artless models. This fact would seem to dispose Richter to let a thematic rule govern his painting practice. The title *Hanged*, for example, would seem to predicate the viewer's recognition of the content on factual knowledge of a historical event that preempts personal perception. Richter seems to count on a viewer's knowledge of the historical event as the exclusive premise of its intelligibility.

But things work differently on the picture plane. In *Hanged* the potentially sentimental figure of the slender girl, head pulled awry from the torso, legs dangling helplessly, is perversely concretized by the painting's emphatically smeared surface. This painterly gesture stymies efforts to orient one's reading to a figure-ground gestalt, as if to obviate the perceptual register altogether. Painting, and especially history painting, traditionally makes perception defer

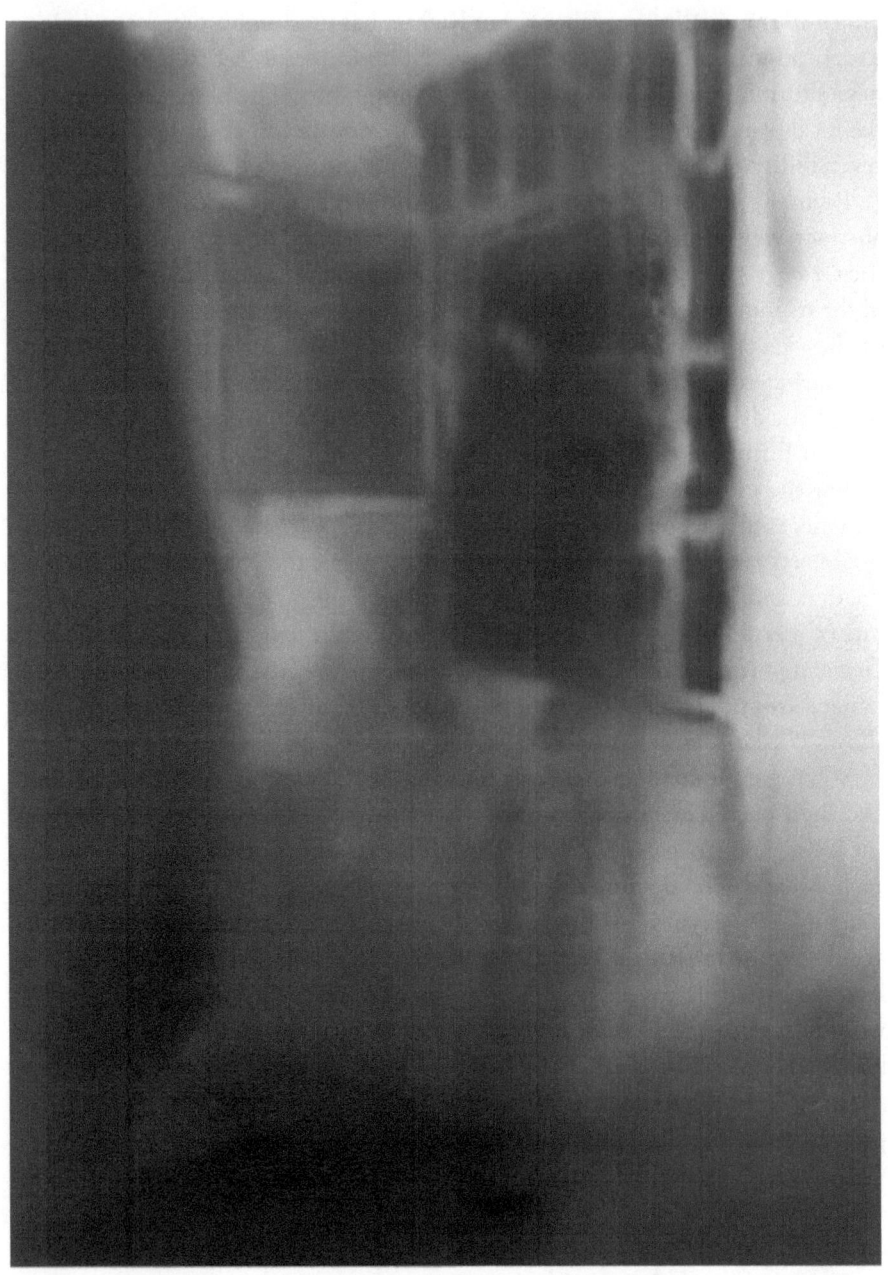

Fig. 6   Gerhard Richter, *Hanged*, from *October 18, 1977*, 1988. The Museum of Modern Art, New York. © Copyright of the artist. Digital Image © The Museum of Modern Art/Licensed by SCALA/Art Resource, N.Y.

to conception, where the stable ratio of figure to ground facilitates a transcendental reading. As Robert Storr characterizes the legacy of history painting that Richter renounces: "Originally the historical component of history painting was broadly defined, often mythic, and generally exclusive of current or even recent events. Instead, painters concerned themselves with noble principles and noble action in magnificent decors often borrowed from antiquity" (Storr, 121). This is a familiar mode of rationalist abstraction that modernist painting reacted against, reasserting perception as the ground of abstraction: Clement Greenberg's clarion valorization of painterly materials over what they might otherwise be deployed to represent.[6] On this basis, it is often said that modernist abstraction sacrifices historical engagement. It is said to sacrifice the political significance of painting to perceptual experience, which the rhetorics of postmodernism in turn decry as a feckless aestheticism—by which they mean, undue concreteness, the fetishism of perception.

Richter himself disarmingly declaimed: "I don't mistrust reality, of which I know next to nothing. I mistrust the picture of reality conveyed to us by our senses, which is imperfect and circumscribed."[7] I believe that in the photo-blur technique of the *October 18, 1977* paintings—in *Hanged* particularly—Richter has clarified this statement by taking the imperfect circumscription of perception to be an untranscendable condition. In the way that the artist makes perception an ineluctable métier of conception, Richter's work here is coherent with the practices of Tintoretto and Wall. More important, with the photo-blur technique Richter escapes the feral debate between modern abstractionists and postmodern historicists by joining the issue of perception to the phenomenon of self-deceiving perspective. Richter makes the self of that self-deception persist as a viable fallibilist or perspectivalist acumen which dutifully serves the circumstance of the viewer standing before the picture plane. The blur itself is the emblem of such fallibilism.

To be explicit, the challenge Richter takes up in the *October 18, 1977* paintings is epitomized this way: the viewer must question the relevant focal plane of perception before the recognitional value of what is clearly pictured in photographic terms (even illegibly) can be read as the pretext for photorealist technique. In *Arrest I* the architecture that outlines the parking lot, in which the capture of the protagonists took place, establishes a focal point that precludes focus on the action, which it can nonetheless be seen to frame.

---

6. See Clement Greenberg, *Art and Culture: Critical Essays* (Boston: Beacon Press, 1971), especially "The Plight of Culture"
7. See "Interview with Rolf Schoen, 1971," in Richter, *Daily Practice*, 73.

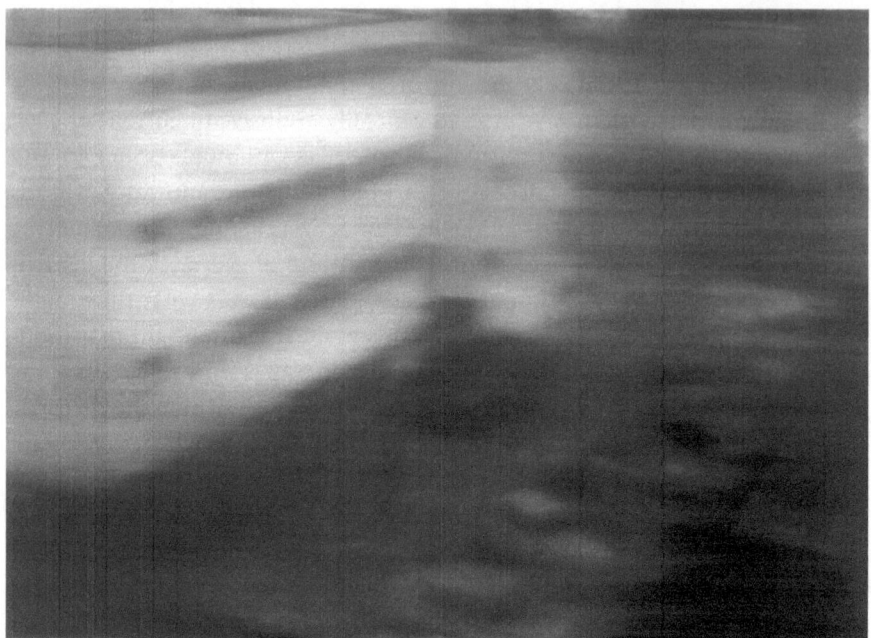

Fig. 7 Gerhard Richter, *Arrest I*, from *October 18, 1977*, 1988. The Museum of Modern Art, New York. © Copyright of the artist. Digital Image © The Museum of Modern Art/Licensed by SCALA/Art Resource, N.Y.

We might say that the eye becomes a camera before the camera becomes a thematic gloss on the formal technique of the picture. But what is the point of technique in this context? And how does painterly technique do justice to the history it invokes as its own practical purposiveness? Richter's paintings answer these questions by imposing a rigorous constraint upon viewing: one that preempts what is otherwise there to be seen too easily as historical event, or what's worse, the image of historical event. In that way the pretentious expectation that artistic technique can do justice to tragic history (its most melodramatic venue, the touchstone of pathos) is made irrelevant.

Instead, I would argue, the scene of tragic history is made more realistic, so to speak, by being reduced to the contingency of the historical subject who is viewing the painting at any particular moment in time. In the triptych *Dead* (not reproduced here) the head of Ulrike Meinhof is presented in three increasingly truncated horizontal views.

The conspicuous mimicry of the telephoto zoom lens disappoints the expectation of a higher optical resolution within or without the frame. We have already seen that in the dynamics of trompe l'oeil painting, where perception elides with self-deception, what is there to be seen is neither reality nor illusion. Rather, the calculation of their differences, or the calculus of their differentiation is what is most conspicuously on display. This is emphatically the case in the métier of the photo-blur. For this reason, I believe the notion of the self-deceiving subject is better attuned to Richter's technique than most other ideas of subjectivity that we might want to correlate with it. Self-deception instantiates the flexibility needed to accommodate incommensurable perceptual registers that are nonetheless continuous in time.

Witness *Confrontation 2* for the way Gudrun Ensslin's shy solicitation of the inquiring camera answers the slippery focal plane of the photo-blur effect, as if to remind us of our anxious perceptual involvement in her historical fate. We might otherwise remain at a safe iconographic distance.

Correlatively, in all of the *October 18, 1977* paintings, the viewer who trespasses too closely to the picture plane suffers the uncanny experience of seeing where the painter has squeegeed the line of the photo-image. We confront the virtually featureless ground upon which the figural definition of the line-to-be-blurred would have been originally encountered by the artist in its most immaculate invisibility. The closer we come to the surface of the canvas, the more we come to realize that the image disappears, qua image. It reappears as a kind of perceptual clay to be molded by increasingly contemplative hands, whose powers of differentiation will not be speculatively freed from perceptual activity. I think it is no exaggeration to say that the tragedy of the hapless political protagonists of the news story behind the paintings was their lack of the very deliberative resources which these paintings purvey: by the dense calculus of differentiations they impose upon a responsive and responsible viewer. In stating that his commentary on the Stammheim prisoners was primarily a response to their misguided idealism, Richter engages the problem of self-deception. He recognizes that any human action, unattuned to the contingencies of action, produces only the image of a deed. Richter leads us to speculate that this would be a truly feckless abstraction.

By pushing the raw material of perception into the foreground of the image as he does perhaps most devastatingly in the *October 18, 1977* paintings, Richter dramatizes the contingency of perception without merely representing it as an image. The self-deception marked in the blurred depth becomes a calibration of distances from the object. This calibration resituates the viewpoint of the subject as a productive enterprise. What makes it thus distinct from the oft-maligned production paradigm of post-Enlightenment idealism—and

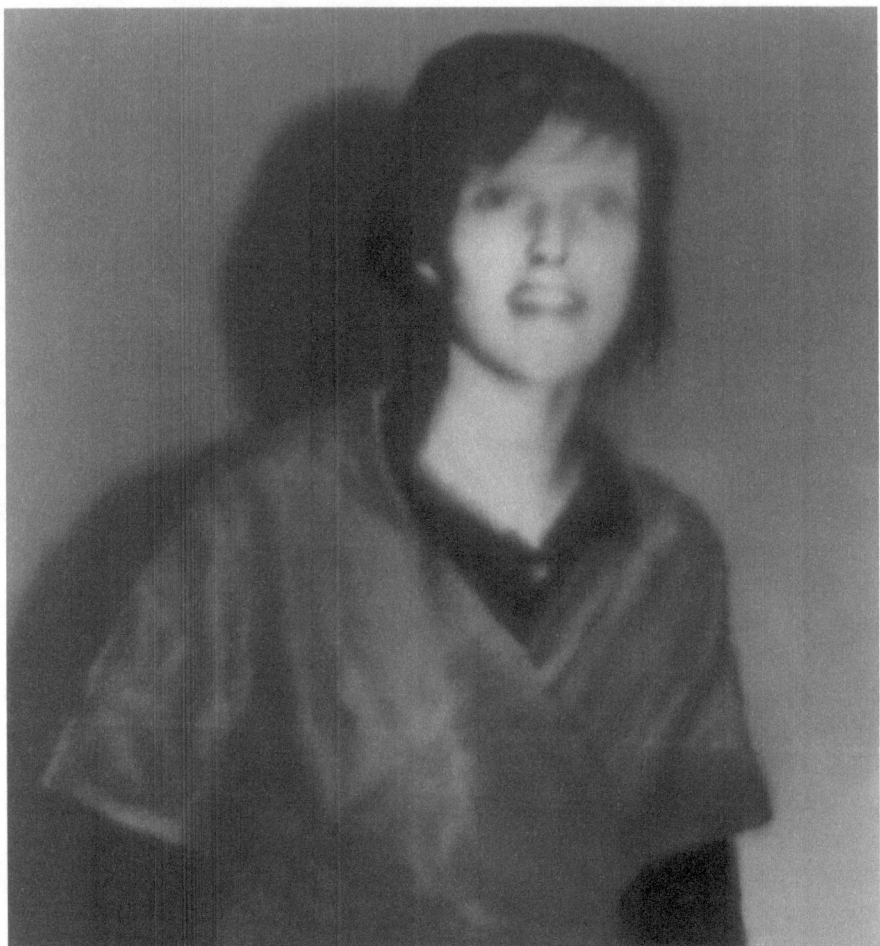

Fig. 8   Gerhard Richter, *Confrontation 2*, from *October 18, 1977*, 1988. The Museum of Modern Art, New York. © Copyright of the artist. Digital Image © The Museum of Modern Art/Licensed by SCALA/Art Resource, N.Y.

the absolute subject, which the Stammheim prisoners ironically perpetuated by their radicalism—is that it does not rest in the plot/image resolution of what is produced.[8] We cannot see what is there to be seen in Richter's paintings—the density of historical time—without *seeing more*, without perpetuating historical time in the act of seeing.

8. See, in particular, Jürgen Habermas's critique of the production paradigm in *The Philosophical Discourse of Modernity: Twelve Lectures*, trans. Frederick Lawrence (Cambridge: MIT Press, 1987), 48–49.

By dissolving subjectivity into immediacy and indeterminacy, postmodern orthodoxy insists that any belief in rational subjectivity is self-deceiving. That insistence raises self-deception to the level of an inescapable transcendental condition. Such heightening is fetishistic, however; like all fetishes, it merely mystifies what it aims to reveal. Given such mystification, it becomes impossible for us to grasp a subject's capacity to differentiate between self-deception and self-complicating cognition. My idea is that self-deception is not a transcendent universal, but a means whereby our rational powers exercise their capacity to discriminate. This would seem to be Richter's idea, and the root of his representational practice. His blurrings are not postmodernism's. Postmodernism's blurrings are unlimited, and therefore untrustworthy. Richter's blurrings are limited and thereby reliably attached to a more vitally rational enterprise. The self-deceived perception that animates Richter's *October 18, 1977* canvases engages historical time in the way that no mere image of the historical moment can keep faith with. In my judgment, there is no more dignifying history for humanity to lay claim to than one in which we are still so persistently involved.

The Moving Image / The Subliming Eye

Wall and Richter both suggest that history must be grasped as entailing an illusoriness that can be worked through by the rationalizing/rationalistic self-deceiver. But this is on the condition that we accept two key propositions. First, we must agree that the self deceiver's commitment to any beliefs depends upon a capacity for spelling things out beyond what content any specific belief makes apparent. Second, we must accept that it is only the taking up of commitments in time that is dispositive for the value of any belief that warrants spelling out. In other words, time is not a touchstone of phenomenological truth or metaphysical aspiration. Both of these attitudes would obviate or sublimate the work of tragic self-realization, which I am alleging is mandated in the circumstance of self-deception as a kind of "second sight," a prompt to seeing again.

The work of the video installation artist Bill Viola and the filmmaker Peter Greenaway give us further incentive for striving to grasp a history that is not merely a scene of retrospective pathos, one that is not simply a fetish of human suffering. Both of these artists deploy devices for representing temporality that conjure perceptual incommensurabilities. More to the point, their aesthetic practices court our attunement with the concept of sublimity. From the time of Longinus, sublimity has been honored above all aesthetic feats as an art of hidden powers, a feeling that ennobles the mind by exceeding its rationalistic grasp. Viola and Greenaway, however, are no ordinary sublimicists. They orchestrate the dynamics of the sublime in a way that encourages us to think about how second sight, that is to say, seeing again, is concordant with the kind of rationalistic and hence normative thinking that I have argued Tintoretto, Wall, and Richter promote. Their attempts to inhabit a tragic history within the purview of the everyday, of document, of the register of proliferating perceptual particulars, privileges the embodiment of experience over the representation of experience. After all, the theory of sublimity, from Longinus, to Kant, to Lyotard, is nothing if not a challenge to the powers of representation. But, and however counterintuitive it sounds, Viola and Greenaway show us how this fact is precisely what connects the sublime to the everyday. More to the point, they do so by means that are practically congruent with the Gombrichean insight about the unrepresentability of ambiguity in illusionistic art. For Gombrich, we will recall, this unrepresentability nonetheless warrants a switching between systems of seeing, which I have argued are de facto modalities of reasoning—inasmuch as they are determined by taking up commitments to specific motivational biases. The activity of switching accrues to subjective experience as an augmenting of the repertoire of reasons out of which one takes up one's commitments to act in a certain way.

Or I might say that unrepresentability doesn't obviate the struggle to represent. This point is already loudly resonant in Kant's supplementation of the theory of sublimity with a theory of genius: one that entails Kant's exposition of aesthetic ideas and aesthetic attributes.[9] By contrast with Kant's absolutist characterization of the supersensible substrate of reason, which the experience of sublimity throws into relief, Kant's positing of aesthetic ideas and aesthetic attributes in his theory of genius portends a comparative and contrastive activity. Aesthetic ideas are presentations of the imagination that prompt "much thought, but to which no determinate thought whatsoever, i.e., no [determinate] *concept*, can be adequate" (Kant, *Critique of Judgment*, 182). Correlatively, an aesthetic attribute is a "concept [that is] provided with a presentation of the imagination such that, even though this presentation belongs to the exhibition of the concept, yet it prompts, even by itself, so much thought as can never be comprehended within a determinate concept" (183). In both instances I want to suggest that Kant's concession to a "spreading out" of the powers

---

9. Immanuel Kant, *Critique of Judgment*, trans. Werner S. Pluhar (Indianapolis: Hackett, 1987).

of imagination entails the kind of alternation between registers of perception that, once again, potentiates the aspectual resources of human notice. These resources, I have already argued, conduce to our construing self-deception as a modality of second sight. It should therefore not be hard to see how the dynamic of hiding and exposing that is native to aesthetic ideas and attributes and is a key animus of sublimity from Longinus to Kant is just as essentially an animus of subjectivity under the constraint of self-deception. Even more important however—and *pace* Kant—I will argue that the spreading out of the powers of imagination, stipulated in Kant's theory of genius, lends itself to narrative reason-giving. This narrative reason-giving joins self-deception to the momentous enterprise of thinking about what to do next.

Bill Viola's *The Greeting* (1995) and Peter Greenaway's *A Zed and Two Noughts* (1985) are in fact both films. *The Greeting* is a video installation piece originally shot on 35mm film in order to record the action at 300 frames per second. Greenaway's film is a theatrical feature and displays itself like a museum piece by its persistent allusiveness to the devices of painting. The two works are, as I have already indicated, most strongly united by their courtship of the tragedy inherent to sublimity. As Horkheimer and Adorno maintain, sublimity opens the horizon of tragic experience—and implicitly the horizon of learning—in a way that mere beauty cannot, because beauty doesn't hide anything. In fact it is the self-acknowledged purpose of the culture industry to conflate beauty with visibility or transparency. Or as Horkheimer and Adorno put it, "tragedy has been dissipated in the void of the fake identity of society and subject."[10] To the contrary, Viola and Greenaway both foreground the sensuous agitation that is the telltale of sublimity and thus guarantees the incommensurability of society and subject, spectacle and subjective spectatorship. This sensuous agitation is the definitive preemption of beauty. In the classical versions of sublimity of course, this sensuous agitation, insofar as it preempts the pleasures of beauty, teases out a process of conceptualization as its anodyne. What is specifically new, in the subliming practices of Viola and Greenaway, is that the tease of conceptualization does not become fetishistic: by turning the concept into a perpetually unreachable horizon. Rather, it promulgates a narrative succession of horizons. Because these horizons are crossable, in the manner encouraged by Tintoretto's crossing of picturing systems, the tease of conceptualization sustains the interests of tragic knowledge. In this regard

---

10. For one of the fullest and most original accounts of this insight, see J. M. Bernstein, *Against Voluptuous Bodies: Late Modernism and the Meaning of Painting* (Stanford: Stanford University Press, 2006), esp. 259.

tragedy is de facto a form of interestedness—the antithesis of Kantian beauty. This explains why it might make sense to think about how artists of sublimity like Viola and Greenaway are naturally the patrons of tragedy and, like Richter, are keeping faith with Horkheimer and Adorno's Enlightenment.

Hiding and Noticing in Viola's *The Greeting*

Viola's installation piece *The Greeting* takes a quintessential mannerist picturing system as its jumping-off point. To say that it is, at least on one level, a filming of Jacopo Pontormo's painting *The Visitation* (1528–29) intimates the seeming inadequacy of the language of painting to capture the spiritual event. Nevertheless, I think this intimation is a useful and perhaps necessary point of departure for appreciating Viola's achievement.

The painting epitomizes the mannerist's investment in color as a modality of presence. Such presence is attuned to the condition of present-ness that I have insisted self-deception subsists upon. Aptly, Pontormo's painting means to represent an instantiation of what cannot be represented except as evidence of what does not readily enough appear. Compositional aspects of the painting dramatize our desire to keep up with the act of seeing, though our powers of notice are seemingly outstripped by the forms of attentiveness through which we are prompted to see ourselves seeing. The painting of the invisible spirit of God visited upon Mary's womb is doubled in the visitation of Mary upon her older cousin Elizabeth. Elizabeth is herself, and belatedly in life, pregnant with a twin miracle.

Jean-Luc Nancy has written astutely of the "unnoticed" details of Pontormo's painting in *The Ground of the Image*,[11] which for me is the vital link to Viola's project. The second sight to which we are recruited by Pontormo's painting of the meeting of the divinely impregnated Mary and her older cousin Elizabeth is signaled, according to Nancy, by the ecclesiastical Latin meaning of the word *visitatio*. *Visitatio* denotes not merely a visitation but "a procedure for becoming aware of something, for examining and experiencing something" (Nancy, 109). Thus Nancy points up a number of formal elements in Pontormo's painting that make us see what we cannot seem to know in advance, by dint of our already possessing a procedure for becoming aware. This is precisely

---

11. Jean-Luc Nancy, *The Ground of the Image*, trans. Jeff Fort (New York: Fordham University Press, 2005).

Fig. 9   Jacopo Pontormo, *The Visitation*, 1528–30. San Michele, Carmignano, Prato, Italy/The Bridgeman Art Library.

the predicament of the two mothers-to-be. Presence, specifically the pregnancy of Christ, is both present and about to be presented. As Nancy sees it then, Pontormo conjures the virginal pubis in a pattern of triangular spaces opened between folds of the womens' gowns where the pregnant bellies kiss. The trinitarian geometry of the female sex is thereby figured as an unnoticed detail of our apprehension of the imminent birthing of divine spirit. Likewise, two figures proffering the Eucharist are shrunken to the stature of children into the background, but are advancing into the very perspectival view that is otherwise contrived to diminish notice of what is present in distances. Nancy points to many other instances where contrastive views arise out of previously unnoticed details.

Nancy's gist, however, is to portend what I want to argue the sublimity of Viola's practice eludes. Nancy is keen for us to come to terms with a sublime incommensurability of views in such a way that we will countenance what he calls a "being there of the beyond" (Nancy, 124), whereby art is understood to be an infinite sharing out of a perhaps too patly Heideggerian Being. More important in this context, Nancy thereby courts a sublimity beyond tragedy. Nancy's purpose is to resist what he thinks is our weakness for imposing a "there" on the beyond, "instead of inscribing the beyond as the 'there'" (124–25). His tolerance for incommensurables, as infinite as it is, therefore ceases to weigh upon our cognitive faculties in the manner that sublimity must, if it is to have bearing on tragedy. Nancy would urge our transcendence of the conditions of presence in order to honor the timelessness of presence.

In his visiting of the visitation, Viola gives us an apt counterpoint to Nancy. Because his 300 frames per second slow-motion camera keeps us well within the ambit of time that is incrementally pregnant with portent, Viola's *use* of Pontormo's painting, holds us to the finitude of knowing what we do not yet know. Our knowledge obtains under a temporal constraint that does not court timeless abstraction. Like Pontormo, Viola is interested in the sublime dynamic of hiding and showing. But his work fosters a disposition that, I would argue, more rigorously attends to the rationalistic duties of *visitation* than Nancy testifies to in his reading of the Pontormo painting. If *visitatio* is indeed a procedure for becoming aware, the extreme slow motion of the image in Viola's installation piece produces a kind of shameless attentiveness—one that carries the Hegelian overtones exploited by Jeff Wall—by stretching forty-two seconds of action to ten minutes of viewing time. The formal persistence of our attention risks a self-conscious voyeurism. But this is precisely the point. As the Hegelianism expressed in Wall's practice intimated, we can see through the failures of seeing in a way that motivates further attention. Such motivation would be obviated by Nancy's "beyond," which effectively evacuates motivation. The two protagonistic women of *The Greeting* are pregnant with what will be known by gestation: a notoriously *slow-motion* modality of human notice and self-knowledge. A woman, after all, *becomes* a mother. Under the spell of pregnancy she knows too much and too little at the same time. This is to say that pregnancy is too fetishistically a visual proposition. One watches for changes with the understanding that the appearance instantiated in birth will be both incommensurable with one's observations and continuous with them. The shameless attentiveness of the viewer of Viola's work—who is most urgently a viewer with respect to what he sees he cannot see beyond—puts him curiously in synch with the artifice of Viola's accelerated film speed. We see the beyond successively in the ever more perspicuously articulated slowness of time. The successiveness is an inescapable warrant for reckoning with motivational bias.

In other words, the shamelessness of our attention bears on the self-deception that Hegel and Wall say we are implicated in under the auspices of Notional truth. It is operative in Viola's *The Greeting* by the increasing pressure we feel to notice—ever more meticulously—what one *wants* (what one is motivated to want) to see beyond. This is the only viable pathway to the beyond. Things are moving too slowly to see otherwise. We seem constrained to know where we are only as an impediment to knowing anything else. By contrast, the intimation of the sublime glossed in Nancy's account of the "there" that is already a beyond obviates attentiveness to the circumstantial constraint of one's knowledge that there is a beyond. In *The Greeting* the prospect that there is a beyond necessitates what, for Nancy, would have to be a counterintuitive struggle with the here and now. Aptly, in Viola's work, the figures of the two mothers-to-be are mediated by a third presence: a woman whose eyes match the gaze of the viewer. This occasions a necessary reckoning on our part with the unreal temporality of the painfully slowly unfolding action.

But is this reckoning achievable? Everything is orchestrated to arouse an anxiety about the possibility of our taking in what is presented so slowly that one easily imagines it is already too apparent to be seen. Viola purveys an incommensurability between the amplitude of the view occasioned by slow-motion cinematography and the viewer's impression that he cannot apprehend the relevance of the image. Our attention is paradoxically too high-powered, too fast to catch up with the lagging pace of what is happening before our eyes.[12] Viola has caught his viewer in the epistemic meshes of the distinction between the painterly image and the moving image.

To put this another way, the time of the painting belongs to us. Our eye roams at its own pace over the finite field of view, confident of an ability to take it all in. Contrastingly, our heightened attunement to the filmic montage of moments in Viola's installation instantiates a time to which we are subordinated by our *in*ability to exercise expectations about what should be the proper object of our attention. Thus when we watch *The Greeting* from beginning to endlessness (it is a continuous loop), we are urged to meet the demands for a form of notice that will be adequate to apparently incommensurable orders of knowledge. Hence, our *visitatio,* our procedure for becoming aware, must accommodate the kind of time-lapse that we associate with montage in cinema, where the simultaneity of hiding and showing is operative, as it is in painterly illusionism. This is of course counter to our natural predisposition to know things prematurely, that is to say, "right away." So there is a strong tension between the conceptual I and the perceptual eye as would be *de rigueur* for any circumstance of sublimity.

Viola makes this dynamic central to the mise-en-scène of *The Greeting.* Initially, we witness a spectacle of greeting that is unrecognizable as such, backgrounded as it is in the retreating space of a street running behind the two women who figure to be protagonists of the composition. In that space of recession two men, like the unnoticed figures recessed in Pontormo's painting, commune in the ceremony of lighting a cigarette. The tableau of the two women in the foreground, whose encounter is already established, their hands almost joined, already greeted, not greeting, is disturbed by a mounting crescendo of wind on the soundtrack. We witness a lively animation of their loose robes. A younger woman, garbed in vermillion and clearly pregnant enters the scene. Mary reaches toward her cousin—if we are so allegorically minded—on a horizontal axis and across the vertical axis of the third woman, now interposed between them. The gesture is the crux of a crossing that, within the iconographic lexicon of a mannerist painter like Pontormo, might have been perceived as nakedly cruciform. But in this context it is more pertinently a crossing of systems of picturing/knowing, much as we encountered in Tintoretto. Mary, or the woman who is plausibly pictured as Mary, whispers into the ear of her friend, who would be Elizabeth, echoing words that register the

---

12. The documentary filmmaker Errol Morris offers a germane commentary with respect to the staging of reenactments in documentaries as fostering new horizons for notice. See "On Re-Staging Action," http://morrisl.blogs.nytimes.com/.

Fig. 10   Bill Viola, *The Greeting*, 1985. Video/sound installation, color video projection on a large vertical screen mounted on wall in darkened space; amplified stereo sound. (Photo: Kira Perov)

distortions of slow-motion sound: "Can you help me? I need to speak to you right away, right away." The blond woman who fills the space between the women enacting the greeting, up to this point pensive and immobilized is encouraged by the older woman to turn her face toward the newcomer and smile. The embracing women disengage and the action repeats.

A kind of tragedy befalls the viewer in the guise of her being forced to see again and again what she is seeing as what eludes the attentiveness of mere perception. Because we are prone to envision the action more rapidly than the eye is constrained to take it in, we are overwhelmed with proliferating but discrepant reasons for registering the meaning of the action that will not cease. What do we see, at what point? These are the questions that press upon the viewer's effort to match perception with cognition. As did Tintoretto, Wall, and Richter, Viola puts us in the presence of an artwork that calls us to account for the relevance of the question as much as for the answer. And, as was the case when we entered the general framework of illusionistic image-making inaugurated in the four styles of Roman wall painting, our task is to mitigate the tragedy of our situation. We must do so in a way that does not escape the duty of temporal duration, which I have characterized in other contexts as diachronic rationality.

Perhaps the question "Can you help me . . . right away?" is the corollary of the question "What do we see at what point?" For here there is no *right away*—that is, nothing of the immediacy of the painted image. The diachronically dense points of time unfolded *right away* in *The Greeting* are distributed with a lucidity that entails the kind of "spreading out of the mind" unfolded by Kant in his "Analytic of the Sublime." The effects displayed here are perhaps kindred to the effects that flow from the spreading out of the milk in Jeff Wall's photograph. In any case, Viola's emphasis on the incremental specificity of time occasioned by slow motion comes into curious accord with diachronic rationality wherein "right away" requires self-consciousness of an inappropriate or an inadequate attentiveness. We might think, for example, how the stasis of painting prompts us to see too quickly (*right away*), to assign a prefabricated allegorical significance, with no other possibility of meaning.

In the filmic modality of *The Greeting*, however, we might say that the dovetailing of sublimity and tragedy amounts to something like a protocol for reason-giving that is not so self-reifying as allegorical reading can be. For in each successive moment of *The Greeting* our reasons for attending warrant new considerations or new commitments. They will have a consequence that will count for us differentially as we take up our commitments to them or not. The mind spreads out in the sense that the movements of the figures in the frame, whose animus is made more portentous by the sound of the wind and the sweep of their garments, occasion an annunciation of something else that is about to happen. But this "something else" is registered as the viewer's acute sense of unwittingness about the grounds for believing its necessity, let alone its sufficiency.

Let me be more specific. The two women become three women in a manner that elicits a doubtfulness about the operant reasons for understanding what was met between the initially poised figures. What did we *not* notice about the expression on the intercessor's face that anticipated the arrival of another, who renders the intercessor such a mediational figure in the first place? What did we miss in the recognition of emotional transport that is signaled in the extension of the arms of the new protagonists reaching across the space of our vision? Their embrace conspicuously eclipses the recessed action of the two men already met, as if to relegate that notice to another register of value. Furthermore, the occluding embrace of the female protagonists is at one moment a seeming occasion for speech and at the next a kiss. In the next moment it reverts to an occasion for anxious speech. The deceleration of our observational powers opens us to doubt about what is about to happen *right away*. We are rooted in a commitment to one way of seeing things only to realize what waywardness of perspective is potentiated in that attentiveness.

My point, of course, is that the waywardness of attentiveness may be a valuable resource of reasoning here. The physical movements of the foregrounded protagonists, in their very slowness, prompt us to think that their bodies move simultaneously but according to discrepant plans. The simple directionality of backward and forward becomes a stage for dramatizing new incommensurabilities. The slow progress of a hand or a foot in space prompts us to anticipate trajectories of action that ensuing perception ultimately belies. The overly manifest presence of the slow-motion body hides its true momentum in the very plenitude of its appearance. Thus the ascribable motives for the incommensurable views of the action are sustained in tandem with each other. Above all we must note that there is no integrative narrative except that which obtains in the time of viewing. This requires what I have been countenancing as a touchstone for self-deceptive viewing: an active tolerance for incommensurables.

With these considerations in mind, the circumstance of the viewer of *The Greeting* is perhaps best epitomized in the hovering movement of the older woman's foot. Our notice of it follows upon the characters' consummation of the climactic embrace. At first the foot seems to signal a withdrawal, a shifting of weight away from the incident of physical intimacy. But, as it prompts our imagining how the whole body might follow the foot, the gesture is plausibly this character's way of better registering the face of the woman who solicits her conversation. By stepping back, the older woman can see better what is to be appreciated in the facial expression of the solicitous other. Presumably this better communication would ultimately carry the older woman forward again into a more intimate embrace. Specifically, as the foot is raised from the ground, we can anticipate it moving in both directions. We see a kind of balancing of the older woman's mind against the weight of the younger woman's body. If the former's movement is a withdrawal from the solicitation "I need to speak with you," the physical gesture might portend an occlusion of the soliciting woman's mind. She would, in turn, fall back into her solitary body. Viola is reminding us that greeting is a modality of communion and, inescapably, a portent of departure. Coming and going are twinned by their temporal successiveness, though we are predisposed to partition their meanings. The ecstasy of meeting would be mitigated by the sorrowful knowledge of inevitable departure, just as the thought of death curdles the vitality of life in the animate moment.

I would of course argue that the slow-motion métier of Viola's installation inhibits such rational partitioning. Or, rather, it is precisely this inhibition that stimulates our most productive reasoning before the "picture plane" of the video monitor. Viola makes an interesting comment in this regard. He notes that images, specifically the images that ordain a rationalistic space, tend to lie about actual perceptual experience.[13] He is critical of how paradigms of perception, that is to say, perceptual languages, eschew the experience of illusoriness and the self-deceptive baffles of more raw perception. Perception otherwise ceaselessly animates the mind in a manner that is deeply suggestive of sublimity. Specifically, Viola is harking back to premodern (pre-Albertian) modes of projection. He asserts that a distinctly "realistic" way of showing obtained for visual artists before the advent of perspectivism. He calls to mind a medieval depiction of a building with all of its sides showing in the same plane. By contrast, Viola points out that artificial images, images that are already rationalized by technologies of vision, "aspire to the image and not to the object, to visual perception and not to the *experiential mind field* [my emphasis].

---

13. See the transcript of Viola's 1989 panel discussion, "The Visionary Landscape of Perception," in *Reasons for Knocking at an Empty House* (London: Thames and Hudson, 1995).

They do not, for example, show all sides of an object that we know from our experience to exist. The camera only sees three faces of a cube, for example, yet our hands can tell us that the other three simultaneously exist" (Viola, 221). The sustaining of incommensurable reasons for the actions that are purveyed by *The Greeting* might be construed as a return to the "mind field" that, curiously enough, is perfectly coherent with perception if we allow illusoriness to prevail. With respect to such "illusoriness" Viola invokes the conceit of a reality conceived of as a high-definition, visual technology. It prompts the eye to more detailed registers of notice, where we assume that reality itself is ultimately resolvable: capable of a highest definition. By contrast, Viola asserts that "reality itself is infinitely resolvable" (222). As with the Kantian sublime, we realize that in the mind's striving for comprehension "there is no maximum" of resolution—as obtains with respect to visual technology. Rather, "you move through planes of meaning: first the familiar world; then the macro, or the ant's eye view; then the microscopic; the molecular; the atomic; etc." (222). This knowledge is vivified in *The Greeting*. It is strikingly similar to what is achieved in Richter's métier of the blur. The blur is not an obstacle to vision or a determinate occlusion of vision, but a threshold of new perceptual counters, new reasons for seeing. So we might say that *The Greeting* is not sublime in its opening of an infinite vista of boundaries to be crossed, but in its showing us that what is hidden (the dynamic of Gombrichean illusionism) is a mode for traversing the "mind field." This is a mode of thought that is otherwise obviated in the lucidity of more instantly rationalized vision.

If greeting and departure are not partitioned, we must succumb to the experience of hypothesis testing, second-guessing our perception by postulating new reasons for noticing what could not have been apparent "right away." If the greeting of the putative cousins eclipses the body of the third woman, whose gaze initially matches our own, can we escape the assumption that we are self-deceived, that we ought to be looking elsewhere for our proper orientation? That is to say, the state of pregnancy is ours, in the sense that we are bound to look for more evidentiary ground for our attentiveness. If Nancy wanted us to take away a notion of the inarticulable timelessness of presence from Pontormo's composition, Viola roots us in the present time with a mandate to *greet* the challenges it presents. The vital truth of greeting is an acknowledgment of what is not meant to be already known, but what imminently solicits knowing. Viola's métier invites us to see how greeting is incipiently a parting of the ways between what is already held sacred—an artifact of what has already been reasoned out of time—and what reasons ensue for the self that persists in time. Such persistence embodies a question about what will be unexpectedly met with, not as a spectral conundrum but as a negotiable circumstance: one that warrants a justificatory will to explain oneself to oneself. This is, above all, a will *to know what one is doing*. As we trace the motions of the bodies in the ever more dynamic space Viola has conjured for them by extreme slow-motion photography, we are accruing a perversely rapid proliferation of orientations, or *visitatae*. To reprise Nancy's understanding of visitation, we might say that we are productively burdened with proliferating procedural cues for becoming aware, examining, and experiencing.

Another way of grasping this would be to say that Viola brings the task of knowing what one is doing strikingly close to understanding that the act of attending is a doing in its own right. Our vivid present-ness to the action is a constant revising of what we know to expect. There will thus be no end to the action, except in the transference of the temporal burden from the register of the picture plane to the viewer who stands before the video monitor. This feedback loop, so to speak, is perhaps the most dramatic effect of Viola's work. I have already noted that we cannot have a cogent sense of human or subjective purpose without a feedback mechanism, as Elster proposed it, "by which the activity in question can be modified as a result of changes in circumstances in accordance with the purposes" (*Sour Grapes*, 107).

Viola bears this out. For we might say that *The Greeting* is a manifest hiding of what is visible via the slow-motion lucidity of showing what would otherwise not be seen. The feedback between the fast temporality of the fixed viewer, hastily thinking past perception, and the slow temporality of the moving image, ever more exhaustively soliciting new thoughts, guarantees that knowing what one is doing will perpetuate doing in the very manner that I have associated with the workings of the self-deceiving mind. It amounts to an ever more animate disposition to greet one's experience, assuming that the self is sufficiently deceived about what is there to be met. As is the case with any feedback mechanism, the self-deception entailed here presumes that the revisability of human purposes is the salient stake of human agency. It is a sine qua non of purposiveness itself. My entertaining a test of the "sufficiency" of self-deception is not a flippancy here. It is rather a testimonial to the necessity for facing up to the temporally complex challenge of knowing what one is doing insofar as one is always doing more than one knows. The truism that one is always doing more than one knows is signaled by classical theories of sublimity. But, as I have indicated in my discussion of Viola and now of Greenaway, the subliming away of reasons does not do justice to the warrant for knowing more. This is what mortal beings incessantly contend with in the time they are bound to account for.

Unframing Notice in Greenaway's *Zoo*

In *A Zed and Two Noughts*, Peter Greenaway takes up the temporally dense challenge to know what one is doing, or *greeting*, on the threshold of mortality. This may, at first, seem merely a willful perversity. Mortality is, after all, the putative vanishing point of the perspective to which the concept of greeting orients us. *A Zed and Two Noughts*, or *Zoo*, is indeed a film about loss. But it deploys those specific formal resources of cinema which belie absence in the very act of presenting the disappearance of physical bodies. More specifically, we might just say that Greenaway's film focuses upon the time of physical decay. Visible putrefaction is its controlling visual conceit. In this instance, however, decay is not loss per se, that is to say, the cancellation of notice, but a transformation and hence a prompt for more perspicuous notice. No doubt Greenaway means for us to notice that decay cannot, after all, be seen with the naked eye; one needs the camera. Greenaway might quibble: one needs the cinema. Cinema is most conspicuously evident in *A Zed and Two Noughts*, in the film's use of time-lapse photography to record the process of decay. More to the point, however, time-lapse photography is the telltale of Greenaway's aesthetic enterprise, just as it was the formal armature of Viola's *visitation* in *The Greeting*. For in many ways it licenses an assumption that all such devices of cinema constitute an imperative of second sight. The theme of "twinness" in *A Zed and Two Noughts* addresses this proposition and inflects the viewer's knowledge of what he is doing. One is, after all, bound to do a double-take when bearing witness to twinness. In a manner of speaking, the double-take is likewise the cognitive reflex of the self-deceiver who is bound to see more urgent reasons beyond the horizon of his seemingly most rational take on things.

Such claims with respect to Greenaway require at least the contextualization of plot summary if they are to carry the weight of argument. Greenaway's scenario joins the time of evolution with the time of decay by orchestrating a visually and conceptually complex grieving process for its central characters: Oswald and Oliver Deuce, twin animal behaviorists. Their respective wives have died in an automobile accident in a car driven by a woman named Alba Bewick, who loses one leg in the catastrophe. She is doctored by a medical practitioner, Van Meegeren, who bears the name of the famous forger of Vermeer paintings (Hans Van Meegeren) and who strives to mimic the artist's career in every aspect of his own life. The action of the film is driven by Oliver's obsessive viewing of a documentary film about evolution. Knowing how life ends, his curiosity about how it begins figures the feedback mechanism that I have posited as the condition of human purposiveness. Asymmetrical knowledge seeks the truth of symmetry. Accordingly, Alba's one-legged asymmetry leads her into Van Meegeren's scheme to amputate her other leg. Thus her body will come to "fit the frame" of his perverse restagings of Vermeer compositions. The inconsolability of the brothers' grief leads them to father twins upon Alba. Spent by that birth, Alba wills her own death. In the end Oliver and Oswald, who are revealed to have been originally Siamese twins, are joined back together in the act of suicide. They die upon a gridded platform set up before a time-lapse camera that they have rigged to record the deterioration of their flesh. But the project becomes a self-parodying casualty of time, of the twenty-four hours that bring on the dew at the dawn of a new day. This short-circuits the electrical devices that are meant to perpetuate the experiment. The cameras, lights, power sources, all become perches for an infestation of decay-promoting snails.

This is the barest outline of Greenaway's project. But it does invite the thought that twinness here is a natural conceit for the way the multiple frames of celluloid are made unitary in montage. We are primed to imagine that Greenaway's cinematic mind will converge upon this theme in the very manner of his constructing the film. In this regard, the conceit of twinness in Greenaway's film is a clear acknowledgment of the susceptibility of human attention to something like the self-deceiving illusion underpinning the essential visuality of cinema. The same illusion one might say, underpins the perverse continuity of evolution and grief that constitutes the drama, such as it is, of Greenaway's film. To attempt to know how things began on the basis of how they end challenges human attentiveness by forcing an impossible adequation of one thing to another. The problem is equivalent to the time-lapse exhibition of the process of decay which unexpectedly augurs patterns of construal that are absolutely incommensurable with the idea of loss. After all, the technological cine-magic of the film repeatedly manifests static deadness as the vital animation of maggots. That is to say, Greenaway's camera shows us that apparently inert mammalian and reptilian corpses are, upon closer inspection, actually armies of decay on the move. As in the case of self-deception, this spectacle calls for a special attentiveness, an alternate spelling out of the viewer's relation to the viewed.

The reasons for believing what we think we know in Greenaway's film—especially under the spell of time-lapse cinematography—depend, once again, upon the Gombrichean facilities for switching between viewing systems that were on display in my reading of Tintoretto. In *A Zed and Two Noughts,* these systems are paradoxically determined by perceptual anomalies. It is, of course, precisely the perceptual anomaly of the sudden unexpected event of mortality that Oswald and Oliver Deuce will not countenance in its incommensurability with the system of life, namely, the process of evolution. Instead, rationalistic reducers that they are, the twins insist upon a single viewing system, so to speak: an objective representation of the eternalizing process of decay, which is ultimately epitomized in their own suicides. In effect, we might say that the Deuces are too rigidly stoical about what can be known. In other words, because they have little tolerance for incommensurables, they ultimately have little imagination for the resourcefulness of mind requisite for switching modes of viewing. The power of Greenaway's film depends upon the artist's imbuing the viewer with this power of self-deceived imagination which the Deuces are lacking. Moreover, this power in Greenaway's film is a reminder that the métier of the visual arts is not so distinct from the métier of the verbal arts when it comes to the deliberative parsing of presentational particulars.

As if he had this point in mind himself, Greenaway seems to set the film in a zoo with heightened awareness of how the phonetically palindromic properties of the word—zoo, ooz[e]—mime the dynamic of enlightened/Enlightenment self-deception embodied by the institution itself. The zoo is a rationalistic hedge against our slipping back into the ooze of the natural past. Like the palindrome, the mind that contemplates the zoo knows the course of its thinking to be backward and forward at the same time. In the zoo the animals succumb to the reduction of the idea. But the idea succumbs, in its turn, to new cage-inspired behaviors. Animals in the zoo do not behave naturally, except as their natures have been altered. What occurs in the cage, which Greenaway does not want us to forget is a kind of film frame, is something like what Jacques Rancière, in *The Future of the Image,* calls a "de-figuration."[14] Rancière is interested in how certain visual strategies orchestrate an "interplay of temporal distances" whereby a displacement of notice becomes an occasion of attention. He is imagining a descriptive modality whereby what one sees is what one has not seen by virtue of what is so urgently visible. Defiguration "constitutes the discursive space that renders novelty visible, which constructs

---

14. Jacques Rancière, *The Future of the Image,* trans. Gregory Elliott (New York: Verso, 2009), 82–84.

a gaze for it in the very discrepancy of temporalities" (Rancière, 83). Rancière's example of defiguration is Gaugin's *Vision du sermon* (also known as *La Lutte de Jacob avec l'ange*). The pictorialization of the sermon entails an inference from the more conspicuously pictured gaze of the parishioners (83–84), though their faces are turned away from our view. Their foregrounded white headgear commands notice over the spatially distant "struggle" of Jacob and the angel, in such a way that that the viewer struggles to find an orientation. This improvisational orientation must bridge foreground and background without the rationalizing givens of a geometrically calibrated perspective. Rancière calls the strategy "mystery making" (84). For obvious reasons, I would be more inclined to call it a challenge to the viewer's tolerance for incommensurables. After all, the tolerance for incommensurables occasions rationally determinative self-deception in lieu of indeterminate mystery making. The challenge yields the kinds of searching rationality that I have already characterized as a skeptical or anxious diachrony of attentiveness.

In Greenaway's film, the strategy of defiguration is plausibly figured in the character of the zoo's resident prostitute, Venus de Milo. Dressed always in black, and so teasing out an all too familiar binary logic, she is nonetheless the antitype to Oliver and Oswald. This is evident in her willingness to know differences inferentially more than differentially. We might say she countenances an Enlightenment that is deferential to rather than differential from the unknown. This is to say, she honors an Enlightenment attuned to the necessity to switch orientations in order to find orientation. She pointedly refuses to answer the zookeeper Van Hoyten's loaded question, "Tell me Milo, do you think a zebra is a white animal with black stripes, or a black animal with white stripes?"[15] Such binary logic is unnatural to Milo. The true token of her epistemic orientation is the cycle of pornographic stories she is writing about animals becoming ever more licentious within their various enclosures. This is a work of imagination that defies the enclosures of the conceptual grid which the zoo is emblematic of.

As we shall see, Greenaway's compositional and editorial métier likewise provokes the viewer to the self-consciousness of being a now self and a then self, in the manner of the self-deceiver who is situated within and without the enclosures of self-understanding. Or at least this is the case when we think of the self-deceiver in pursuit of other orientations that portend better reasons for taking up commitments to them. Such enclosures, like all duly pornographic

---

15. See Peter Greenaway's scenario for *A Zed and Two Noughts* (London: Faber and Faber, 1986), 28.

stories of animal behavior, paradoxically figure openings or orifices. Oswald and Oliver, and indeed the institution of the zoo itself, are contrarily invested in a more orthodox Enlightenment regime of legislative reason, where framing excludes everything not within the frame. Finally, it needs to be pointed out that the visual strategy by which Greenaway works through the difference between the inferentially disposed Venus de Milo and the binary compulsions of the twins is keyed to a kind of foregrounding of aspect dependency. In fact, I might best describe Greenaway's aesthetic practice, in Rancière's terms, as self-deceivingly defigurative. The new status of the visible in painting, which Rancière claimed is made apparent by defiguration, is made operative on the cinematic register by Greenaway's assiduously painterly orchestration of the film frame.

Greenaway's compositional métier is crystallized in an early scene of *A Zed and Two Noughts*. The entire episode is, in part, a troping of the foundational self-deception of cinema that I have already analyzed. We are conventionally seduced by the twenty-four frames per second of the celluloid strip that are miraculously unified in the moving image emitted from the lens of the projector. Not coincidentally, in the scene I wish to discuss, Greenaway deploys an architectural artifice to frame the question of the framability of experience.[16] This occurs at the commencement of the Deuce brothers' drama of grief. The camera finds the twin figures within a colonnaded porch of the church to which they have come to mourn. They are discussing both the unbearable idea of their wives' putrefaction and the proliferation of bacteria—the onset of biological history—that must have occurred upon the site of Eve's first bite of the apple. As the camera tracks backward, our focus is fixed upon the retreating figures standing still in the midst of their dialogue. It is a conversation about inception. The retreating camera is ostensibly keeping the Deuce brothers in proper perspectival view, as vanishing ends. But it simultaneously calls our attention to precisely what we are *not* meant to see by that mode of picturing. Indeed, within the Albertian picturing system we are not meant to see into the vanishing point. We are rather meant to know ends at the expense of seeing. Greenaway's mobile perspectivalism (the tracking camera) mimes the temporality inaugurated in Eden, where we are similarly meant *to know* paradoxically, only at the end of history. In other words, Greenaway's tracking shot shows us that even the representation of timelessness entails the temporality

16. Here I believe Greenaway is alluding to the late quattrocento and baroque practice of *quadratura*: the use of architectural structures, often in states of ruination, to set off views of nature within a framework of rational purposiveness. *Quadratura* is of course a prop of tromp l'oeil illusionism.

of motion. Aptly, the architecture of the colonnade is an archetype both of rational construction, the human bulwark against nature, and of the seemingly counterrational desire not to decide whether one is inside or outside the architectural frame.

The architecture of the colonnade, in its very permeability, expresses an open-ended speculation upon the project of enclosing Nature, even a tolerance for the incommensurability of nature and culture. And yet the colonnade is nonetheless a mode of enclosure and a mode of framing. In other words, like all of the other paradoxes invoked here, it warrants the alternation of subjective commitments. It opens us to growing doubt about what we are seeing as *most significant.* This is indeed always the case given the incommensurability of inside and outside that *flickers,* so to speak, when we pass through any colonnaded space. It is, of course, a flickering that calls to mind, once again, the movement of celluloid through the gate of a movie projector. The point of this passage of the film, however, is not to present incommensurability per se. It is instead to make the possibility of framing into a provoking question. How can we find our commitments to viewpoint in relation to the knowledge that viewpoint is contrastively reasoned? This, for Greenaway, might be the essential task of cinema. From Greenaway's viewpoint, it is the task that too many filmmakers lamentably forget.

Greenaway is, after all, a cinematic artist well known for his strident polemicism against cinema. He notoriously declared its demise on September 23, 1983.[17] This is the date of the coming into currency of the television remote control unit. In Greenaway's mind cinema's demise arises from the knowledge that cinematic framing, and particularly the illusionistic temporal framing of twenty-four frames per second, precludes other modalities of notice: particularly ones that entail viewing systems that are inferable from what is within the frame but are nonetheless incommensurable with the viewing system of that frame. The remote control unit is, for Greenaway, a counter for thinking aspects of a framed view that obtain as competing commitments of the viewer. Greenaway is very much like the artist Bill Viola imagines himself to be in seeking to recover the devices of pre-Renaissance painting. We will recall Viola's enthusiasm for modes of projection that permit incommensurable views in contravention of the rules for image-making—views that circumscribe an otherwise open "mind-field." Viola's touchstone for the mind-field

---

17. See Peter Greenaway, "Cinema Militans Lecture: Towards a Re-Invention of Cinema" (paper presented at the Netherlands Film Festival, Utrecht, September 28, 2003), http://petergreenaway.org.uk/essay3.htm. This is his most complete account of the current state of the medium.

was the representation of a building that permits our viewing it in accordance with possibilities of perception that are, nonetheless, precluded by the lucidity of the rationalistically spatialized image. Greenaway is similarly insistent that the cinematic frame is illusionary in ways that must be exploited—rather than forgiven—for making forays into something like Bill Viola's "mind-field." Such *thinking as seeing* is otherwise obliterated by the cinematic viewer's capitulation to the binary of illusionism and realism. This is merely an aesthetic reverberation of the Cartesian dualism of thinking and sensing. According to Greenaway, it is, not surprisingly, also a modern legacy of painting practices and of the devices of the theatrical stage, which, the director protests, have handicapped the development of cinema as an art form. The cinematic viewer has been rendered incapable of seeing that the distinction between the illusionistic and the realistic is itself merely illusory. Or we might say that the failure to notice this liability is self-deluded—rather than self-deceiving in my terms—when it does not denote something like the Gombrichean impulse to switch from one system of viewing to another.

This calls to the fore a controlling assumption behind my assertion that ethical learning is entailed by self-deception. I am assuming that for one to know the shortcomings of one's commitments—in the present context I am referring to commitments denoted in a system of viewing—one must know more scrupulously what one is doing in affirming one's commitments. To this end, or so it might seem, Greenaway's *A Zed and Two Noughts* gives us a view of the *barred* world of a too theatrically framed cinema. The medium is a zoo unto itself in this respect. Indeed the notion is starkly figured in Greenaway's repeated tracking of the camera across barred fields of vision, like the view through colonnaded space. This camera movement disposes the viewer to a yet unrealized spelling out of the conditions of viewing. Such conditions—the flickering of one scene through the bars of another—are nothing less than a mandate to undertake the contrastive work of noticing what escapes our attentiveness. I have been arguing all along that Enlightenment knowing is the official blind spot of rational viewing, guaranteeing that something will escape our attentiveness. In a complementary way, the institution of the zoo is the premier Enlightenment institution: it combines a bid for the human mastery of Nature with the anxious self-mastery of taxonomic knowledge. The inevitable failure of the taxonomic grid, in the face of our inevitable discovery of new species, redounds to the de facto mastering of humanity by Nature. Now I'd like to suggest that Greenaway's "defiguration," his framing/de-framing mise-en-scène in *A Zed and Two Noughts,* might be specifically exploited as a corrective to the blind spots of Enlightenment rationalism. Within the space of Greenaway's vision, however, we might check the excesses of rationalism without sacrificing the activity of reasoning. For Greenaway shows us something we are not ordinarily predisposed to see or think: the process of visual reasoning, by which we are ever better apprised of what escapes our attentiveness, underwrites our commitments to other views.

One could say that Greenaway uses the painter Vermeer as a counter for visual reasoning that quite explicitly entails the kind of contrastive work I have just acknowledged as Greenaway's enlightening métier. Vermeer is a painter who is notorious for his modest output: maximally, thirty canvases. Hence his extraordinary susceptibility to the notice of would-be forgers. Forgers play upon the public's imaginative appetite for resemblances that would foster new commitments to augment the famous painter's small body of work. The forger incites belief in the widening of the repertoire by enticing notice of ever more rationalizable likenesses to what does not exist. Similarly, Vermeer is a painter who is notorious for confecting compositions that depend upon multiple vanishing points. These constitute a touchstone for the kind of incommensurability the detective of art forgeries would be bound to espy.[18]

The defigurational impact of Greenaway composing the scenes of his film by mocking Van Meegeren's métier belies the ambition of the Deuce brothers. Their thinking subsists on twinness, doubling, and symmetry, where commensuration is all. Over the course of Greenaway's film, the brothers come into closer accord with each other's appearance to reveal the secret of their origin. They were Siamese twins separated at birth: the advent of a history that dooms them to suffer from a Platonist nostalgia. Quite to the contrary, whether discerning the deceptions of a forger or proving out the truth of twinness, the viewer of Greenaway's film is tutored to develop antithetical powers of notice. These powers must be capable of discovering points of contrast beyond the presumptuous integrative rules of picturing systems that are blind to the emerging logics of asymmetry. The contrastive logic of multiple vanishing points in Vermeer is a corollary of the kind of notice that Greenaway inculcates by scenes in which his own "forgeries" of Vermeer are purveyed as conspicuously failed gambits of simple deception.

In considering such compositional stratagems as this, we must of course remember that twinness is the ultimate self-deception. From the point of view

---

18. See Philip Steadman, *Vermeer's Camera: Uncovering the Truth Behind the Masterpieces* (Oxford: Oxford University Press, 2002). Also see David Hockney's increasingly influential extrapolation of these insights in *Secret Knowledge: Rediscovering the Lost Techniques of the Old Masters* (London: Studio, 2006).

of the twin, one must assume that the self is always self-consciously something to be examined for certainty of its identity vis-à-vis the other twin. From the point of view of the viewer one can simply ask: who does not look with special acuteness to notice the hidden differences between apparent twins, especially if those differences do not exist? Greenaway shows sympathy for these impulses by, in effect, juxtaposing two widely recognizable Vermeer compositions: the *Art of Painting* and *The Girl in a Red Hat*. We see Van Meegeren's wife posing for the photographer, sporting the sackbut prop of the former painting and wearing the red fur hat of the latter. But she is also naked, unlike the figures featured in either of the paintings. When she brusquely exits the frame after accusing Van Meegeren of infidelity with Alba Bewick, we are reminded that fidelity in representation is a counter of the viewer's attentiveness more than of the painter's exactitude in twinning the painting with the *original* reality. The disparate temporalities of Ranciere's defiguration whereby *a displacement of notice becomes an occasion of attention*, once again accrue to the viewer's experience as a mandate to look askance at appearance. One can only do so meaningfully with contrastive rigor.

If mortality is the ultimate antagonist of notice because it cancels appearance, it might also be seen as the perverse correlative of Enlightenment rationality, which likewise sacrifices appearance to a deadening thought. As Jeff Wall makes plain in his own version of montage, thought deadens and becomes

Fig. 11   Alba and the Deuces, from *A Zed and Two Noughts*, 1985, directed by Peter Greenaway. Reproduced by permission of Peter Greenaway.

abstract when it is no longer tethered to the specifically Hegelian baffles of appearance. Aptly enough, Greenaway's film is emphatically a resuscitation of the rationalistically mortified body of appearances. Or we might say he urges us to reanimate the corpse with renewed faith that appearance is what cannot be rationalistically framed, except by reframing one's view. This is a nod to self-deception insofar as Greenaway's viewer is prompted to do what the Deuces cannot do: to see again, rather than to look steadily at the problem of the changeability of appearances in mortal time. *Seeing again* is the hallmark of Greenaway's mise-en-scène insofar as the Deuces' progressive self-coalescence is thwarted by the viewer's cognizance of what he is not noticing. The twins end up inhabiting a single suit of clothes, which taunts us to examine the invisible seams that otherwise suture difference.

This denotes a mental process made properly figurational in the time lapse spectacles of physical decay that the film purveys as its dominant motif. The latter are conspicuously made visible by strobe lights clicking on and off in synch with the stopping and starting of the camera. It is as if one could not see without the prosthesis of a disorienting blindness. This is the kind of ellipsis of attention that I have been suggesting intrudes upon the self-deceiver's consciousness. Likewise, it vividly tropes the kind of contrastive work the viewer is recruited to by Greenaway whenever the view is seen to be evolving in response to what is exhibited outside the frame of attentiveness. The final scene of Greenaway's film is a spectacle of contrasting black lines and white spaces. It is, if nothing else, starkly emblematic of contrastive work. As I have already mentioned, the Deuces' suicides are meant to be graphed in time on this gridded surface. The black and white grid, not coincidentally a collection of frames, enframed by the experimental apparatus meant to commensurate what evolves in time with the timelessness of death, becomes the most exemplary compositional gambit of Greenaway's film.

Like the good Enlightenment reasoners they are, the Deuces seek to close the logical circuit of meaning between life and death at the end of *A Zed and Two Noughts*. As their evening progresses, the mechanisms of strobe lights and multiple cameras are short-circuited by an infestation of snails, brought on presumably by the ambient temperature's arrival at the dew (another rationalistically determinative grid). Snails, of course, subsist on decay. The snail is perfectly emblematic of the Deuces' goal. But it is technically the nemesis of their technological project. The conceptual order of the grid, disfigured by the incursion of snails, constitutes a defiguration inasmuch as a temporal distance intrudes on the occlusion of the gridded line of sight. Not only does the viewer do what the Deuces cannot, but, more important, the viewer knows what he or she is doing in a way the Deuces cannot.

Greenaway's viewer is compelled to view inferentially because the figures that must be made intelligible are dislocated from the representational grid upon which they are otherwise meant to be mapped. This means the viewer knows that other reasons for what appears apply as features of the experience. Specifically, these are reasons that are inextricable from the warrant to be a viewer in the first place. We must think of the viewer here as one who submits to the succession of temporal frames. We might say that, in this circumstance, one has a warrant to be a viewer out of the predicament of not knowing one's best reasons for acknowledging the object one has plainly in one's sights. Thus, we might judge that the Deuces do not see because their reasons for seeing are too presumptive with respect to what they want to see.

It is important to realize that what one has not presumed to see is automatically subsumed to perceptual contingency. And this is, perhaps counterintuitively, the reason one cannot say that no reasons apply in the circumstance of an unrationalized perception. Indeed, such is the real meaning of the activity of notice: the presumption that perceptions are inextricable from reasons potentiates our understanding of how the inadequacy of reasons to perceptions might be a strong imperative of knowledge. This invites the diachronic narrative expectations of better reasons and the corollary imperative that something more is to be done next. In this way we are still keeping faith with the Bachean question that, for me, underpins the essential human condition. This claim is sustainable where mental action and physical action are irreducibly bound, as I'm suggesting they are in perceptual contingency. The question "What do I do next?" is strikingly alive in Greenaway's work.

At the conclusion of *A Zed and Two Noughts,* the snails' corruption of the grid is correlative with the viewer's predicament throughout. The viewer is caught in a de facto avowal of commitment by dint of a self-deceiving perception. The Albertian grid, no less than the rationalizing grid for which the Deuces die, presupposes after all a perceptual accord with the world that brooks no perceptual contingency. But the grid itself becomes a perceptual contingency in inverse proportion to what the perceptual plenitude it purveys occludes notice of. Inasmuch as the Deuces' decomposing bodies will merge with the conceptual lines of sight projected by the grid, one will see the grid in all of its nonschematic, that is to say, nonsignifying, particularity. The insight does not evoke a ratio of schematizing concept to percept, but a ratio of percept to percept. Because we see the failure of reasons for avowing knowledge of what we see, for example, the failure of the grid to map time or space, we are bound to reason otherwise. This is especially true as we are led by perceptual contingency. We are thus acutely responsive to the question "What do I do next" because we know how irresistibly the question presses upon us. In effect, knowing how the question presses is an answer to the question. Most conspicuously, we know that our avowals to know our perceptual commitments in the world entail our experience of the consequences of avowing such commitments. Moreover, these avowals entail our imagining terms of fitness between the two temporal realms denoted by act and consequence. This is the significance of notice *par excellence.* It liberates us from the Kant-inspired presumption that our performances are derived from a priori laws. If, to the contrary, we allow for the fact that performances arise from the will to avow commitments, we affirm the present-ness of subjectivity as the salient touchstone of character. It would likewise be the preeminent value denoted in character development. Correlatively, the teleology of character development is not the presumption of a reason to be realized because it is the right or best reason. Rather, it is the realization that reason-giving is de rigueur wherever the temporal circumstance of character is a threshold for our self-consciousness of self-deception.

Tintoretto, Wall, Richter, Viola, and Greenaway are visual artists whose investment in the temporal circumstance of character is fully proportionate to their sense of what constitutes visuality in the first place. They show us with extraordinary starkness how, on the register of visuality, the most relevant character is that of the viewer. The viewer's susceptibility to perceptual illusion elides with the time of viewing. It thus makes the obligation to acknowledge self-deception as integral to self-realization an all the more urgent reason for knowing what one is doing. The agency-arresting tragedy of not knowing what one is doing is obviated when the activity of knowing what one is doing becomes a self-sustaining proposition. For Tintoretto, Wall, Richter, Viola, and Greenaway, the spelling out of the viewer's condition of intelligibility, as an ever richer prospect for intelligibility, is just such an activity. It earns the self-respect that I have argued the self-deceiver is entitled to by his or her unusually resourceful habitation of the conflictual space of tragic *peripeteia.*

7

Shameless Self-Deception

Self-Deception as Practical Experiment

Throughout this book I have maintained that the beneficent value of self-deception inheres in the way it makes self-realization into a reason-giving enterprise with respect to the contingencies of knowing what we are doing. We might therefore think of it as a modality of practical experimentation. Along these lines, Annette C. Baier has written a useful essay entitled "The Vital but Dangerous Art of Ignoring." Baier invokes René Descartes's willful doubting of everything as a corollary of the self-deceiver's dogged willfulness to know what he or she is doing. Baier confirms that Descartes is something of a forerunner of the late twentieth-century thinking on this topic, which strives to discover the rationalistic underpinnings of self-deception. Descartes famously anticipates the strategic efficacy of acting "as if" things were otherwise, as if the body did not exist. The argumentative lever of what Baier credits Descartes with exploiting is roughly consistent with my own emphasis on the discipline of notice. Descartes's willingness in the *First Meditation* to act as if the body did not exist is predicated on an anxiety that he has not noticed what contingencies of the belief that the body does exist have not been observed. When Descartes declares, "I think it will be a good plan to turn my will in completely the opposite direction [vis-à-vis dogmatic belief], and deceive myself, by pretending for a time that these former opinions are utterly false" (Baier, 59, quoting Descartes), he convincingly makes a bid to engage the experimental practicality of self-deception.

I would go so far as to say that Descartes is acknowledging a pride in his own cleverness with respect to the daunting task of self-knowledge. Baier herself concedes the possibility that self-deception is an occasion for mental attunements to the self that would otherwise be precluded in the blind faith of mere self-assertion. When Baier concludes from Descartes's performance that "we risk self-deception whenever we engage, as we constantly do, in more or less voluntary sharpening of our mental focus on some matters, along with a consequent blurring of focus on others" (54), she is intimating that the risk is an investment in the self. The currency of this investment is, not coincidentally, time. Baier characterizes the variability of mental focus as a "temporal stretch" (60). Here, once again, is the persistent orientation of the self-deceiver to a now self and a then self. A temporal stretch is entailed by Descartes's denial of the existence of things: what he is bound to deny becomes a variable of his distance from earlier denials. This is another way of reckoning with a fact that I have tried to keep foregrounded throughout this book: self-deception is, above all, for and about the self.[1] The self is not rendered nugatory in the act of self-deception. We see this clearly in Descartes's example. The "temporal stretch" that occasions Descartes's transition from thinking of self-deception as self-willed to thinking of self-deception as something induced by the postulate of an evil genius is far from an abandonment of self. It is emphatically an acknowledgment of shifting motivational biases. I have maintained these shifting grounds to be foundational for appreciating self-deception as a métier of self-realization, that is to say, as an enhancement of our powers of notice.

Now it is important to tease out more shamelessly the counterintuitive dignity that might be credited to the self-deceived character. We will see this more starkly by putting the self-deceiver in direct opposition to the self-heroizing Enlightenment reasoner, for whom the self-deceiver is a patently discreditable antagonist. The authority of this Enlightenment reasoner inheres in his pretense to sustain a timeless autonomy that brooks no self-deception. It brooks no self-deception because the postulate of selfhood is dogmatically principled and deontologically authorized. This state of affairs precludes the subjective capacity of heightened notice without which, I have been arguing, any work of art would be rendered too systematically subservient to a rationalism without revisable reasons. On the contrary, I am trying to evoke a self-deceiving aspect of aesthetic experience, which is to say, a mode of aesthetic learning that deploys reasons without dogmatic rationalism. The shifting grounds of motivational biases, upon which I am claiming the self-deceiving mind subsists, constitute the precondition of this realm of experience. It is this cognizance that should encourage us to view self-deception without the shameful

---

1. For a full-scale consideration of what this means, see Amélie Oksenberg Rorty, "Self-Deception, Akrasia and Irrationality," in *The Multiple Self (Studies in Rationality and Social Change,* ed. Jon Elster (Cambridge: Cambridge University Press, 1987), 115–32, especially 125.

stigma of irrationality that is otherwise attached to it by more immovably grounded rationalists.

There is no question that certain instances of self-deception do warrant shame and an acknowledgment of culpability, especially outside the realm of aesthetic experience with which I have been preoccupied. The driver who convinces himself that he is fit to drive because he can touch his nose with the tip of his finger, when he knows that he has been drinking heavily, makes a bad driver notwithstanding. But dogmatic applications of reason can be just as destructive and blameworthy. We have seen that the instrumentalism of dehumanizing technologies is the notorious touchstone of the critique of modernity that was launched by Horkheimer and Adorno in *Dialectic of Enlightenment*. In any case, my purpose here has not been to make invidious judgments about the advisability of self-deception with respect to the dicta of reason. Rather, I am simply considering the proposition that the mental dispositions entailed by the circumstance of self-deception conduce to our exploiting experience as a mode of discovery. Since, for the self-deceiver, belief is determined by what one notices, and notice itself is a function of the desire to see more fully what might constitute the evidence for belief, truth does not mediate between self-deception and reason. We might say instead that where truth cannot be hypostatized knowledge becomes more daring.

In keeping with these observations, I launched this book by noting how the mental and affective traits of self-deception might come to be appreciated as unlikely assets of human inquiry. In my initial survey of current debates on the topic I was indebted to the work of theorists of self-deception like Amélie Oksenberg Rorty, who touted the proposition that self-deception is "a disease only the presumptively strong minded can suffer."[2] Through the "readings" of works of art that make up the substance of this book, I have been trying to make explicit how strengths of mind, such as that attributed to the self-deceiver by Rorty, are strikingly coherent with the very fact of mindedness itself, without which our sense of rational modernity would be relatively incoherent. It is not a coincidence that Descartes and Hegel have been seen as exemplars of rationalism for whom reasoning entails elements of self-deception. Jeff Walls's presumption upon the shameless self-deceptions of self-consciousness that vindicate the Hegelian "distraught soul" (analyzed in the *Phenomenology*) occasions a self-realization that is only too well complemented by contemporary theorists

---

2. Amélie Oksenberg Rorty, "The Deceptive Self: Liars, Layers, and Lairs," in *Perspectives in Self-Deception*, ed. Brian P. McLaughlin and Amélie Oxenberg Rorty (Berkeley and Los Angeles: University of California Press, 1988), 25.

of self-deception. For them a kind of shamelessness in the act of self-deception has decidedly beneficent consequences.

So I might say that the conceit of shame accurately captures the complexities of self-deceiving experience, precisely because it teases out the temptation to embrace shamelessness. In some way then, what I am proposing is a view of artistic appreciation that presupposes a stance of shamelessness. I take self-deception to be the métier of that stance. Above all an anxious disposition, vis-à-vis the reasons one does not yet possess for acting in any particular instance of sensuous engagement with the world, has been the starting point for all of the aesthetic gambits I have valued in these pages. Like shame, anxiety has its pros and cons. It can be a register of weakness and a resource for counteracting the many unforeseen consequences that menace human activity. I have already invoked the speculations of Annette Baier and Adrian Piper with respect to how self-deceivers are self-preservers. They are anxiously hedging against fears that whatever reasons they possess for self-realizing action will be inadequate to changing circumstances. It is now worth spelling out the inferences of this self-consciousness more exhaustively. This will involve a review of contemporary theorists of self-deception for whom anxiety cultivates a practical idealism.

Anxiety and Strength of Mind

The fact is, anxiety—which we have seen to figure in the strategic illusionism of artists like Lotto, Nabokov, Tintoretto, Greenaway, and others—is a recurrent term of art in the work of theorists of self-deception who have attempted, in some part, to tease out Rortyan strengths of mind. For such theorists such strengths of mind are intrinsic to self-deception despite our most well motivated skepticism about egging the self-deceiver on. I will freely admit that the aesthetic stratagems examined in these pages seem to implicate us in egging the self-deceiver on. Yet there is more to the story. After all, the anxieties aroused by and addressed by the artworks discussed in these pages constitute an enterprise of finding reasons for beliefs whose warrant is discoverable only on the threshold of anxiety about not knowing enough. Consequently, the self-deceiver in question is not incompatible with idealism about human reasoning. That is to say, for theorists like Annette C. Baier, Annette Barnes, Adrian Piper, and Mark Johnston there is a rough consensus that anxiety-driven self-deception need not be invidiously and antagonistically judged against principled rationalism. It is for this reason that I wish to reprise a view of the consensus about self-deception that has formed around anxious knowledge about the limits of knowledge. This may be the strongest premise for indicating what dignity shamelessness can tutor.

We have of course already engaged Annette C. Baier's notion, out of Descartes, that the will to self-deception is not just a will to ignore the facts. It is, more urgently, a recognition of the doubtfulness that one knows all the facts, or at least those facts sufficient to the desire to achieve self-understanding under the pressures of narrative temporality. Similarly, Annette Barnes in her book *Seeing Through Self-Deception,* Adrian Piper in "Pseudorationality," and Mark Johnston in "Self-Deception and the Nature of Mind" agree that the act of mind constitutive of self-deception is uniquely resourceful.[3] Its resources derive from the exigency of facing its own limitations without giving up on prospects for productive agency. Given the interpretative challenges posed by the artworks taken up in this book, we might argue that aesthetic experience most significantly constitutes a laboratory for the mind facing its limitations. Cognizance of these limitations arouses precisely the fear—epitomized in the emotional/affective fallout from tragic *peripeteia*—that anxiety theorists of self-deception count so significantly. For all of the theorists I have just mentioned, the anxiety that their operative desire that P will turn out *not* to be the case, commits them to defend against the circumstance of not-P. This constitutes an inducement to prevail upon mental strengths that are indistinguishable from the most stringent standards of rationalistic continence. As we have seen in multiple encounters with artworks, these strengths include attentiveness, responsiveness to stimuli, resourceful deduction, vigilance to the possibility of error, and a self-protective, self-revising perspectivalism.

To appreciate the point, we need only focus more closely upon how Baier's attention to the "temporal stretch" of Cartesian mind necessitates a mind-sharpening disposition to ignore or forget what is immediately the case. The benefit of this forgetting is the Cartesian subject's permission to acknowledge motives that would be more conducive to desires respecting what might otherwise—and more fruitfully for the subject—be the case. This relationship with oneself, which we might call a metaself-deception, allows us to "ponder the rationality of the decision that it will be a good plan to deceive oneself for

---

3. Barnes, *Seeing Through Self-Deception;* Adrian M. Piper, "Pseudorationality," in *Perspectives on Self-Deception,* ed. Amélie Oksenberg Rorty and Brian P. McLaughlin (Berkeley and Los Angeles: University of California Press, 1988), 297–323; Mark Johnston, "Self-Deception and the Nature of the Mind," in ibid., 63–91.

some indeterminate period [and thereby] . . . ponder the criteria for judging its success" (Baier, 79). Given this prospect, Baier unashamedly asks the question "Who is more self-deceived?" Is it the philosopher who dismisses self-deception as a paradoxical instance of irrationality, or is it the Cartesian who accepts the inevitability of self-deception as a superior rationality, whereby learning to live with it means "milking it for all that it can yield" (70)? Because self-deception ceases to be a zero-sum game, the possible winnings may be claimed by all.

In a similar vein, Adrian Piper concedes that the self-deceiver is, no doubt, a little mad. But the self-deceiver's mania for noticing what other theories she might take up, respective of a given circumstance that threatens the fulfillment of her desire, is nonetheless rationalistically motivated. As Piper puts it, the motivations that cause a self-deceiver's investment in a theory of action that instantiate his or her commitments "involve a desire to buttress another theory, namely an honorific self-conception" (315). In my reading of Nabokov's *Lolita*, I have already alleged the applicability of Piper's definition of "pseudo-rationality" as the highest-order disposition to literal self-preservation. But it is now perhaps easier to take seriously her notion that such self-protectiveness inculcates an order of personal vigilance: one which intensifies scrutiny of one's shortcomings. Notice of one's shortcomings has the perverse virtue of instilling a humility, as Piper sees it, like that exhibited by fictional "characters: Uriah Heep or even St. Augustine" (Piper, 318). There is of course a certain shamelessness entailed in the willfulness to attend so vigilantly to shortcomings that are so vulnerable to exposure. Shamelessness in this case is tantamount to the kind of self-revisionary mandate that I have argued gives ethical urgency to the self-deceiving mind.

Accordingly, and as we saw in chapter 1, Annette Barnes's view of self-deception is almost exclusively coupled with the desire for anxiety reduction as a broadening of the horizon of intelligibility. It prompts her to see self-deception as an occasion for unusually detailed scrutiny of what we care about insofar as there is warrantable evidence for that concern, however inappropriately biased it might be (Barnes, 87). Inappropriate bias notwithstanding, the self-deceiver is deeply interested in exploring a diverse range of motivational grounds. In this regard, Barnes aptly references David Sanford's notion of the self-deceiver as one who is actively engaged in marking the distinctions between ostensible and anxiously anticipatory reasons for action. Barnes, however, insists upon our recognition that all of this acknowledges an extraordinary imaginative reach and speculative vigor. In appreciating the scope of such activity, we entertain a broader range of rational commitments than any simple distinction between truth and falsity might allow.

Finally, Mark Johnston goes so far as to characterize self-deception as "adopting a cognitive attitude" (Johnston, 89). With this statement, he denotes the act of taking the world in a way that matches one's desires. In other words, self-deception may be characterized as a kind of wishful thinking. But the operative wishfulness here is not self-trivializing. Johnston encourages us to see some parity between reason and self-deception insofar as both are adaptive forms of mental process. Johnston is a strong defender of the proposition that we can treat self-deception the way we treat a tropism: it is a "purpose serving mental mechanism" (Johnston, 67). Like the others, Johnston doesn't see self-deception in shamefully reductive terms: as alternative or even contrary to rational thinking. By assuming that rational thinking means preeminently that causal relations are in effect between mental states, one of which could be characterized as a reason for another, Johnston is able to go a step further. He embraces the notion that mental tropisms "(blind but purpose-serving connections between mental state types) are not peripheral phenomena but are the basic connections that constitute rationality and irrationality alike. Rational connections are not constitutive and exhaustive of the mental" (Barnes, 88). In other words, some human actions warrant a modality of cognition that is acutely responsive to extenuating circumstances of a mind that knows itself to be inferentially purposive. Purposiveness obtains on the basis of what comes to the mind in the course of its efforts to sustain "hopeful belief" (Barnes, 89) in the fulfillment of its desire. Hopeful belief, in this context, is a variable of noticing what else there is that will make oneself better known to oneself.

While all of these anxiety theorists concede to self-deception a degree of cognitive and imaginative resourcefulness, like Rorty's "strengths of mind," there is a clear dispute between them with respect to the ultimate beneficence or culpability of the self-deceiving mind. The central dispute seems to be the belief that anxiety itself can be handled in ways more compatible with principled rationality. Piper and Barnes, who both see self-deception as epiphenomenal of states of mind one would ideally eschew, clearly reprove the self-deceiver for not standing up rationalistically to the motivating fear. Piper advocates a policy of "epistemic audacity" (Piper, 319). Piper admonishes that one ought to possess the courage of one's convictions. One ought to be willing to "test one's favored theory of one's experience more generally, as well as of oneself, against circumstances or aspects of one's own behavior that one perceives as challenging or threatening it" (Piper, 319). Both Piper and Barnes clearly imagine a normative rationality that, for the most strong minded of us, ought to be bootstrapped out of an ever more scrupulous vigilance respecting the motives for one's fears. But this call to a more principled vigilance about motives for anxiety aptly enough recapitulates the logic of self-deception. It depends, after all, upon a disposition to be vigilant, that is to say, to notice, that transcends contextually bound motives. This disposition to notice induces the self-deceiver to know more, motivationally speaking. It is a kind of warrant to take up commitments in which one is not already invested by virtue of one's previous actions.

On the other hand, Baier and especially Johnston would seem to accept the proposition that some situations of reasoning are simply intractable with respect to the ideal of best reasons. These are situations where the shamelessness, so to speak, of self-deception cannot measure up to a demand for epistemic audacity. Baier's Descartes, for example, never resolves his doubts about the advisability of doubting that he has a body. He never ceases to be a strategic self-deceiver. In the late pages of the "Sixth Meditation" we should note that Descartes is still fretting about "errors of nature,"[4] like phantom limb experiences, that he concedes are bound to deceive us over the course of time. Similarly for Johnston, the unpredictable course of time seems to be what is most dispositive for his insistence that, given an extraordinary complexity of circumstances, some states of mind simply do not rise to the occasion of rationalistic self-monitoring (89). His assertion that other adaptive forms of mental process inevitably take over accords with my own stance: we have no reason to imagine that, given the course of time, the anxiety that occasions the self-deceiver's resourcefulness of mind is ever conclusively reduced to principles, or ever definitively resolved. As I have been attempting to show in these pages, this points to a state of mental attentiveness that is not easily held up for invidious comparison with rational deduction from principles.

Let me be clear. I am not discouraging the idealism of epistemic audacity. I am suggesting instead that there is perhaps a distinction without a significant difference between epistemic audacity and the capacity for notice entailed by self-deceiving mind. I would argue that what those who make invidious comparisons between self-deceiving mind and some ideal of rational continence count as a weakness is, on the contrary, an unequivocal strength. I would say

---

4. René Descartes, *Discourse on Method and Meditations on First Philosophy*, 4th ed., trans. Donald A. Cress (Indianapolis: Hackett, 1980), 99.

that this is especially the case where one respects the Razian idea that in classical, as opposed to "contemporary" rationality, the aspect-dependency of reason-giving cannot be ignored. Baier and Johnston seem particularly sensitive to the fact that where anxiety is not quelled by a sufficient reason, nonetheless some adaptive reasoning ensues. One always comes to see more in the course of becoming a more vigilant inspector of the context of one's choices.

Self-Deception and the Contextualist Imperative

This is, to be sure, a contextualist argument, one which warrants its own brief contextualization. As Stephen Turner has acknowledged, the classical rebuttal to contextualism is that it relativizes our knowledge of problems.[5] It does so in a way that is irrelevant to the conventions of intelligibility that make the problems recognizable to us in the first place. But Turner intimates that contextualism already comprehends what an acknowledgment of aspect-dependency disposes us to: the wisdom that in applying doctrines we are at risk of ignoring features of the doctrine that would augment the scope of its applicability. The self-deceiver's anxiety about such oversight comports well with the contextualist's unapologetic presentism. Presentism is of course, another point of criticism against contextual reasoning: one which I argued in chapter 1 is the existential underpinning of self-deception as well. But this criticism need not succeed.

As Turner admits, there are at least two notions of contextuality to contend with (*Brains,* 144). The standard contextualist might be said to see a classical problem as solvable or as interpretable according to classical terms, from which present-day contextualists are necessarily alienated. The contextualism that Turner seems most interested in, and that I wish to align with the heightened notice of the self-deceiver, is different. This contextualism does not see a problem in classical terms: namely, what could the problem have meant to those who first noticed it to be significant? Rather, it sees the problem in terms of *what can be made of it* under the exigencies of circumstantial notice in the present moment of one's attentiveness. Turner knows that when we subscribe to the first contextualism, by stressing the dependency of meaning on "local circumstances and motives, dead traditions of discourse, and dead conventions," we are estranged from ourselves in the very act of taking up the problem. But

---

5. See Stephen Turner, "Teaching Subtleties of Thought / The Lessons of Contextualism," in *Brains/Practices/Relativism,* 142–59.

he argues that the self-consciousness of this estrangement "allows us to see things that we can alter and replace. Distinctions that were for them [contextualists of the past] distinctions without a difference may well be, for us, very useful distinctions indeed. And if contextualism does not provide a formula for discovering which distinctions do make a difference in our context, it nevertheless encourages us and in a way trains us *to look for these distinctions*" (Turner, *Brains,* 149–50; my emphasis). The result is that we develop an ability to more richly understand what kind of problem we are contending with. We are consequently equipped to deal with it in new ways. We need only contemplate the artworks examined in these pages to appreciate the point. They are united by the common experience of the reader's/viewer's ability to take up commitments that otherwise seemed unimaginable. That is to say, those commitments would have seemed unimaginable except as conditions of misunderstanding the text we were reading or the picture plane with which we were interacting.

Turner exemplifies this thinking. He points out how Max Weber's definition of "the state" in 1922 is a kind of second sight with respect to his predecessor Rudolph Von Ihering's definition of the state in 1877. Weber calls the state a "compulsory political association . . . [that] upholds the claim to the monopoly of the legitimate use of force" (Turner, *Brains,* 146–47, quoting Weber). Ihering defines the state as "the sole owner of social coercive force—the right to coerce forms, the *absolute monopoly* of the state" (147, quoting Ihering). Turner notes that a small difference, Ihering's use of the phrase "social coercive force" as opposed to Weber's "legitimate use of force," is disproportionately significant with respect to the context of knowledge it fosters. Weber's altering and replacing of the phrase "social coercive force," Turner says, is a way of picking out the "less obvious features of a doctrine" (149). Ihering's notion of the state is revealed to be teleological. Weber's ignoring of that teleological aspect permits him to make legitimation the salient determinant of the state instead of teleology. Turner characterizes Weber's maneuver in contextualist terms as relativizing a problem to "a richer 'context' of conventions, literary models, and whatnot" (149).

The works of art examined here, under the aspect of self-deception, similarly prompt a seeking after "less obvious" distinctions—distinctions otherwise obscured by the more obvious features of a problem. As Turner wants to persuade us, the relativizing for which contextualism is typically discredited—on the basis of the incommensurability of the contextualist's analysis with the norms constitutive of an original framework of knowledge or belief—can unexpectedly become a tool of critical thinking. Such contextualism becomes a tool of critical thinking by fostering the kind of contrastive work—with all of the Hegelian overtones touted by Jeff Wall—that the anxious self-deceiver cannot shake himself free of. Specifically, in the Hegelian context, I have said that self-deception obtains as a critical tool because the dialectical disposition of self-consciousness toward otherness is coordinate with a discipline of notice. Both the anxiety-bred reasoning of the self-deceiver and the relativizing reasoning of the contextualist open us to a mode of learning about oneself without being bound to a self-preempting theory of self.

From the beginning of this work I have maintained that the aesthetic experience—which I have characterized as sustainable by practices akin to self-deception—suspends the idea that self or character has any epistemic anchorage except the capacity for self-preserving self-examination. This capacity is made exigent by the circumstance of temporality. It is this *uncharacteristic* characterization of the self that all of the artworks considered here give animus to, whether within the framework of fictional narrative or within the narrative framework of reading and viewing. To be sure, a certain shamelessness always obtains in the willingness to act out of character. But, at the same time, we must understand that the all too confident pride of self can become an epistemic obstacle to experience. This is especially true when one must take up a commitment to act on the basis of knowing what one is doing: especially when one is doing something unprecedented with respect to one's already rationalized commitments.

I began this book by positing an *uncharacteristic character* because I wanted to make the temporal predicament of the artifice/device of character in the novel a springboard for speculation. I wished to speculate upon the way in which all works of art are, in one way or another, character building for the audiences that engage them out of the cognizance of a common temporal predicament. This continuity between character and reader—or viewer, or any responsive sensibility—is a presupposition of everything that has been at stake in my argument so far. I think it is fair, in fact, to generalize that the theorists of self-deception, and the artists whom I have adduced as collaborators in the investigation of the world of the self-deceiver, treat self-deception as a proactive métier. The realm of activity is, without question, the sine qua non of all explanatory reasoning.

Thus we have seen how the *uncharacteristic character* labors to explain him- or herself in time as a way of joining explanation with the game of giving and receiving reasons. All explanatory problems presuppose this exigency of active subjectivity and the emplotments by which it is instantiated to itself as an object of reflection. The inherent normativity of that circumstance makes it possible to posit ethical ramifications for the kinds of self-deceptions that aesthetic forms compel us to work through. Because those self-deceptions relate to character as a stake of activity, character remains a work in progress, so to speak. Self-deception is norm-producing in the way that actions foster their own regularity: always on the assumption of the inevitable *in*applicability of the rules implicit in them. Where the fostering agency is rendered self-explanatory, under the pressure of mistaken assumptions, normativity is the effective ground of ethos. Ethos is grounded in effect.

This is, I believe, a beneficently shameless proposition. For it does not presuppose a moral code or mandate a codification of value beyond the circumstance of one's learning to give reasons that will be better received, even with respect to one's need to be self-justifying. After all, the relevant self is not a bastion of belief but a self-comprehending acquirer of beliefs: one acquires beliefs on the basis of the notice one gives to warrantable reasons. We might say that the modalities of self-deception exhibited by the artists discussed in these pages gain their powerful effect insofar as they are nurturing the intrinsic shamelessness of such a noticing self.

It is important to understand what is being challenged here. The well-honored piety that says the self-deceiver ought to be ashamed of himself or herself for his or her lack of something like Piper's "epistemic audacity" implies the kind of self-heroizing ego that is so well indoctrinated by post-Enlightenment culture. Its cultural authority is tethered to a normativity that is indistinguishable from truth claims. Shame attaches to the lack of notice that there are norms for which evidence is presumed to be adequate. What is marginalized in this understanding is the kind of Hegelian learning that I have associated with contrastive work, whereby what constitutes evidence is a variable of what one is prompted to notice without presumptive norms. As we have just seen, norms are fostered in the course of noticing that warrants for reasoning secure an understanding of what one is doing only with respect to what one worries one doesn't yet comprehend.

So the artwork experienced in these terms is perhaps most exhaustively characterized as an unapologetic inducement to greater notice, rather than as a representational end in itself. Contemplation of one's relation to the explanatory problem instantiated in an artwork, so characterized, is a humbling proposition—as one might argue, all serious learning is and ought to be. But this is not to invite mere capitulation to the necessity for adaptation. Learning is a labor like that understood by the anxiety theorists of self-deception. Vigilance prevails as a cognitive pressure upon the mind to resituate itself with respect to a self-superseding perceptual horizon. The prospect for relativizing what one knows to richer contexts, as Turner might have it, is sustained in the sensuous form of presentation itself, by what Gombrich formalistically claims to be the essential "incompleteness" of the visual image. I am of course suggesting that such incompleteness obtains in all instances of aesthetic experience where self-deception is a formalistic imperative, where illusionism is implicitly afoot, where spelling out one's reasons for attending is thus made unusually urgent.

So I am proposing, in effect, that the work of art that imperils perceptual certainty makes the self-recognition of character a contingency of whatever reflective labor is entailed by that contingency. I have said that illusionism in art, visual or verbal, has been an important touchstone of this proposition. But illusionism is too easily conflated with trompe l'oeil where we take it to be a cognitively inert affective predicament. I have therefore proposed that by observing the epistemic complexity of self-deception, we supply a necessary supplement to our understanding how the affective predicament of illusionism/trompe l'oeil, may be *developed* if not, albeit provisionally, resolved. The narrative dynamic of self-deception, by contrast, gives a necessarily wider scope to the cognitive processes that ensue from the sensuous dilemma. The audience/viewer can take the sensuous dilemma of illusionism as a point of departure for intuiting norms, instead of invoking the precept of an already instantiated ethos. This would render the proffering of norms simply grist for the mill of hypothesis testing. The nurturing of inferential thought that goes along with this protocol of hypothesis testing allows us to see normativity as something we establish in the course of our becoming active: once again, with the purpose of better understanding what we are doing.

All of this activity, noted by theorists of self-deception as vigilance, cleverness, resourcefulness of reason-giving, and so on, is of course complementary to qualities that are generally valued in aesthetic experience. They are likewise—under different theoretical accounts of the aesthetic—considered to be elemental to the formal integrity of the artwork. What is the work of art for but to be attended to? If we can dispense with the notion that self-deception is simply paradoxical, and so rationalistically nugatory at best, we might see that the challenges of self-deception are quite similar to those posed by the notion of paradox in aesthetic theorizing generally. Paradox is integral to most accounts of modern aesthetic experience. We need only acknowledge the centrality of paradox to the aesthetic norms of the New Criticism, which still hold sway in the close reading of literary texts. Aesthetic paradox is not an obstacle to sense-making or reason-giving because it is so crucial to the distinctive ways in which the artwork makes sense of the experience of human reasoning.[6] The paradoxical dimension of self-deceiving sense is the occasion it gives for reasoning against one's seeming best reasons. This is especially true when we notice, conatively, what evidence our reasons do not support that we nonetheless want to count as worthy of our belief. Such paradox gives occasion for what David Pears might call a necessary "latitude."[7] One gives oneself latitude where one wants to hold out the possibility that one's belief will be right with respect to evidence that is self-sustaining through the experience of taking up new commitments. I am claiming that the self-deceiver and the artist are both adepts of this experience.

Of course, Pears and the more epistemically audacious critics of the self-deceiver assert that one does see at some point that one is self-deceived, that the evidence for one's action is mere wishfulness in Johnston's terms. As a result, the whole thought process of self-deception is discredited and vacated. On the contrary, the self-deceiver as I have given account of him or her, and the artist as I have represented him or her in the works I have read as self-deceiving, is inextricable from the thought process that produces self-deception. The self-deceiver is caught up in the possibility that one is never able to see that one is self-deceived with respect to a finite evidentiary ground. For the evidentiary ground is perceived to be extensible in ways that are inexhaustibly self-unfolding. In other words, the dynamic of self-deception that animates much aesthetic experience holds faith with an ideal of self-knowledge that is not a pretext for the dogmatic Enlightenment hypostatizing of the self. It is, rather, an arena within which the self finds terms for experiencing its inescapable contingency. Those terms are susceptible to rational assessment and responsive to the pressures of experience that warrant more adequate reasons for self-assertion.

This personal, historical, unfolding, for all of the Hegelian baggage it carries, does not involve a *Geist*-inspired telos. Rather, for the artists whom we have engaged in these pages, the discernment and impingement of unanticipated

---

6. Here the standard dicta of American New Critics like Brooks and Warren, Beardsley, and Crane still have currency. See Frank Lentricchia, *After the New Criticism* (Chicago: University of Chicago Press, 1981).

7. See David Pears, "The Goals and Strategies of Self-Deception," in *The Multiple Self (Studies in Rationality and Social Change)*, ed. Jon Elster (Cambridge: Cambridge University Press, 1987), 59–78, especially 61.

motivational biases is the most urgent, most present, register of experience. The drama of this higher-order responsiveness to the world is conspicuously akin to what aesthetic theorists commonly valorize as the imagination. Specifically, we might think of the Kantian, and subsequently, the Coleridgean investments in the concept of productive imagination, wherein the constructing of a sense-image depends upon an inferential penumbra of retinal stimuli: that is to say, beliefs, memories, expectations are coordinate with perception. As Kant explains in the Third Critique, the governing law is not that of the understanding, abstract from perception, but one internal to the improvisational or playful harmonizing of presentational and conceptual powers: imagination and understanding (Kant, *Critique of Judgment*). An extraordinary elasticity of thought is featured here, in terms that make the boundedness of experience subject to an initiative for altering one's circumstance. In other words, we are bound to second-guess the relevance of our responsiveness to the cultural surround with respect to potentially richer contexts of response.[8] I would argue that in our experience of the most challenging works of art, this second-guessing, or to put it squarely in the parlance of the current discussion, *seeing again, anxiously noticing, wishing to know better the reasons according to which one's beliefs/desires are sustainable,* is a sine qua non of aesthetic valuation. Such second-guessing is likewise one of the simple existential pleasures of involving ourselves in the work of art. For the self-deceiver's second-guessing is the guarantee that our disposition to know what we are doing is never decoupled from the doing itself. Reciprocally, it is the guarantee that whatever we are doing will not be decoupled from an imperative to know what it is.

If the inducement to notice is nothing but the endorsement of these guarantees, we can see the good warrant for treating self-deception as a rationalistic resource for understanding the artwork and its relevance to an ever more vivid life-work. The surprisingly creative dispositions of the self-deceiving mind, modeled and exercised in the artworks we have discussed here, might give us confidence that the high unlikelihood of rational minds ever completely escaping the circumstance of self-deception is duly compensated. This compensation endures in the proposition that self-deception lends itself to forms of reason-giving that are uniquely suited to the narrative pressure of changing circumstances in time. These conditions give rationality its motive and urgency in

---

8. Paul Ricoeur's magisterial *Time and Narrative*, especially volume 3, offers a thorough unpacking of this point. Ricoeur exposes the implicit narrative or diachronically rationalistic ramifications of the embrace of productive imagination by post-Enlightenment thinkers.

the first place. The self-deceptions that we have seen to be integral to the artwork are topoi of learning. Without them our hopes that character (whether in fiction or in the exigent circumstances of physical existence) can purposively *go on* might well be both unrecognizable and unrealizable. In other words, the power of self-realization that is at stake in learning to accept the responsibilities of the self-deceiving mind is a métier of experience fully attuned to the challenges of an existential incompleteness. It is the promise of coherence upon which only the most imaginative character can imaginably subsist.

Bibliography

Althusser, Louis. *Lenin and Philosophy.* Translated by Ben Brewster. New York: Monthly Review Press, 1971.
Aristotle. *The Basic Works of Aristotle.* Translated by Richard McKeon. New York: Random House, 1941.
Armato, Rosario, and John M. Spalek, eds. *Medieval Epic to the "Epic Theater" of Brecht: Essays in Comparative Literature.* Los Angeles: University of Southern California Press, 1968.
Arnheim, Rudolph. "Perception of Perspective: Pictorial Space from Different Viewing Points." *Leonardo* 10 (1977): 283–88.
Ashbery, John. *Self-Portrait in a Convex Mirror: Poems.* New York: Penguin, 1990.
Audi, Robert. "Self-Deception, Rationalization, and the Ethics of Belief." In *Moral Knowledge and Ethical Character.* Oxford: Oxford University Press, 1997.
Bach, Kent. "(Apparent) Paradoxes of Self-Deception and Decision." In *Self-Deception and Paradoxes of Rationality,* ed. Jean-Pierre Dupuy, 163–89. Stanford: Center for the Study of Language and Information, 1998.
Baier, Annette C. "The Vital But Dangerous Art of Ignoring: Selective Attention and Self-Deception." In *Self and Deception: A Cross-Cultural Philosophical Enquiry,* ed. Roger T. Ames and Wimal Dissanayake, 53–72. Albany: State University of New York Press, 1996.
Bakhtin, M. M. *Problems of Dostoevsky's Poetics.* Translated by Caryl Emerson. Minneapolis: University of Minnesota Press, 1984.
Baltrušaitis, Jurgis. *Anamorphic Art.* New York: Harry N. Abrams, 1977.
Barnes, Annette. *Seeing Through Self-Deception.* Cambridge: Cambridge University Press, 1997.
Barthes, Roland. *Camera Lucida.* Translated by Richard Howard. New York: Hill and Wang, 1982.
Beckett, Samuel. *Nohow On: Company, Ill Seen, Ill Said, Worstward Ho.* London: Calder, 1989.
———. *Three Novels: Molloy, Malone Dies, The Unnamable.* New York: Grove Press, 2009.
Berger, Harry, Jr. *Fictions of the Pose: Rembrandt Against the Italian Renaissance.* Stanford: Stanford University Press, 2000.
Bernstein, J. M. *Against Voluptuous Bodies: Late Modernism and the Meaning of Painting.* Stanford: Stanford University Press, 2006.
Bersani, Leo, and Ulysse Dutoit. *Caravaggio's Secrets.* Cambridge: MIT Press, 1998.
Besançon, Alain. *The Forbidden Image: An Intellectual History of Iconoclasm.* Translated by Jane Marie Todd. Chicago: University of Chicago Press, 2009.
Brandom, Robert B. *Articulating Reasons: An Introduction to Inferentialism.* Cambridge: Harvard University Press, 2001.

———. *Making It Explicit: Reasoning, Representing and Discursive Commitment.* Cambridge: Harvard University Press, 1994.
Bryson, Norman. *Looking at the Overlooked: Four Essays on Still Life Painting.* Cambridge: Harvard University Press, 1990.
Cascardi, Anthony J., ed. *The Cambridge Companion to Cervantes.* Cambridge: Cambridge University Press, 2002.
Cervantes, Miguel de. *Don Quixote.* Translated by Tobias Smollett. New York: Modern Library, 2004.
Davidson, Donald. "Two Paradoxes of Irrationality." In *Philosophical Essays on Freud,* ed. Richard Wollheim and James Hopkins, 289–305. Cambridge: Cambridge University Press, 1982.
De Armas, Fredrick A. "Cervantes and the Italian Renaissance." In *The Cambridge Companion to Cervantes,* ed. Anthony J. Cascardi, 32–57. Cambridge: Cambridge University Press, 2002.
Deleuze, Gilles. *Cinema I: The Movement Image.* Translated by Hugh Tomlinson and Barbara Habberjam. Minneapolis: University of Minnesota Press, 1986.
———. *Difference and Repetition.* Translated by Paul Patton. New York: Columbia University Press, 1995.
———. *Pourparlers.* Paris: Minuit, 1990.
Demos, Raphael. "Lying to Oneself." *Journal of Philosophy* 57 (1960): 588–95.
Descartes, René. *Discourse on Method and Meditations on First Philosophy.* 4th edition. Translated by Donald A. Cress. Indianapolis: Hackett, 1980.
———. *The Philosophical Writings of René Descartes.* Vol. 2. Translated by John Cottingham, Robert Toothoff, and Dugald Murdoch. New York: Cambridge University Press, 1984.
Dewey, John. *Art and Experience.* New York: Perigee, 2005.
Diderot, Denis. *Rameau's Nephew / Alembert's Dream.* Translated by Leonard Tancock. New York: Penguin, 1966.
Dilthey, Wilhelm. *Leben Schleiermachers.* 2 vols. Edited by M. Redeker. Berlin: Walter de Gruyter, 1870.
Doris, John M. *Lack of Character: Personality and Moral Behavior.* Cambridge: Cambridge University Press, 2002.
Dupuy, Jean-Pierre, ed. *Self-Deception and Paradoxes of Rationality.* Stanford: Center for the Study of Language and Information, 1998.
Ekserdjian, David. *Parmigianino.* New Haven: Yale University Press, 2006.
Eldridge, Richard. *The Persistence of Romanticism: Essays in Philosophy and Literature.* Cambridge: Cambridge University Press, 2001.
Elkins, James. *Visual Studies: A Skeptical Introduction.* New York: Routledge, 2003.
Elster, Jon. *Alchemies of the Mind: Rationality and the Emotions.* Cambridge: Cambridge University Press, 1999.
———, ed. *The Multiple Self (Studies in Rationality and Social Change).* Cambridge: Cambridge University Press, 1987.
———. *Sour Grapes: Studies in the Subversion of Rationality.* Cambridge: Cambridge University Press, 1983.
Fingarette, Herbert. *Self-Deception.* 2nd edition. With a new chapter. Berkeley and Los Angeles: University of California Press, 2000.

Flaubert, Gustave. *Madame Bovary*. Translated by Paul de Man. New York: W. W. Norton, 1965.

———. *The Selected Letters of Gustave Flaubert*. Translated and edited by Francis Steegmuller. New York: Farrar, Straus, and Giroux, 1953.

Frankfurt, Harry. *The Importance of What We Care About*. Cambridge: Cambridge University Press, 1988.

Franklin, David. *The Art of Parmigianino*. New Haven: Yale University Press, 2004.

Galassi, Peter. *Jeff Wall*. New York: MoMA, 2007.

Gombrich, E. H. *Art and Illusion: A Study in the Psychology of Pictorial Representation*. Princeton: Princeton University Press, 1989.

Goodman, Nelson. *Languages of Art*. New York: Bobbs-Merrill, 1968.

Greenaway, Peter. *A Zed and Two Noughts*. London: Faber and Faber, 1986.

———. "Cinema Militans Lecture: Towards a Re-Invention of Cinema." Paper presented at the Netherlands Film Festival, Utrecht, September 28, 2003. http://petergreenaway.org/essay3.htm.

Greenberg, Clement. *Art and Culture: Critical Essays*. Boston: Beacon Press, 1971.

Gregory, R. L. "Analogue Transactions with Adelbert Ames." *Perception* 16 (1963): 277–82.

Habermas, Jürgen. *The Philosophical Discourse of Modernity: Twelve Lectures*. Translated by Frederick Lawrence. Cambridge: MIT Press, 1987.

Hawkes, John. *Humors of Blood and Skin: A John Hawkes Reader*. New York: New Directions, 1984.

Hegel, Georg Wilhelm Friedrich. *The Phenomenology of Spirit*. Translated by A. V. Miller. Oxford: Oxford University Press, 1977.

———. *The Phenomenology of Mind*. Translated by J. B. Baillie. New York: Harper and Row, 1967.

———. *Hegel's Science of Logic*. Translated by A. V. Miller. Atlantic Highlands, N.J.: Humanities Paperback Library, 1969.

———. *Encyclopedia of Logic*. Edited by H. S. Harris et al. Indianapolis: Hackett, 1991.

———. *System of Ethical Life (1802/3) and First Philosophy of Spirit (Part III of the System of Speculative Philosophy (1803/4)*. Edited and translated by T. M. Knox. Albany: State University of New York Press, 1979.

Hockney, David. *Secret Knowledge: Rediscovering the Lost Techniques of the Old Masters*. London: Studio, 2006.

Hollman, Eckhard. *A Trick of the Eye: Trompe L'oeil Masterpieces*. Translated by Jürgen Tesch. New York: Prestel Publishing, 2004.

Horkheimer, Max, and Theodor W. Adorno. *Dialectic of Enlightenment*. Translated by John Cumming. New York: Continuum, 1990.

Hume, David. *Of the Standard of Taste and Other Essays*. New York: Bobbs-Merrill, 1965.

Jay, Martin. *Downcast Eyes: The Denigration of Vision in Twentieth-Century French Thought*. Berkeley and Los Angeles: University of California Press, 1994.

———. "Scopic Regimes of Modernity." In *Vision and Visuality*, ed. Hal Foster, 3–23. Seattle: Bay Press, Dia Art Foundation, 1988.

Johnston, Mark. "Self-Deception and the Nature of the Mind." In *Perspectives on Self-Deception*, ed. Amélie Oksenberg Rorty and Brian P. McLaughlin, 63–91. Berkeley and Los Angeles: University of California Press, 1988.

Judovitz, Dalia. "Vision, Representation, and Technology in Descartes." In *Modernity and the*

Hegemony of Vision, ed. David Michael Levin, 63–86. Berkeley and Los Angeles: University of California Press, 1993.
Kant, Immanuel. *Critique of Judgment.* Translated by Werner S. Pluhar. Indianapolis: Hackett, 1987.
———. *Political Writings.* Edited by H. S. Reiss and translated by H. B. Nisbet. Cambridge: Cambridge University Press, 1970.
Korsgaard, Christine M. *The Sources of Normativity.* Cambridge: Cambridge University Press, 1996.
Lacan, Jacques. *The Four Fundamentals of Psychoanalysis.* Translated by Alan Sheridan. New York: W. W. Norton, 1973.
Langdon, Helen. *Caravaggio: A Life.* Boulder, Colo.: Westview Press, 2000.
Lentricchia, Frank. *After the New Criticism.* Chicago: University of Chicago Press, 1981.
Lobeira, Vasco de. *Amadis of Gaul.* Translated by Robert Southey from the Spanish version of Garciodonez De Montalvo. London: John Russell Smith, 1872.
Lopes, Dominic. *Understanding Pictures.* Oxford: Oxford University Press, 1996.
Lukács, Georg. *Theory of the Novel.* Translated by Anna Bostock. Cambridge: MIT Press, 1971.
Makkreel, Rudolph A. *Dilthey: Philosopher of the Human Studies.* Princeton: Princeton University Press, 1975.
Mastai, Marie-Louise D'Otrange. *Illusion in Art: Trompe L'Oeil, A History of Pictorial Illusionism.* New York: Abaris Books, 1975.
Mele, Alfred. *Autonomous Agents: From Self-Control to Autonomy.* Oxford: Oxford University Press, 2001.
———. *Self-Deception Unmasked.* Princeton: Princeton University Press, 2001.
McElroy, Joseph. *Actress in the House.* New York: Overlook, 2004.
McLaughlin, Brian P., and Amélie Oksenberg Rorty, eds. *Perspectives on Self-Deception.* Berkeley and Los Angeles: University of California Press, 1988.
Mondzain, Marie-José. *Image, Icon, Economy: The Byzantine Origins of the Contemporary Imaginary.* Translated by Rico Franses. Stanford: Stanford University Press, 2004.
Moran, Richard. *Authority and Estrangement: An Essay on Self-Knowledge.* Princeton: Princeton University Press, 2001.
Morris, Errol. "On Re-Staging Action." http://morrisl.blogs.nytimes.com/.
Nabokov, Vladimir. *The Annotated Lolita: Revised and Updated.* Edited by Alfred Appel Jr. New York: Vintage, 1991.
Nancy, Jean-Luc. *The Ground of the Image.* Translated by Jeff Fort. New York: Fordham University Press, 2005.
Nietzsche, Friedrich. *On the Genealogy of Morals and Ecce Homo.* Translated by Walter Kaufmann and R. J. Hollingdale. New York: Vintage, 1989.
Parsons, Talcott. *The Structure of Social Action.* New York: McGraw-Hill, 1937.
Pascoe, David. *Peter Greenaway: Museums and Moving Images.* London: Reaktion, 1997.
Pears, David. *Motivated Irrationality.* Oxford: Clarendon Press, 1984.
———. "The Goals and Strategies of Self-Deception." In *The Multiple Self (Studies in Rationality and Social Change),* ed. Jon Elster, 59–78. Cambridge: Cambridge University Press, 1987.
Piper, Adrian M. "Pseudorationality." In *Perspectives on Self-Deception,* ed. Amélie Oksenberg Rorty and Brian P. McLaughlin, 297–323. Berkeley and Los Angeles: University of California Press, 1988.

Pippin, Robert. *Hegel's Idealism: The Satisfactions of Self-Consciousness.* Cambridge: Cambridge University Press, 1989.

———. *The Persistence of Subjectivity: On the Kantian Aftermath.* Cambridge: Cambridge University Press, 2005.

Plato. *Euthyphro, Apology, Crito, Phaedo.* Translated and edited by Benjamin Jowett. New York: Prometheus Books, 1988.

———. *The Republic.* Translated by G. R. F. Ferrari and Tom Griffith. Cambridge: Cambridge University Press, 2000.

Puglisi, Catherine. *Caravaggio.* London: Phaidon, 2000.

Rancière, Jacques. *The Future of the Image.* Translated by Gregory Elliott. New York: Verso, 2009.

Raz, Joseph. *Engaging Reason: On the Theory of Value and Action.* Oxford: Oxford University Press, 1999.

———. *The Practice of Value.* Edited by R. Jay Wallace. Oxford: Oxford University Press, 2003.

Richter, Gerhard. *Atlas.* Edited by Helmut Friedel. New York: D.A.P., 2006.

———. *The Daily Practice of Painting.* Edited by Hans-Ulrich Obrist and translated by David Britt. Cambridge: MIT Press, 1998.

Ricoeur, Paul. *Time and Narrative.* 3 vols. Translated by Kathleen McLaughlin and David Pellauer. Chicago: University of Chicago Press, 1984–88.

Robb, Peter. *M: The Man Who Became Caravaggio.* New York: Picador Press, 1998.

Rondeau, James. "Interview with Jeff Wall." In *Jeff Wall: Selected Essays and Interviews.* New York: MoMA, 2007.

Rorty, Amélie Oksenberg. "The Deceptive Self: Liars, Layers, and Lairs." In *Perspectives in Self-Deception,* ed. Brian P. McLaughlin and Amélie Oxenberg Rorty, 11–28. Berkeley and Los Angeles: University of California Press, 1988.

———. "Self-Deception, *Akrasia* and Irrationality." In *The Multiple Self (Studies in Rationality and Social Change),* ed. Jon Elster, 115–32. Cambridge: Cambridge University Press, 1987.

Sanford, David. "Self-Deception as Rationalization." In *Perspectives on Self-Deception,* ed. Brian P. McLaughlin and Amélie Oksenberg Rorty, 157–69. Berkeley and Los Angeles: University of California Press, 1988.

Sartre, Jean-Paul. *Being and Nothingness: An Essay on Phenomenological Ontology.* Translated by Hazel E. Barnes. New York: Washington Square Press, 1973.

Shakespeare, William. *Othello.* Edited by Stephen Orgel. New York: Penguin, 2001.

Singer, Alan. *Aesthetic Reason: Artworks and the Deliberative Ethos.* University Park: Pennsylvania State University Press, 2003.

Spike, John T. *Caravaggio.* New York: Abbeville Press, 2001.

Steadman, Philip. *Vermeer's Camera: Uncovering the Truth Behind the Masterpieces.* Oxford: Oxford University Press, 2002.

Storr, Robert. *Gerhard Richter: October 18, 1977.* New York: MoMA/Abrams, 2000.

Tietze, Hans. *Tintoretto: The Paintings and Drawings.* London: Phaidon, 1948.

Townsend, Chris, ed. *The Art of Bill Viola.* London: Thames and Hudson, 2004.

Turner, Stephen. *Brains/Practices/Relativism.* Chicago: University of Chicago Press, 2002.

———. *The Social Theory of Practices: Tradition, Tacit Knowledge and Presuppositions.* Chicago: University of Chicago Press, 1994.

Vasari, Giorgio. *Vasari's Lives of the Painters, Sculptors, and Architects.* Translated by Edmund Fuller. New York: Dell, 1968.
Velleman, J. David. *The Possibility of Practical Reason.* Oxford: Oxford University Press, 2000.
———. *Self to Self: Selected Essays.* Cambridge: Cambridge University Press, 2006.
Vernant, Jean-Pierre, and Pierre Vidal-Naquet. *Myth and Tragedy in Ancient Greece.* Translated by Janet Lloyd. Cambridge: MIT Press, 1988.
Viola, Bill. *Reasons for Knocking at an Empty House.* London: Thames and Hudson, 1995.
Wall, Jeff. *Jeff Wall: Selected Essays and Interviews.* New York: MoMA, 2007.
Walton, Kendall L. *Mimesis as Make-Believe: On the Foundations of the Representational Arts.* Cambridge: Harvard University Press, 1990.

Index

Adorno, Theodor, 11, 160, 162, 165–67, 179, 205
aesthetic paradox, 215–16
agency: choice-driven, 99; classical, 99, 117–18; hierarchical model of, 9, 62; perception and, 138–45; practical, 60–65
Alchemies of the Mind (Elster), 23
Althusser, Louis, 146 n. 9
Altieri, Charles, 75 n. 6
Ames, Adelbert, 11, 141, 146
Ames transformation, 141–42
anamorphic projection, 51
anxiety: self-deception and, 111; strength of mind and, 206–8
appearance, Hegel and, 48, 53
Aristotle, 122–23
Arnheim, Rudolph, 147–48
art: deception and, 3; literary, 4–5; second-guessing of, 217; self-deception as bridge between life and, 2
Ashbery, John, 9, 66, 75–86, 96; source of unique powers of, 90
Audi, Robert, 6, 17, 17 n. 2, 20, 22, 27–28, 42, 43, 98

Bach, Kent, 17, 18–20, 21, 23, 31, 32, 43, 52, 58, 95, 96, 98
bad faith, Sartre and, 37–39
Bahktin, Mikhail M., 26 n. 10
Baier, Annette C., 111, 203–4, 206–8, 210, 211
Baltrušaitis, Jurgis, 84 n. 10
Barnes, Annette, 111, 206–7, 209
Barthes, Roland, 153–54
Beckett, Samuel, 44, 97
becoming of the self, 3
belief, suspension of, 42
Berger, Harry, 100, 101–2, 101 n. 6, 102 n. 7, 104
Bildungsroman, 108–9

Brandom, Robert B., 8, 65, 74, 79, 80, 80 nn. 8–9, 94, 96; on inferentialism, 56–60
Bryson, Norman, 139 n. 3

capacity rationality, 98–100
Caravaggio, Michelangelo da, 9, 66–67, 86–96; source of unique powers of, 90
Cervantes, Miguel de, 10, 16, 105, 112–18
character: compulsive notice and, 109–12; condition of present-ness in, 14–16; in fiction, 14–15; Fingarette and, 26–27; the novel and, 14; self and, 13–14; self-deceiving, 13; uncharacteristic, 15, 96, 100, 213–14
choice-driven agency, 99–100
classical agency, 99, 117; notice as crux of, 117–18
cogito, 51–52
compulsive notice, character and, 109–12
Confrontation 2 (Richter), 175, 176
Conrad, Joseph, 16
conscientious consciousness, 42
consciousness, reflective, 61
consequential commitment, rules of, 58
contextualism, self-deception and, 211–18

Daily Practice of Painting, The (Richter), 168–69
Davidson, Donald, 6, 111
De Armas, Fredrick A., 114
defiguration, 193–94
Deleuze, Gilles, 92–96
Demos, Raphael, 2 n. 1
Descartes, René, 51, 203–4, 210
Dewey, John, 67 n. 1
Dialectic of Enlightenment (Horkheimer and Adorno), 11, 205
Diderot, Denis, 10, 105, 115–25
Discovery of the Body of St. Mark, The (Tintoretto), 11, 146–53
Dilthey, Wilhelm, 108–9
Don Quixote (Cervantes), 10, 105, 107, 112–18

double truth, 114, 115
doxastic gaps, 57, 60, 79

Eisenstein, Sergey, 92–93
Eldridge, Richard, 3 n. 3
Elkins, James, 145
Elster, Jon, 22–23, 23 n. 7, 144, 190
emotion, 23
enlightenment: fables during, 26; Horkheimer and Adorno on, 165–67; self-deception and reason during, 10; treatment of heroes in, 103
epics, pervasiveness of self-deceiving mind in, 4
epistemic audacity, 209–11, 214
error, 105
essence, Hegel and, 48, 53

Fingarette, Herbert, 6, 26–27, 29, 31, 38–43, 43, 51, 61, 111, 143
Flaubert, Gustave, 8, 16, 28–43, 104
Ford, Ford Madox, 16
formalism, modern, 167
Frankfurt, Harry, 9
Freud, Sigmund, 167

Gombrich, Ernst, 10–11, 60–61, 60 n. 15, 138–41, 138n1, 139, 143–44, 215
Goodman, Nelson, 149
Greek tragedy, 164–65
Greenaway, Peter, 11, 12, 145, 146, 177–80, 191–202
Greeting, The (Viola), 179, 180–91
Griffith, D. W., 92–93

Hamartia, 165, 167, 169
Hanged (Richter), 171–73
Hawkes, John, 44–45
Hegel, Georg W. F., 3, 6, 8, 65, 96, 106–7, 158–59, 205; appearance and, 48, 53; essence and, 48, 53; the Notion of, 47–48, 52, 53, 55; syllogism and, 54
heroes: Nietzsche's treatment of, 103; treatment of during Enlightenment, 103
heroic hypocrisy, 114
hierarchical model of agency, 9
higher-order motivations, 62, 63
Horkheimer, Max, 11, 160, 162, 165–67, 179, 205
hypothesis testing, 21–22, 23, 27–28

iconoclasm, 49–50, 58
"identification as," 27–28, 39

Ihering, Rudolph von, 212
illusionism, 8, 10–11, 48, 51, 59
inferentialism, 9, 55–60; the Notion and, 62; work of Brandom on, 56–60
interiority, 100–101
irony, 30
irrationality, self-deception and, 16

Jay, Martin, 90 n. 18
Johnston, Mark, 206–7, 209, 210, 211
Joyce, James, 16
Judovitz, Dalia, 51 n. 10

Kant, Immanuel, 48, 97, 105 n. 12, 178–80, 217
knowing, paradox of, 167
Korsgaard, Christine, 105 n. 12

Lacan, Jacques, 50, 50 n. 8
learning, self-deceptions as topoi of, 217–18
Lehman, David, 75 n. 6
life, self-deception as bridge between art and, 2
linquistic texts, 138–39
liquid intelligence, 160
literary art, self-deception as thematic crux of, 4–5
Lolita (Nabokov), 10, 105, 107, 125–37, 208
Longinus, 179
Lopes, Dominic, 138 n. 1, 142–43
Lotto, Lorenzo, 101–2
Lukács, Georg, 107–8

Madame Bovary (Flaubert), 8, 28–43
Manet, Edouard, 159
Mau, August, 139
McElroy, Joseph, 44–46
Medusa (Caravaggio), 9, 66–67, 86–96
Mele, Alfred, 6, 17, 17 n. 2, 20, 21, 31, 43, 98
Milk (Wall), 157–63
mind, powers of, Descartes and, 51–52
mirror anamorphosis, 51
modern formalism, 167
Mondzain, Marie-José, 50 n. 5
Moran, Richard, 61–62
Morris, Errol, 184 n. 12
motivations, higher-order, 62, 63
movement image, 92–93

Nabokov, Vladimir, 10, 16, 105, 125–37
Nancy, Jean-Luc, 180–83
New Criticism, 215–16
Nietzsche, Friedrich, 103, 167
normativity, 97

notice: compulsive, character and, 109–12; as crux of classical agency, 117–18
noticers, self-deceivers as, 2
noticing, 66, 106–9; costs of missing, 68
notion, 8, 47–48, 52, 53; inferentialism and, 62
novels: aptness of, for noticing, 107; character and, 14; pervasiveness of self-deceiving mind in, 4; plot and, 104; self-deception in, 106

October 18, 1977 (Richter), 171, 173–77
Odoni, Andrea, 101–2
Othello, 17–18, 22

painters: ideal viewpoint and, 74; self-deception and, 4–5
paintings, 9
paradox, 215–16; of knowing, 167
Parmigianino, 9, 66, 68–74, 96; source of unique powers of, 90
Parsons, Talcott, 152
Pears, David, 111, 216
Peripeteia, 106, 165, 202, 207
Perloff, Marjorie, 75 n. 6
photo-blur paintings, 168–77
Piper, Adrian M. S., 129, 206–7, 208, 209–10, 214
Pippin, Robert, 47, 48 n. 3, 53, 54–55, 103
Plato, 24, 61, 70–71
plot-making, literary, 104–5; Aristotelian precept of, 106
poems, 9
point of view, Flaubert and, 34
Pontormo, Jacopo, 180–82
Portrait of Andrea Odoni (Lotto), 101–2
portraiture, reasons for, 100–106
presentism, 211
present-ness: condition of, in character, 14–16; condition of, self-deception and, 17; Flaubert and, 33; in *Madame Bovary,* 39–40
Proust, Marcel, 103
pseudorationality, 129
punctum image, 153

Quintilian, 60 n. 15, 61

Rameau's Nephew (Diderot), 10, 105, 107, 115–25
Rancière, Jacques, 193–94
rational agency, 99–100
rationality, 19; capacity, 98–100; self-deceiver and, 1; self-deception and, 17; self-deception as tool for, 36–37

rationalization: self-deceiver and, 2; self-deception and, 20–21, 44
Raz, Joseph, 98–101, 114, 117
reason-giving, 97, 99
reflective consciousness, 61
remote consequences, 160
Richter, Gerhard, 12, 117, 145, 146, 164, 168–77, 202
Ricoeur, Paul, 217 n. 8
Roman wall painting, 139–40
Rorty, Amélie Oskenberg, 6, 17, 31–32, 38, 94, 205, 209

Sanford, David, 24–26, 29, 36, 141, 208
sapience, 57
Sartre, Jean Paul, 37–39, 40
score-keeping, 58, 59, 74
second-guessing, of art, 217
self, self-performative, 22–23
self-assertion, 23–24, 107
self-control, 98
self-deceivers: as motivated and purposeful, 19–20; narrative texts and, 16; as noticers, 2–3; rationality and, 1; rationalization and, 2; rationalizing needs of, 21; as self-enhancing agencies, 22; traditional treatment of, 6; truth and, 19–20
self-deception: anxiety and, 111; anxiety-driven, as life-preserving skill, 111; as arena, 18–19; artistic creation and, 3–4; artworks and, 3; assumptions abandoned for, 22; bear the costs and, 49; as bridge between life and art, 2; conditions for, 22; contextualist imperative and, 211–18; counterintuitive propositions regarding, 7; Enlightenment reason and, 10; as fulcrum of learning, 5; irrationality and, 16; in life and art, 1; as life-preserving skill, 111–12; normativity and, 214; in novels, 106; orthodox view of, 6; painters and, 4–5; pedagogical resources of, 66–69; pervasiveness of, in histories of epic and novel, 4; Plato on, 24; as practical experiment, 203–6; present-ness and, 17; rationality and, 17; rationalization and, 2, 20–21, 44; revising, in *Madame Bovary,* 28–43; risks of self-determination and, 49; Sanford's version of, 24–26; as self-preservation, 129–30; significance of, as art form, 4; stigma of, 1; as thematic crux of literary art, 4–5; as tool of rationalistic enterprise, 36–37; as topoi of learning, 217–18

"Self-Portrait in a Convex Mirror" (Ashbery), 75–86
Self-Portrait in a Convex Mirror (Parmigianino), 9, 66, 68–74
self-preservation, 129–30
Sellars, Wilfred, 80 n. 9
Singer, Alan, 13 n. 1
skepticism, 64
social practices, 63–64
Socrates, 70–71
Solaris (Tarkovsky), 158
spelling out, 146
Sterne, Laurence, 16
Storr, Robert, 169
studium image, 153
sublimity, theory of, 178
suspension of disbelief, 42
syllogism, Hegel and, 54

Tarkovsky, Andrei, 158
Tintoretto, Jacopo, 11, 145, 146–53, 158, 202
Tönnies, Ferdinand, 64 n. 19
tragedy, Greek, 164–65
trompe l'oeil, 48–51, 58, 59

truth, self-deceivers and, 19–20
Turner, Stephen P., 63–65, 152 n. 13, 211–12, 214

uncharacteristic character, 15, 96, 100, 213–14

Velleman, J. David, 62–63, 65, 68–69, 75, 75 n. 7, 77, 77 n. 7, 94, 95–96, 96, 102 n. 8, 104 n. 11, 121, 122 n. 24
ventriloquism, 121–22
Vico, Giambattista, 167
Viola, Bill, 11, 12, 145, 146, 177–91, 202
visitatio, 180, 182
Visitation, The (Pontormo), 180–82
visual artists, 11–12
visuality, 138

Wall, Jeff, 11, 12, 145, 146, 157–63, 182, 202, 205, 213
Walton, Kendall, 139
Weber, Max, 212
Wirklichheit, 49

Zed and Two Noughts, A (Greenaway), 179, 191–202

www.ingramcontent.com/pod-product-compliance
Lightning Source LLC
Chambersburg PA
CBHW021402290426
44108CB00010B/347